STUDIA POST-BIBLICA

VOLUMEN SEXTUM

STUDIA POST-BIBLICA

EDIDIT

P. A. H. DE BOER

VOLUMEN SEXTUM

LEIDEN
E. J. BRILL
1962

A LIFE OF
RABBAN YOHANAN
BEN ZAKKAI

Ca. 1-80 C.E.

BY

JACOB NEUSNER

Research Associate in Jewish History
Philip W. Lown Institute of Advanced Judaic Studies
Brandeis University

LEIDEN
E. J. BRILL
1962

In Memory of my Father
Psalm 91.11

CONTENTS

PREFACE

I gratefully acknowledge the assistance of the following teachers and colleagues in writing this book: Professor Salo W. Baron of Columbia University, who supervised my research, generously giving both learning and effort; and Professor Morton Smith of Columbia University, who read the manuscript in several successive drafts, offering detailed and rigorous criticism of each in matters of both substance and style; many of their comments are noted, but the true measure of their valuable criticism is by no means exhausted by these notes; Rabbi Neil Gillman of the Jewish Theological Seminary of America, who was in many ways a partner in writing this book, discussing and contributing to its development with me page by page from its inception to its conclusion; Professor W. D. Davies of Union Theological Seminary, who offered extensive comments; and Rabbi David Weiss of the Jewish Theological Seminary, who read and criticized this essay with particular reference to the use of rabbinic materials.

Since this is an essay in Jewish history, it bears witness to my teachers and rabbis of the faculty of the Jewish Theological Seminary of America, in particular Professor Louis Finkelstein, Chancellor, and Professor Saul Lieberman, Dean of the Rabbinical School, who taught me the basic disciplines of Jewish learning. In addition, the Seminary granted me a fellowship in the Special Program of Talmudic Studies, in which, guided by Professor H. Z. Dimitrovsky, I was able to pursue more intensive study of rabbinic literature. Most important, members of the Seminary faculty, specifically Professors Moshe Davis, Abraham S. Halkin, Abraham J. Heschel, and Seymour Siegel, exemplified in their friendship for me the highest ideals of fellowship created by the study of the Torah. To them, their colleagues, and my fellow students at the Seminary, I have been deeply and gladly indebted.

It is appropriate to note also the less obvious, but no less significant contribution of other teachers, colleagues, and friends, who have played important parts in my education in writing, historical research, and Jewish studies. Their personal interest, encouragement, and instruction contributed materially to this and all future research. They include the following: Miss Ardis B. Chase, Dr. Henry J. Rives, and Mrs. Elma C. LeBlond of the public schools of West Hartford, Connecticut; Professor Thomas McGann, formerly of Harvard University, now at the University of Texas; Professors Oscar Handlin and Harry A. Wolfson of Harvard University; Dr. Cecil Roth of Oxford University; Professor Richard T. Vann, formerly of Harvard University, now at Carleton College; Rabbi Abraham J. Feldman of West Hartford, Connecticut; Professors Brevard S. Childs and Judah Goldin of Yale University, John A. Hutchison of Claremont Graduate School, William A. Johnson of Trinity College, and James Ross of Drew University; Professor and Mrs. Peter Gay of Columbia University; Rabbis David Clayman, Ben Zion Gold, Manuel Gold, Jules Harlow, Joel Kraemer, Shmuel Leiter, Yohanan Muffs, Bernard Och, Jack M. Rosoff, Sheldon Schiffman, Matthew Simon, Solomon Spiro, Daniel Thau Teitelbaum, and Eugene Weiner; Mr. Donald P. Edelstein of Quincy, Massachusetts; and Dr. Abraham Goldberg of the Hebrew University in Jerusalem.

Finally I thank those institutions and foundations which provided financial support for my education during the past decade, namely, Harvard College, the Trustees of the Henry Fund, the Board of Foreign Scholarships of the Department of State, the Graduate Faculties of Columbia University, the Jewish Theological Seminary of America, and the National Council on Religion in Higher Education. I am especially indebted to the Fellows of the National Council for their intellectual fellowship and personal friendship, indispensable to meaningful scholarship in any subject.

I had hoped to dedicated this book to the honor of both my parents, Samuel and Lee B. Neusner, but my father's death last December prevents it, and the essay that follows stands as a memorial to his name. One cannot sufficiently describe, much less acknowledge, the debt he owes to his parents in every enterprise of life, and I shall not attempt it.

Erev Pesah, 5721   JACOB NEUSNER
March 31, 1961.

I wish to tank the Jewish Theological Seminary for awarding the Abraham Berliner Prize in Jewish History to *A Life of Rabban Yohanan ben Zakkai.*

Erev Shavuot, 5722   J. N.
June, 1962

CHAPTER ONE

WOE IF I TELL IT...

In the first century, men generally regarded religion as an irreducible historical reality. They did not, for the most part, try to explain it as a consequence of economic, social, or psychological causes. For Jews, Scripture embodied the record of man's genuine religious experience. They therefore looked into its ancient literature to find paradigmatic instruction on the nature of religion. They did so through the medium of disciplined exegesis, called *midrash* (from *darash*, to search). The word of God was like fire, the Jewish sages taught, and like the hammer that breaks the rock into pieces. No word of Scripture could, therefore, fail to yield a particular nuance of light, and, properly understood, none was irrelevant to events at hand.[1]

Some men were prepared to give their lives for Scriptural imperatives. If today men die for nation or class, one turns legitimately to study the sources of nationalism or class loyalty. In the first century, men died for faith. One wonders, therefore, what was the content and direction of that faith. He asks, in particular, how Jews mediated between the unchanging word of Scriptural religion and the inconstant world in which they lived, and turns therefore to the lives of those who exemplified the religion of their time, for from the perspective of a later day, a few men appear to have embodied major elements of Scriptural faith and experience, providing a living *midrash* of Scripture by re-enacting a part of the biblical drama in their own age and idiom.

One such man was Yohanan ben Zakkai. His direct religious experience apparently drew, in part, on the Scriptural symbols provided by Ezekiel's vision of the chariot. His social and political thought finds significant parallel in the teachings of Jeremiah at the fall of the First Temple. His response to the destruction of the Second Temple in 70 C.E. recalls the capacity to seize upon disaster to transform the religious understanding which was exhibited by Hosea before the fall of Samaria and by the Second Isaiah in the Judean Exile in Babylon. His constructive activity at Yavneh bears comparison to that of Ezra in Jerusalem. While there is absolutely no evidence that Yohanan ben Zakkai saw himself from such a perspective, one must keep in mind how deeply the biblical record had marked the consciousness of his

---

[1] Jeremiah 23.29, Cf. Babylonian Talmud (hereafter – TB) Sanhedrin, 34a.

age, and how immediate and genuine Scripture appeared to him and his contemporaries. Hence, Yohanan ben Zakkai provides an interesting example of the structure of a Scripturally-centered religious experience. He has, moreover, held a central place in Jewish history. He was one of the leaders of the Pharisaic community in Jerusalem before the destruction of the Temple, and afterward he undertook the work of reconstruction. Who he was, what he taught, and how he met the perplexities of religion in his time – all this needs to be recovered from the rather scanty remains of his life, scattered throughout Talmudic and midrashic literature.[1]

These remains were transmitted in a long process of literary tradition. One does not know whether this tradition was at first primarily oral or written, but this is not relevant to a biography of Yohanan ben Zakkai. What is relevant is that the tradition has drastically reshaped the stories of Yohanan's life, and imposed on them forms which the stories probably did not exhibit to begin with. Striking examples of these forms include the recension of Yohanan's disputes with the Sadducees and his various conversations with his students. Study of the way in which biographical materials have been shaped by the process of tradition has had striking success in scholarship on the Gospels. One would expect, therefore, that such criticism of the forms of recension might throw light on the way in which material on Yohanan ben Zakkai has been shaped and developed or diminished by the process of tradition. Rabbinic literature certainly has a precise set of forms in which material is cast. These forms are clearly marked, for instance, in various sections of the Mishnah, and material is manifestly bent to fit the forms. Study of forms and of the way in

---

[1] Aside from brief articles in encylopedias, three longer monographs have been written on Yohanan ben Zakkai, M. Landau, "Bilder aus dem leben und Wirken der Rabbiner: Rabbi Jochanan ben Sakkai," *Monatschrift für Geschichte und Wissenschaft des Judenthums* (hereafter – MGWJ), I (1852), 163-176, 283-295, 323-335; J. Spitz, *Rabban Jochanan ben Sakkai* (Berlin, 1883), and A. Schlatter, "Jochanan ben Zakkai, der Zeitgenosse der Apostel" (Guetersloh, 1899) in *Beiträge zur Förderung Christlicher Theologies*, III, 4. Schlatter's article should be read in the light of L. Blau's critical review, "Jochanan ben Zakkai in christlicher Beleuchtung," *MGWJ*. VII (1899), 548-561. There are a number of articles on particular aspects of Yohanan ben Zakkai's career, cited below. The essay that follows is the first comprehensive consideration of all sources relating to Yohanan ben Zakkai, including that in Midrash Tannaim unknown to Landau, Spitz, and Schlatter, and includes consideration of the more recent speculations of Allon, Stein, Kaminka, and the insights of Goldin, and hence is to be defended as an effort to state what is positively known about Yohanan ben Zakkai at this time in the light of contemporary understanding of first century Judaism.

which material has been adapted to them, and discovery of the traces
of adaptation, might help in estimating more accurately the historical
reliability and the original content of the stories about Yohanan ben
Zakkai. Such a study requires, however, more fundamental research
on the historical processes and forms of transmitting rabbinic traditions
than has been done to date. A biography of Yohanan ben Zakkai is too
narrow a frame of reference for such form-criticism, and I have not
undertaken it. My effort has been rather to focus on the content of
the traditions relating to Yohanan ben Zakkai, and to recover as much
of his intellectual biography as one can in the absence of more accurate
means of form-criticism. This attempt has entailed collection and
organization of all the extant information on Yohanan ben Zakkai.
Further critical evaluation of it must await the definition and historical elucidation of the forms of recension applying to rabbinic traditions.[1]

---

[1] Cf. Vincent Taylor, *Formation of the Gospel Tradition* (London, 1953), 207-8.
I have found few points of explanatory or inferential character added to earlier
accounts; slight tendency, in spite of additions, for the accounts to become shorter;
no place where direct speech is replaced by indirect; and no evidence that the form
of later versions became perceptibly rounded and less detailed. While all these
processes of recension may have taken place, there is no specific and obvious
evidence in the sources on Yohanan ben Zakkai that they *have* taken place.
Yohanan's teachings were clearly transmitted by those who heard them, cf. for
example Mishnah Eduyot 8.7, TB Sotah 5. (cf. TP Sotah 5.6.; TB Ketuvet 14a;
TB Hagigah 3b (Mishnah Yadayim 4.3, Tosefta Yadayim 2.16); Tosefta Hagigah
3.36; Sifra Parashat Shemini 7.12 (Wess ed. 54a), etc. In such instances, Yohanan's
teachings were transmitted directly by, and for the purposes of, the next generation,
and not by means of an edited collection of sayings. For evidences that some of
Yohanan's sayings were edited and transmitted in very particular forms, cf. Louis
Finkelstein, *Mavo LeMasekhet Avot de Rabbi Natan* [Introduction to Tractate Avot
and Avot de Rabbi Nathan] (New York, 1950), 38-43, 60-61; Y. N. Epstein, *Mavo-ot
LeSifrut HaTannaim* [Introduction to Tannaitic Literature] (Jerusalem, 1957),
40-41, 295-6, 399-401 (on the Mishnah of Sotah chs. 8-9). By the time of Abba
Shaul, the material in Avot and Avot de Rabbi Natan relating to Yohanan's
conversations with his students was certainly edited in its final form, for Abba
Shaul presents traditions directly contradictory to those in the texts. Certainly in
the lifetime of Eleazar ben Arakh, and possibly even before the death of Yohanan
ben Zakkai, Yohanan's high praise of Eleazar must have been written down or
given a final form for oral transmission, for it is doubtful that he could have been so
praised after he separated from the Yavneh consistory. It is doubtful that the
confusion between Eliezer ben Hyrkanus and Eleazar ben Arakh could have
persisted, if Eleazar's days of great learning had passed. Other consistent markings
of traditions about Yohanan include the following forms: "'amru 'alav" cf. TB
Sukkah 28b, TB Baba Batra 134b, TB Pesahim 26a; but compare TP Avodah Zara
3.11, which does not preserve the same form for the same teaching; the midrashim
in the manner of the *homer* in Tosefta Baba Kamma 7.3-7 are clearly a recension of
some of the same teachings which appear in different forms elsewhere, cf. the

Since Yohanan ben Zakkai died shortly after the destruction of Jerusalem, possibly about the year 80, and since he was credited with extraordinary longevity, one may well assume that he was born shortly after the end of the reign of Herod the Great, at about the beginning of the Common Era. Who was this Zakkai, who named his son "Yohanan," *the Lord gave graciously*, the sources do not say. The shred of information is the name Zakkai. What can one learn from this? Zakkai was the Aramaic equivalent of the Hebrew *zadik*, righteous, upright. This much is clear from the Aramaic translation of Scripture, for in Genesis 6.9, the Hebrew reads, "These are the generations of Noah. Noah was a *righteous man*, blameless in his generation," and the Aramaic translator used the word *zakkai*. It was also the name of a clan that returned from Babylon; listed among those who came back to Judah were "the sons of Zakkai, seven hundred and sixty" (Ezra 2.9, Nehemiah 7.14). It was a sib of commoners, among the "men of the people of Israel," and not among those distinguished by the inherited status of priests, Levites, Temple servants, sons of Solomon's servants, singers, or gatekeepers. Yet the clan must have amounted to something; in a group of less than 45,000, a family of more than seven hundred fifty members must have been prominent. Heirs of the name Zakkai appeared again in rabbinic literature. A tanna, Rabbi Zakkai, was contemporary of Judah the Prince (ca. 200 C.E.) and a Babylonian Amora of the third century was known to have emigrated to the land

---

comparisons in ch. 5. Some of the midrashim which were apparently in the manner of the *homer* were never so designated, cf. for example Sifre Deut. 194, TB Sotah 44b, TP Sotah 8.9. Note also that the forms of Avot and Avot de Rabbi Natan manifest a consistent order of discourse: Eliezer ben Hyroanus, Joshua ben Hananiah, Yosi the Priest, Simeon ben Nathaneel, and Eleazar ben Arakh. The principle of arrangement is certainly not based on seniority, for Eliezer came after Joshua and Simeon. Placing Eleazar last has an effective, literary consequence: it makes possible Yohanan's praise of Eleazar as the climax of the lesson. I should conclude that Eleazar is placed last for that reason. Eliezer may precede Joshua because Shammaitic opinions are very often placed before Hillelite opinions, the former being a Shammaite and the latter a Hillelite. Not enough is known about Yosi and Simeon to explain why one takes precedence, except perhaps that Simeon was ignorant when he came to Yohanan, and may have therefore given way to Yosi, who might not have been, and who was a priest. Other clearly marked collections in which Yohanan was included are 1. Ketuvot 13; TP Sotah 9.16 (parallel in TP Avodah Zarah 3.1; the accounts of the trip with Eleazar ben Arakh in TB Hagigah 14b, TP Hagigah 2.1, Mekilta de R. Simeon bar Yohai, ed. Melamed-Epstein, 158 1. 13 through 159 1. 21, etc. In addition, note Birger Gerhardsson, *Memory and Manuscript: Oral Tradition and Written Transmission in Rabbinic Judaism and Early Christianity* (Uppsala 1961), trans. by Eric J. Sharpe [Acta Seminarii Neotestamentici Upsaliensis, XXII], p. 21-189.

of Israel, where he became chief lecturer at one of the leading academies, and was called "the Babylonian." Otherwise, however, the name does not occur.[1]

Yohanan's[2] father, one may assume, had witnessed much of Herod's reign. Herod, who had hoped to build a realm for the dynasty he founded, allied himself with Rome.[3] Imperial policy at Herod's time was to exert authority through territorial monarchs, petty kings ruling frontier territories still too unruly to receive a Roman viceroy. Later Rome came to govern the protectorates through her own agents, and finally to incorporate the subjugated lands into the normal provincial structure.[4] Thus in Armenia, Cilicia, and other territories on the Parthian frontier, Rome established kings, ethnarchs, and tetrarchs, governing through a friendly, subservient agent in lands where Rome herself did not choose to rule. Honored by Rome with the titles *socius et amicus populi Romani* (associate and friend of the Roman people), and, in the East, *Philo-Romaos* and *Philo-Kaisar* (friend of Rome, friend of

---

[1] F. Brown, S. R. Driver, C. A. Briggs, *Hebrew-English Lexicon* of the Old Testament (Oxford, 1955) s. v. Zakkai. M. Jastrow, *Dictionary of the Talmud Babli*, etc. (New York, 1950), s. v. Zakkai. A. Kohut, ed., *Aruk Completum* (New York, 1955), s. v. Zakh. Cf. also M. Seligsohn, "Zakkai," *Jewish Encyclopedia* (New York, 1906, hereafter – JE), XII, 731; S. E. Lowenstam, "Zakkai," Encyclopedia Mikrait (in Hebrew; Jerusalem, 1954), II, col. 919. Lowenstam suggests that the name is an abbreviation of *zekher*, though he cites the Accadian root *zaku*, pure; the *Aruk* preserves the latter etymology, listing the word under *zakh*. The name Yohanan was also in use in the first commonwealth, cf. *inter alia*, Jer. 40.16, 41.11, II Kings 25.23, etc.

[2] I have mostly dispensed with the honorific "R." or "Rabbi" or "Rabban," because it is anachronistic to employ such titles before the Destruction. Cf. I. Broyde, "Rabbi," *JE*, X, 294. No disrespect is intended, and where the sources use the title, as they almost invariably do in referring to him, I have, of course, followed in literal translation. I do not, on the other hand, use "Ben Zakkai," since this usage was considered disrespectful in Talmudic times, cf. TB Sanhedrin 14 a-b.

[3] Surveys of Herod's reign include the following: Josephus, *Jewish War* and *Jewish Antiquities*, tr. H. Thackeray and R. Marcus (London, 1926 et seq., 7 vols.; hereafter – *War*, *Ant.*; F. M. Abel, *Histoire de la Palestine* (Paris, 1951, 2 vols.); A. H. M. Jones, *Herods of Judaea* (Oxford, 1938); S. Perowne, *The Life and Times of Herod the Great* and *The Later Herods* (Nashville, 1959); E. Schurer, *A History of the Jewish People in the Time of Jesus Christ* (Edinburgh, 1890, 5 vols., hereafter – Schuerer), Division I, vols, 1 & 2; for rather different viewpoints, cf. J. Klausner, *Historia shel HaBayit HaSheni* [History of the Second Temple] (Jerusalem, 1954; 5 vols.; in Hebrew), vol. IV; and A. Schalit, *Hordos HaMelekh, HaIsh u-Pa-alo* [Herod The King, The Man and His Work] (Jerusalem, 1960; in Hebrew).

[4] A. Schalit, *Ha-Shilton Ha-Romai be-Erez Yisrael* [Roman Administration in Palestine] (Jerusalem, 1937; in Hebrew). Cf. also Henri Daniel-Rops, *Jesus and His Times* (New York, 1958), I, 141-151; M. S. Ginsburg, *Rome et la Judee* (Paris, 1928), p. 121.

Caesar), Herod governed efficiently, collecting revenues, contriving
public works to develop vast tracts of land and to eliminate unemployment, and constructing a magnificient temple in Jerusalem. He
built several large cities, fortresses, and palaces, including Herodion
in the south, Sebaste in Samaria, and Caesarea, a seaport in the Sharon.
Herod stabilized political life, which had been in turmoil during the
reign of the last Hasmonean monarchs. Indeed, under him there was
no politics at all, only palace intrigue and slaughter of potentially
dangerous wives, sons, and servants. Most Jews simply could not
participate in public affairs, and retired from the stage of history.
Earlier institutions of political life were either transformed into
instruments of state (such as the high priesthood) or outlawed, or
apparently ignored (like the Sanhedrin). During Herod's reign, the
commercial economy likewise entered the hands of Hellenist and
Roman businessmen, *pragmateuontes*, who were money lenders. Official
culture also came more and more under Hellenistic domination, as
court history was written in Greek by able Syrians, and the Temple cult
was managed by agents of the monarchy, men who purchased the high
priesthood at a price, held it at the king's pleasure, and handed it on
in the accepted Greek manner, enriched by the priestly dues, to the
next appointee.[1]

After Herod's death, the people begged for direct Roman government,

> They implored the Romans... to unite their country to Syria and to
> entrust the administration to governors from among themselves. The
> Jews would then show that, calumniated though they now were as
> factious and always at war, they knew how to obey equitable rulers.[2]

The Romans tried to keep Herod's sons in power, but when this
led to further difficulties, they acquiesced, and appointed the first in a
line of procurators, Sulpicius Quirinius. The procurators did not
share Herod's interest in developing the national resources, but were
mainly concerned with the imperial welfare, if not, first of all, with
their own. They lived in Hellenistic Caesarea, went up to Jerusalem
when masses of pilgrims came up to celebrate the festivals, and were
glad to return to the more cosmopolitan capital as soon as possible.
When, in the spring of 66 C.E., one of them, Cestius, did not survive
a bloody ambush on the road back, the revolution began, and procu-

---

[1] G. Allon, "On the History of the High Priesthood at the End of the Second
Commonwealth" (in Hebrew), *Tarbiz*, XIII, 1. f. [Articles in Hebrew are listed by
the English title only, with the journal notation indicating the Hebrew.]
[2] *War* II, 92.

ratorial government ended abruptly as it had begun. The first act of procuratorial government was normally to divide the conquered territory into municipal districts; the second was to take a census, determining the rate at which cities could be expected to contribute to the treasury. Taxes were applied to men, houses, animals, sales, imports, exports (at a moderate rate), and were collected by an efficient bureaucracy.[1]

Besides these taxes, men paid to another sovereignty as well, that which was imposed by the ancestral faith. The Bible had detailed many kinds of priestly dues, Levitical offerings, and animal sacrifices, to support the expensive Temple cult. Under a priestly government, these taxes would certainly have supported a large administration, and perhaps this was the economic rationale for the multitudinous tithes and offerings. If, however, the priests had ceased to rule, they still claimed their dues, and with Roman help got some of them from the majority of Jews, and all of them from the particularly pious. Thus, throughout these years, Jews were paying a two-fold tax, and the extent of civil and religious taxation has been estimated at from thirty to forty per cent of the gross national income, but it was probably considerably lower since the majority of the Jews paid only a small part of the religious imposts.[2]

Roman rule opened the way for adventurous men to undertake vast enterprises in commerce and travel. Many took advantage of the opportunities of the Empire to move to more prosperous lands; and throughout this period, one discovers Jews settling in the most remote corners of the empire. Those who stayed at home benefited from economic stability, and among them, Yohanan ben Zakkai may have profited, for one source records that he was a tradesman,

> One hundred and twenty years he lived. Forty years he spent in business, forty years he studied, and forty years he sustained all Israel.[3]

[1] F. Grant, *Economic Background of the Gospels* (London, 1926), 105; and G. Allon, *Historia shel HaYehudim be-Eretz Yisrael biTekufat HaMishnah ve-HaTalmud* [History of the Jews in the Land of Israel in the Period of the Mishnah and the Talmud] (Tel Aviv, 1954, 2 vols.; hereafter – Allon, Historia), I, 40–42.

[2] Grant, *loc. cit.*, estimates that 30–40% of the gross national income went for secular and sacerdotal taxes. However, the existence of such extraordinary pious groups as the *havurah*, which devoted great effort to paying the proper clerical dues, would indicate that those not so pious were also not so meticulous in paying the biblical dues; and cf. my discussion in "The Fellowship *(Havurah)* in the Second Jewish Commonwealth," *Harvard Theological Review*, LIII, 2, 125-142, and particularly p. 126, note 5.

[3] Bereshit Rabba, 100.24. Midrash Tannaim, ed. D. Hoffman (Berlin, 1909), 226.30. TB Rosh Hashanah 31b, Sanhedrin 42a, Sifre Deut. 357.

Precisely when he was in business, one does not know; this like the circumstance of his birth does not receive illumination even from legend. If, however, he did make his living in some urban trade, he enjoyed the advantage of the stable currency which Rome introduced. The land did not produce precious metals; it had been praised in Scripture for its good wheat, oil, dates, wine, and honey. Without precious metals, however, it had to depend on foreign coinage for most of its currency. The value of the currency depended on external factors; it might be withdrawn, debased without warning, or its purchasing power might diminish in the fluctuation of foreign commodity markets. The Romans, holding the right to make copper, silver, and gold coins,[1] incorporated the land into the advanced economy of the eastern Mediterranean, and made possible the extensive exploitation of the trade opportunities there. Situated on the trade routes to the East and South, the coastal cities, which contained large Jewish minorities, imported new wares for sale in the bazaars and markets of back country towns like Jerusalem. Thus the Jewish economy in the land flourished; Roman peace, Herodian enterprise, the natural endowment of the land, and broad economic opportunities combined to yield an adequate subsistence in a relatively stable economy for a very large population.[2]

Living standards were, nonetheless, modest. Archaeologists have not turned up treasures of gems or rich pottery or furnishings dating from the first century. Life was simple. People ate cheap foods such as salted fish, bread made from low grades of local wheat, grain imported from Egypt, or barley; they drank beer, wine diluted with water, and sweetened their food with honey, and, as today, dates were a staple food. Judah was famed for its date palms, and the palm tree was sometimes engraved on coins as the emblem of the land. Most men lived by farming or petty handicrafts. Contemporary parables borrow the imagery of fishing, agriculture, and petty trade; few related to large-scale commerce, and riches were defined as a longterm food supply, or a good wife. Almost no parables refer to sophisticated problems of government, but many to a majestic, exalted monarch, much magnified from the viewpoint of the mute populace.[3]

---

[1] Cf. M. Narkiss, Matbect Erez Yisrael [Coins of the Land of Israel] (Jerusalem, 1938).

[2] Cf. S. W. Baron, *Social and Religious History of the Jews* (Philadelphia, 1952; 2 vols.; hereafter – Baron), I, 245 f.

[3] Besides the works of Grant and Baron cited above, economic history of the land is discussed in the following: L. Finkelstein, *The Pharisees* (Philadelphia, 1946,

One piece of evidence indicates that Yohanan did know the intricacies of small business: he was well informed about how men falsify weights and measures. In a discussion on what constitutes an object susceptible to uncleanness, that is, an object which has a receptacle, the question arose whether the beam of a balance or leveling rod that contains a secret receptacle to receive false weights was susceptible on that account to uncleanness. So too, was a carrying yoke with a secret receptacle for money, or a stick with a secret place for pearls, considered a legitimate vessel? All of these shady devices were declared capable of becoming unclean, and of all of them Yohanan ben Zakkai was reported to have said,

> Woe is me if I speak, woe is me if I do not. If I speak, I may teach the deceivers, if I do not, the deceivers will say that the scholars do not know about our schemes.[1]

Class divisions were complicated by the regional variations of the

---

2 vols; hereafter – Pharisees), I, 1-43; M. Avi-Yonah, "Trade and Industry in the Land of Israel in the Roman-Byzantine Period," in B. Maisler, et al., *Mishar, Taasiah, ve-Omanut be-Erez Yisrael* [Commerce, Industry, and Crafts in the Land of Israel] (Jerusalem, 1937), p. 85 f.; J. Klausner, *Bemei Bayit Sheni* [In the Days of the Second Temple] (Jerusalem, 1964), p. 82 f., and Jesus of Nazareth (New York, 1953, tr. H. Danby), p. 173 f.; M. Rostovtzeff, *Social and Economic History of the Roman Empire* (Oxford, 1926), pp. 248-249 notes that the so-called cities of Judea were purely religious and administrative centers, "chefs lieux of rural districts," and that the land was mainly agricultural throughout this period.

[1] Kohelet Rabbah 6.1. The expression was cited in several instances, cf. also TB Baba Batra 89b, "One must not make a measure press that is thick on the one side and thin on the other, nor should he press with one movement, for he would harm the seller and benefit the buyer, nor should he smooth little by little, for he would harm the buyer and benefit the seller. On all these, Rabban Yohanan ben Zakkai said, "Woe is me if I say, woe is me if I do not say. If I speak, the deceivers may learn from me, if I do not speak the deceivers will say, the scholars are unfamiliar with our devices." Cf. also Mishnah Kelim 17.16 (Tr. H. Danby, Oxford, 1933; citations to the Mishnah mainly follow Canon Danby's translation), "A beam of a balance or a levelling rod... [as in Koh. R.], or a beggar's cane that has a receptacle for water, or a stick that has a receptacle for a mezuzah and for pearls – these are susceptible to uncleanness. And of all these, Rabban Johanan ben Zakkai said, "Woe is me if I speak of them, and woe is me if I speak not of them." Cf. also Tosefta Kelim Baba Metziah 7.9, "... are not unclean unless they are used for such a purpose, and of all of them Rabban Yohanan ben Zakkai said, "Woe is me if I say it, and woe is me if I do not say it; if I say it, now I am teaching and deceivers to deceive, if I do not say it now, I hold back the learning, and I shall make unclean the cleannesses; another matter, that the deceivers should not say, the sages are not well informed about their deeds." Cf. also Y. N. Epstein, *Mevo-ot le-Sifrut HaTannaim*, pp. 132, 236, 401. Epstein (p. 401) suggests that Yohanan ben Zakkai "arranged" a collection of mishnaiot (for his students), citing also Mishnah Kelim 2.2, in which an opinion of Yohanan ben Zakkai is also included.

land.[1] Jerusalem, "navel of the universe," was the metropolis of the Jews; its populace included a significant number of wealthy men, both absentee landlords and great merchants, as well as many priests who lived on the priestly dues and Temple endowments, and performed the cultic rites, the city's chief industry. The city also contained a smaller class of Levites, who performed certain non-sacrificial tasks in the sanctuary, provided music in the services, and managed the buildings, as well as artisans whose skills were indispensable in the building and maintenance of the Temple, petty traders, a large urban proletariat, and unskilled laborers. The lower classes were mainly very poor, but after the educational reforms of the first century B.C.E., many of them received an education in the main disciplines of Jewish tradition. This education, centering on religious learning, was sufficiently broad to impart civilizing and humanizing lessons. Jerusalemites tended to separate themselves from the Judean provincials for both social and ritual reasons. Living in close proximity to the sanctuary, the men of the city were more concerned to observe the requirements of ritual cleanness which residence in the holy place imposed than the provincials, who purified themselves mainly for the festal pilgrimages.[2] The provincials did not often have the benefit of education, and the animosities between urban and rural residents were complex. The provincials themselves were by no means united. The country gentry, landowners holding considerable property in the lowland, had less in common with their highland neighbors than with the urban upper bourgeoisie. On the other hand, the rural yeomen and proletariat formed submerged classes, divorced from the main issues of national life. They welcomed the ministry of powerful personalities, sometimes sages empowered by learning, but more often wonderworkers able to heal mind and body. Jericho and the Southern Plain were the main centers of the rural gentility, and the rocky Judean hills, of the rural yeomen and proletariat. In the Galilee, likewise, class divisions between wealthier and poorer peasants were manifest. Hundreds of rural villages, large and small, clustered in the fertile hills and valleys of then orth; but only Sepphoris and Tiberias were large urban centers, and they did not dominate the province as Jerusalem did Judah.[3]

---

[1] Finkelstein, *Pharisees*, I, 1-43, especially the chart on pp. 4-5.

[2] *Ibid.*, 26-27. Note also the attitude of Eliezer ben Hyrkanos' father, for example, who said his son did not require an education; and the antagonism of Akiba ben Joseph in his earlier years to the urban men of learning, TB Pesahim 49b.

[3] Cf. the extended analysis of Finkelstein, *Pharisees;* and the specific criticism

The main social and religious events of this period held little interest for contemporary historians. Josephus, for one, paid very little attention in his rich narrative of politics and war to the inner life of Israel. In truth his histories provide evidence that the masses of men had turned away from public affairs. They may have responded to changes in their political situation; they may have felt growing impatience with social inequity or with the alien government, whose benefits were not obvious to them. Only in the riots and continuous unrest toward the end of this period, however, does such a response become entirely evident. Some, however, did indicate their disapproval of the course of events by withdrawing from the common society; a few became hermits, or fled to other lands, or entered monastic communities in which contact with the outside world was minimal. Thus, for instance, the men who settled in the Qumran commune ordained,

> This is the regulation for the men of the commune, who devote themselves to turn away from all evil, and to hold fast to all that he has commanded as his will, to separate themselves from the congregation of men of iniquity to be a commune in Torah and property.[1]

---

leveled by G. Allon, "Sociological Interpretation of Halakhah," in *Mehkarim be-Toldot Yisrael* [Essays in Jewish History] (Tel Aviv, 1954, 2 vols., In Hebrew; henceforth – Allon, *Mehkarim*), II, 181 f.; and I. Sonne, "Schools of Shammai and Hillel seen from Within," *Louis Ginzberg Jubilee Volume* (English section, New York, 1945), 275 f. Cf. also L. Ginzberg, "The Significance of the Halakhah for Jewish History," *On Jewish Law and Lore* (Philadelphia, 1945), 77 f. The imputation of social or economic motives where the sources are not explicitly so concerned is certainly open to question; consistency in the matter is impossible. Many decisions, as Sonne and others point out, were necessitated by the exigencies of midrash, or by conscious decision on juridical consistency, rather than by social or economic concern. Also, as I have noted, one must be cautious indeed in reducing "religious" matters to economic or social motivation. Still, I have followed Finkelstein in specific cases, where I do not think one can find a more cogent explanation than his.

[1] Manual of Discipline 5.1. On the sects, cf. *inter alia*, Josephus, Life, 2; Antiquities, Books XIII and XVIII; War II 119-166; Philo, *That Every Good Man Is Free*, XII; Pliny, *Natural History*, V. 17, 73; and the relevant passages in the Gospels of Matthew, Mark, and Luke. The most convenient edition of the relevant Qumran literature is A. M. Haberman, *Megillot Midbar Yehudah* (Tel Aviv, 1959, in Hebrew); on relevant rabbinic sources, cf. S. Lieberman, "Discipline in the so-called Dead Sea Manual of Discipline," *Journal of Biblical Literature* (henceforth – JBL), LI, 199 f.; and "Light on the Cave Scrolls from Rabbinic Sources," *Proceedings of the American Academy for Jewish Research* (henceforth – PAAJR), XX, 395 f. The secondary literature is enormous, the most convenient surveys on the Qumran discoveries being M. Burrows, *Dead Sea Scrolls* (New York, 1955) and *More Light on the Dead Sea Scrolls* (New York, 1958) and J. T. Milik, *Ten Years of Discovery in the Wilderness of Judaea* (London, 1959), all of which provide extensive bibliography. On the Pharisees, there are three particularly complete bibliographies: R. Marcus, " A

Likewise the psalmist of their commune prayed,

> Only as you draw a man near will I love him,
> And as you keep him far away, so will I abominate him...[1]

The members of the wilderness communes described by Josephus as Essenes likewise avoided the settled society of town and city, "because of the iniquities which have become inveterate among city dwellers, for they know that their company would have a deadly effect upon their own souls."[2] The communards sanctified themselves by meticulous observance of the rules of ritual purity, and tried to found such a society as they thought worthy of receiving God's approval.

Other men, called Pharisees, who also believed that all was not in order with society, chose another way. They remained within the common society, in accordance with the teaching of Hillel, "Do not separate yourself from the community."[3] The Pharisaic community thought to rebuild society on its own ruins, and with its own mortar and brick. They differed among themselves on many questions. Some, called Zealots, accepted their interpretation of tradition, but thought to restore the fortune of Israel through political action,[4] while others focused their efforts on the spiritual reform of the nation. The Pharisees actively fostered their opinions on tradition and religion among the whole people, and, according to Josephus

> ...they are able greatly to persuade the body of the people; and whatsoever they do about divine worship, prayers, and sacrifices, they perform according to their direction; insomuch that the cities give great attestations to them on account of their entire virtuous conduct, both in the actions of their lives and their discourses also.[5]

Selected Bibliography (1920-1945) of the Jews in the Hellenistic-Roman Period," PAAJR, XI, 97 f.; Finkelstein, *Pharisees*, II, 711 f.; and E. Schuerer, *Geschichte des jüdischen Volkes im Zeitalter Jesu Christi* (4th ed., Leipzig, 1907), 447 f. For discussion of the parallels between the Qumran community and the Havurah, cf. C. Rabin, *Qumran Studies* (Oxford, 1956), pp. 1-21. The sociological comparison of the *havurah* and *yahad* suggested in the following paragraphs is based on my "Qumran and Jerusalem, Two Jewish Roads to Utopia," *Journal of Bible and Religion*, XXIII, 284-290.

[1] Thansgiving Scroll, 14.20-21.

[2] Philo, *That Every Good Man Is Free*, XII, 76.

[3] Avot 1.5.

[4] On the Zealot group, cf. C. Roth, *Historical Background of the Dead Sea Scrolls* (Oxford, 1958); "Simon bar Giora, Ancient Jewish Hero," *Commentary*, XXIX, 52 f.; "The Zealots, a Jewish Religious Sect," *Judaism*, VIII, 33 f.; and "The Zealots in the War of 66-73," *Journal of Semitic Studies*, IV, 332 f. Cf. also W. R. Farmer, *Maccabees, Zealots, and Josephus, An Inquiry into Jewish Nationalism in the Greco-Roman Period*, New York, 1956.

[5] *Antiquities*, 18.1.3.

Though Josephus appears to exaggerate,[1] the Pharisees certainly exerted considerable influence in the religion of Israel.

Among the larger group of men sympathetic to the Pharisaic cause, a smaller number entered into an urban religious communion with one another, through a largely unorganized society known as the fellowship" *(havurah)*. The foundation of this society was meticulous observance of laws of tithing and other priestly dues, and ritual purity even outside the sacerdotal rites; thus the members undertook to eat even profane foods (not sacred tithes or other offerings) in a state of levitical cleanness. These rules tended to set apart the members of the fellowship as a social entity, for they limited commensality and other kinds of social intercourse. Thus the fellows mediated between the obligation to remain within the common society, and the equally important precepts on religious observance. By keeping the rules of purity, the fellow was separated from the common man; but by remaining within the towns and cities of the land, he preserved the possibility of teaching others by example. Thus within the common life, the fellowship formed a separate, if inchoate, society. The fellows lived among, but not with, the people of the land. With neither formal structure nor officers and by-laws, as at Qumram, the fellowship represented the polity of groups of people who recognized one another as part of the same community of observant and pious men. They formed a new, if limited, society within the old. They were men who kept what they held to be the faith in the company of others who did not.

Upper class opinion coalesced in the viewpoint of still another group, the Sadducees, who stood for strict adherence to the written word in religious matters, and conservatism in both ritual and belief. They differed from the Pharisees especially on the doctrine of revelation. They acknowledged Scripture as the only authority, and denied that its meaning might be elucidated by ancient traditions or modern devices of exegesis and scholarship. The Pharisees claimed that Scripture and the traditional interpretation were one; to the Sadducees, such a claim of unity was spurious, and masked innovation. They differed also on the eternity of the soul; the Pharisees believed in the survival of the soul, the revival of the body, the day of judgment, and

---

[1] Yohanan's disputes with the Temple authorities (chapter three) indicate that some cultic practices did not meet his satisfaction. Cf. also M. Smith, "Palestinian Judaism in the First Century," M. Davis, ed., *Israel, Its Role in Civilization* (New York, 1956), 67-81. See also Chapter Eight.

life in the world to come; the Sadducees found nothing in Scripture which, to their way of thinking, supported such doctrines. They ridiculed both these ideas and the exegesis which made them possible. They won over the main body of officiating priests and wealthier men, but with the destruction of the Temple, their ranks were decimated, and very little literature remained to preserve their viewpoint. It is difficult indeed to compare them to the other sects; they may have manifested no such social institution as the Pharisaic and Essene groups at all. In their day, however, they claimed to be the legitimate heirs of Israel's faith, and holding positions of power and authority in the land, they succeeded in leaving so deep an impression on society that even their Pharisaic, Essenic, and (later) Christian opponents did not wholly wipe out their memory.[1]

While the several groups do not present common grounds for close comparison they do appear to have gained support mainly from particular social classes, the Sadducees, as noted, from upper class landholders and merchants; the Pharisees from the middle and lower urban classes; the Essenes from the disaffected of the same classes.[2] These class and sectarian divisions manifested a vigorous inner polity, with politics revolving about issues peculiarly Jewish, such as matters of exegesis, law, and doctrine. The vitality of Israel would have astonished the Roman administration, and did, when it burst forth.

A peculiar circumstance of Roman imperial policy facilitated the growth of such vigorous inner life, and permitted the development of non-political institutions to express it. Roman law respected Jewish rights to limited self-government. The people was governed by its own law, and its quarrels were adjusted by its own judges.[3] Rome had particular and clearly defined purposes for the empire, and its policies could be adequately effected without totalitarian interference into the inner affairs of the conquered peoples. The same indifference to local sensitivities that permitted a procurator to bring his military standards into a city pure of graven images likewise encouraged him to ignore territorial affairs of considerable weight. Thus the national tribunal, called variously the Sanhedrin (council) and High Court, acted with a

---

[1] Cf. G. F. Moore, *Judaism* (Cambridge, 1954, 3 vols.), I, 68-70, S. W. Baron, *History*, I, 271-275. For bibliography on the Sadducees, cf. the works cited by Finkelstein and Marcus, p. 11 n. 1

[2] R. Marcus, "Pharisees, Essenes, and Gnostics," *Journal of Biblical Literature* (hereafter – JBL), LXXIII (1937), 157-161.

[3] Baron, *History*, I, 245 f. Cf. also J. Juster, *Les Juifs dans l'Empire Romain* (Paris, 1914, 2 vols.) on the civil position of Jews and Judaism in the Roman Empire.

measure of freedom to determine internal policy in religion, ritual, cult, and law. While the tribunal probably lost authority to inflict capital punishment, it is generally assumed, shortly after Judah became a part of the Syrian provincial administration (whether in fact it had exerted such authority earlier in Herod's reign is not entirely clear), the court allegedly maintained the right to direct Temple affairs, to adjudicate matters of civil and commercial law and torts, to define family status and marriage procedure, to apply the biblical levies, and to determine the sacred calendar. The tribunal thus represented the one abiding institutional expression of Israel's inner autonomy during the procuratorial regime. Its history has by no means been recovered completely, and many details remain unsettled. It is clear, however, that both the Pharisees and Sadducees took an active interest in the religious, social, and economic administration of Israel's life; that the Sanhedrin provided a means to express these interests, and that the leaders of both major viewpoints played a considerable part in its autonomous affairs.[1] One of the Pharisaic leaders, in many ways the most important, was Hillel the Elder, who, with his colleague Shammai, received the "Torah" from Shemaiah and Avtalion, and handed it on, according to the Pharisaic chain of tradition, to Yohanan ben Zakkai.[2]

---

[1] Extensive bibliography on the problem of the Sanhedrin is provided by S. Hoenig, *The Great Sanhedrin* (Philadelphia, 1953; hereafter – Hoenig, Sanhedrin), 217 f. Hoenig also summarizes relevant sources, and many theories on the subject. Cf. also, C. Tchernowitz, *Toldot HaHalakhah* (History of Jewish Law, New York, 1945), IV, 217-276. Also, Hugo Mantel, *Studies in the History of the Sanhedrin* (Cambridge, 1962).

[2] For an analysis of the chain of Pharisaic tradition relating to Yohanan ben Zakkai, cf. L. Finkelstein, *Mavo Le-Massekhet Avot de Rabbi Natan* (New York, 1950; hereafter, Finkelstein, *Mavo*), p. 38 f.

CHAPTER TWO

FILLING THEIR TREASURIES...

"Rabban Yohanan ben Zakkai took over from Hillel and Shammai."[1]
He received from the earlier leaders of the Pharisees, and transmitted
to his disciples and thence to posterity, a religious tradition concerning
God, the world, and man. This tradition held that God had created
the world, cared for what happened in it, had therefore told man his
will, demanded that man obey it, and had an ultimate purpose for
human history which man might discern. Scripture was the vehicle for
transmitting his will and plan, and together with ancient traditions
about its meaning, was the source of all instruction.[2] Scriptural concerns
extended to every aspect of the life of a "kingdom of priests and holy
nation," and Pharisaism interested itself in affairs today regarded as
secular.[3] Thus the Pharisees proposed policies to guide political action,
and social, economic, and ritual affairs. Viewed in their social setting,
the Pharisees represented one among competing sects, for their coalition included only part of the nation, but their doctrines and breadth of
interests applied to national and, in some ways, universal questions.

Before the destruction of Jerusalem, the Pharisees apparently did
not, however, administer more than their own sectarian affairs. They
did so through a central institution, a kind of central committee on
which the chief sages held places.[4] The institution is said to have united
the chief factions among the Pharisees, the substantially bourgeois
element and the mainly proletarian.[5] At the turn of the first century,

---

[1] Avot 2.9. Cf. Finkelstein, *Mavo*, 39-44.

[2] The content of ancient Jewish faith in the Tannaitic period has been subject of
many comprehensive studies. Cf. the following, together with their bibliographies:
J. Bonsireen, *Le Judaisme Palestinien au Tempes de Jesus Christ* (Paris, 1934, 2 vols.);
G. F. Moore, *Judaism in the First Centuries of the Christian Era* (Cambridge, 1954,
3 vols.); S. Schechter, *Some Aspects of Rabbinic Theology* (New York, 1936); M.
Kadushin, *The Rabbinic Mind* (New York, 1952); and L. Finkelstein, *Pharisees*, I,
145-442; II, 443-627.

[3] G. Allon, "The Attitude of the Pharisees toward Roman and Herodian Rule
Mehkarim, I, 26-30.

[4] L. Finkelstein, *HaPerushim ve-Anshe Kenesset HaGedolah* (New York, 1950; in
Hebrew; henceforth – Finkelstein, *Perushim*) *passim*. I have not entered into the
question of the Pharisaic institutions, which is (for my purposes) peripheral to the
life of Yohanan ben Zakkai. Cf. also Hoenig, *Sanhedrin*, 1-121, *pass.*

[5] Finkelstein, *Perushim*, 16-39. Cf. also L. Finkelstein, *Akiba* (New York, 1936),
294-299.

Hillel and Shammai stood at the head of the Pharisaic Sanhedrin. After the death of Hillel, his son Gamaliel I succeeded him.[1] Simeon ben Gamaliel and Yohanan ben Zakkai apparently succeeded him, possibly two decades[2] before the rebellion of 66-70 C.E.[3]

Shammai left relatively few sayings, and on the whole did not receive a good press in the traditions, which were mainly written by disciples of Hillel's followers. Thus Shammai was remembered for his petulance and was presented as foil to the implacably patient Hillel. We are told that Hillel was blessed by a convert,

> May all the blessings of the Torah rest on thy head! For hadst thou been like Shammai the Elder, I might never have entered the community of Israel. The impatience of Shammai the Elder well nigh caused me to perish in this world and in the world to come. Thy patience has brought me to the life of this world and of the world to come.[4]

While Yohanan was supposed to have succeeded Shammai as well as Hillel, he probably did not study with him. Shammai left only three identifiable Scriptural exegeses, which do not exhibit a characteristic

---

[1] The only evidence (TB Shabbat 15a) that Hillel had a son Simeon is not corroborated elsewhere; I have treated Gamaliel I as Hillel's son and not grandson.

[2] Finkelstein (*Akiba*, p. 298) provides the following table:

Nasi (President)	*Av Bet Din* (vice president)
20 B.C.E. – 20 C.E. Hillel	Menahem
	Shammai
20-50 C.E. Gamaliel I	(Associateship offered to
	Akavyah ben Mehalalel)
50-70 C.E. Simeon ben Gamaliel	Yohanan ben Zakkai.

[3] I cannot date these events with any degree of close accuracy, but do suggest the sequence of Yohanan's life on the basis of the little evidence available. The only certain date is 70 C.E., by which time Yohanan was certainly at Yavneh. On the specific position of Rabban Yohanan ben Zakkai in the Jewish autonomous institutions of first century Jerusalem, see especially H. Mantel, *Studies in the History of the Sanhedrin* (Cambridge 1962), p. 28-35, "R. Johanan b. Zakkai and the Title *Nasi*". I do not think that the evidence on R. Yohanan's debates with the Sadducees is sufficiently contemporary or internally so consistent as to permit Mantel's conclusion that "he was appointed the presiding officer of the Priestly Bet Din when it became Pharisaic." First of all, it is by no means certain that he was a *kohen* at all. Second, the evidence does not support the conclusion that the "Priestly Bet Din" was ever in the hands of the Pharisees before 70 C.E. The reports on the "Water of Ordeals" and the "eglah ha-arufah" may indicate, as Epstein points out, merely a record of actions taken by others. As to the putative title "Rosh Bet Din" which Mantel thinks R. Yohanan held, the only evidence he cites, namely, the Mishnah Rosh Hashanah 2.7, does not indicate this as an official title at this time.

[4] Avot de Rabbi Natan, Text A (ed. S. Schechter, New York, 1945; hereafter – ARNa), ch. 15, p. 31a Tr. J. Goldin, *The Fathers According to Rabbi Nathan* (N.H., 1955), pp. 81-82. All translations of ARNa are Goldin's, and will be designated by page in his translation.

method or viewpoint. The only common element one can discern in the teachings of Shammai and Yohanan is a superficial similarity of emphasis on cheerfulness and study of Torah, common to all the sages at this period. Thus Shammai said, "Fix a period for thy study of the Torah. Say little and do much, and receive all men with a cheerful countenance," and Yohanan taught likewise.[1]

Tradition claims explicitly that Hillel was Yohanan's teacher. Hillel had "come up' from Babylon about the last third of the first century B.C.E., and died in Jerusalem during the first quarter of the first century C.E. He taught a methodology of interpreting Scripture which revolutionized, in time, the intellectual life of Pharisaism. These principles, known to exegetes of Greek classic texts as well, included the following: 1. Inference *a minori ad majus;* 2. Inference by analogy; 3. Constructing a family on the basis of one passage (extending a specific regulation of one biblical passage to a number of passages); 4. The same rule as the preceding, constructing a family on the basis of two biblical passages; 5. The General and the Particular, the Particular and the General; 6. Exposition by means of another, similar passage; 7. Deduction from the context.[2] These principles, which extended the potentialities of the given text, made possible a broad construction of Scripture. One can, indeed, hardly overestimate the importance of this method of study. Criticism today commonly uses the systematic principles of analogy, inference, association, and deduction. Before such principles became available, however, men were

> like primitive chemists deprived of catalytic agents. Phenomena surrounded them, but they suggested nothing new. Facts existed, but

---

[1] Avot 1.15. Cf. J. Bruell, *Mavo LaMishnah* [Introduction to the Mishnah] (Frankfurt a.M., 1976; in Hebrew; hereafter – Bruell, *Mavo*), 33-39; Z. Frankel, *Darkhe HaMishnah* [The Ways of the Mishnah] (Tel Aviv, 1960; in Hebrew; hereafter – Frankel, *Mishnah*), 39-41; W. Bacher, *Agadot HaTannaim* [Legends of the Tannaim] (Berlin, 1924; in Hebrew; hereafter – Bacher, *Agadot*), I, i, 9-11. Bacher discusses the exegesis of Shammai. Parallel teachings of Yohanan ben Zakkai will be discussed below. Sources on Shammai will be found in the following: TB Shabbat 14b, 15a, 17a, 19a, 30b, 31a; Bezah 16a, 20a; Hagigah 16a; Yoma 77b; Sukkah 28a; b; Yevamot 15a; Gittin 57a; Kiddushin 43a; Sotah 47b; Nazir 52b; Baba Batza 133b; Sanhedrin 88b; Avodah Zara 36a, 39b; Hullin 36b, 107b; Niddah 2a, b, 3a, b, 4a, b, 15a; Palestinian Talmud (hereafter – TP) Maaser Sheni 2.2, 2.3; Orlah 2.3; Shabbat 1.4; Pesahim 1.6; Sukkah 2.9; Hagigah 2.2; Ketuvot 8.11; Nadarim 5.6; Niddah 1.1. Cf. J. Umansky, *Hokhme HaTalmud* [Sages of the Talmud] (Jerusalem, 1949; in Hebrew) and *Hokhme HaYerushalmi* [Sages of the Palestinian Talmud] (Jerusalem, 1952, in Hebrew), s.v. (hereafter – Umansky, *Talmud;* and Umansky, *Yerushalmi*).

[2] S. Lieberman, *Hellenism in Jewish Palestine* (New York, 1950), 53-54.

were incapable of reproducing anything surpassing themselves. Hillel recognized that tradition by itself was insufficient... Its components had to be united... so that men would not be helpless when history was silent and they were left to their own resources.[1]

As head of the Pharisees, Hillel promulgated a series of emergency ordinances *(takkanot)* to meet the crises of his time. (The device of issuing such decrees was also employed by Gamaliel I and by Yohanan ben Zakkai.) One such decree was his circumvention of the effect of the Sabbatical year on outstanding loans. This law (Deut. 15.2) had commanded that in the seventh year of the septennial cycle, all outstanding loans and other debts were automatically annulled. Originally a protection for the debtor, the law apparently intended to prevent his becoming burdened with an endlessly multiplying debt, by limiting the tenure of financial obligation. Its effect by the time of Hillel had been to limit the availability of loans in the final years of the cycle; the poor could not, therefore, obtain the loans absolutely necessary for subsistence in the seasonal agricultural economy. Hillel enacted a legal instrument called *prozbul*, by which the lender gave into the hands of a court, to which the biblical injunction did not apply, the record of all his loans. The loans were then not annulled by the seventh year. A second such ordinance dealt with the biblical decree that houses sold in ancient cities might be reclaimed by their original owners within a year of the sale, by restoring the purchase price. The new owners resorted to a ruse, hiding out during the end of the period of grace so that the seller could not return their money. Hillel decreed that the court might act in behalf of the original owner even in the absence of the purchaser. He thus showed himself keenly aware of the interplay between law and social order.[2]

---

[1] On the life and work of Hillel, cf. J. Goldin, "Hillel the Elder," *Journal of Religion*, XXVI, 263 f. Quotation is on pp. 268-9. Cf. also N. N. Glatzer, *Hillel the Elder, The Emergence of Classical Judaism* (New York, 1957); C. Tchernowitz, *Toldot HaHalakhah*, IV, 197-214; W. Bacher, *Agadot*, I, i, 1. On Hillel's exegesis, cf. D. Daube, "Rabbinic Methods of Interpretation and Hellenistic Rhetoric," *Hebrew Union College Annual*, XXII, 239 f., and the same author's "Alexandrian Methods of Interpretation and the Rabbis," *Festschrift Hans Lewald* (Basel, 1954), p. 27 f.; and S. Lieberman, *Hellenism*, pp. 47-82. Biographies of Hillel also include, *inter alia*, W. Bacher, "Hillel," *JE*, VI, 397-401; A. Kaminka, "Hillel's Life and Work," *Jewish Quarterly Review* (hereafter – JQR), n.s. XXX, 107 f.; Frankel, Mishnah, 39-42; Bruell, *Mavo*, 31-39.

[2] Cf. Mishnah Shevi-it 10.3; Arakhin 9.4, and parallels. Cf. also Goldin, "Hillel the Elder," 277 and n. 105. For further sources on Hillel, Hillel the Elder, and Hillel the Babylonian, cf. Umansky, *Talmud*, 66; and Umansky, *Yerushalmi*, 45. On the enactments cf. also M. Bloch, *Die Institutionen des Judenthums* (Budapest, 1905, 3 vols.; in Hebrew), II, 92-118.

If, as tradition alleged, Yohanan studied with Hillel, one understands certain salient qualities which characterized both men. It would have been from Hillel that Yohanan acquired his dedication to the ideal of peace,[1] for Hillel had said, "Be of the disciples of Aaron, loving peace, pursuing peace, loving mankind, and drawing all men to Torah."[2] From Hillel Yohanan would have learned, second, that the sage has the responsibility to concern himself with pressing social problems. Moreover, Hillel had laid the foundation for his public career through many decades of study, and Yohanan did likewise.[3] He also would have learned the usefulness of the special decree, as we have seen, to deal with a crisis, for he decreed changes in law which were far more substantial than the social ordinances of Hillel. He struck out provisions of the Temple cult which men believed were of Mosaic origin, and took into account by further enactments the profound transformation of the liturgical life after the destruction the Temple.[4] Hillel had taught, "One who does not study deserves to die," and Yohanan said that man was created on condition that he study Torah.[5] Hillel admonished, "Do not trust yourself until the day you die," and both Yohanan and his student Eliezer ben Hyrkanos developed this idea in their parables.[6] Of both Hillel and Yohanan, fabulous feats of learning were reported, and to both, a life span of one hundred twenty years was ascribed.[7] Finally, Hillel's teaching "In a place where there is no man, strive to be a man" epitomized Yohanan's conduct during the revolution and afterward.[8]

Hillel was said to have had eighty students, the eldest of whom was Jonathan ben Uzziel, and the youngest, Yohanan ben Zakkai.[9] Jonathan mastered mystical lore, and it was reported that when he would sit and study Torah, birds flying overhead would be burned up [in the heat of his concentration].[10] He also translated the prophetic books of the Bible into Aramaic, but his work has not survived. He

---

[1] Parallel teachings of Yohanan ben Zakkai will be cited below.

[2] Avot 1.12. Compare Yohanan's teachings in Tosefta Baba Kama 7.3, Mekhilta BaHodesh 1; TB Berakhot 17a, etc.

[3] Cf. p. 23-25.

[4] Cf. chapters three and eight.

[5] Avot 1.13, 2.9.

[6] Chapter five.

[7] Cf. below.

[8] Avot 2.7, cf. also Soferim, ch. 8 (ed. M. Higger, New York, 1937).

[9] Cf. note 23.

[10] TB Megillah 3a. Cf. Chapter Five, on reports of Yohanan's mystical speculations. Cf. also TB Sukkah 28a, TB Baba Batra 134b, TP Nedarim 5.6, all of which are cited below.

was however, evidently criticized, for a heavenly voice was heard to proclaim, "Who is this that reveals the Lord's secrets to man?" Jonathan answered,

It is I who have revealed God's secrets to man, but I have not done this for my own honor, nor for that of my father's house, but for the honor of God, that dissension may not increase in Israel.

By translating and explicating prophecy, Jonathan apparently had hoped to win a consensus of opinion on the meaning of crucial texts. He intended to translate the Writings as well, but another voice went forth and shouted, "Enough!" With his disciples, Yohanan carried on the tradition of theosophic speculation.

Hillel and Shammai gave their names to two schools of thought within Pharisaism, the school of Hillel and the school of Shammai.[1] Three hundred and sixteen controversies between the two schools were recorded, with the Shammaites on the strict side in all but fifty-five of them. The debates covered ritual and legal questions; but one, at least, reflected on a more fundamental question, whether it was good that man had been created, or whether it might have been better if he had been left uncreated. The schools spent "two and one half years on the question." The Hillelites argued the affirmative, the Shammaites, the negative; they finally agreed that it would have been better if man had not been made, but once he has been created, he ought to watch his actions.[2] Of the students of Shammai, only three are known by name, Baba ben Butah, Dositai of Kefar Yatma, and Zadok; the second is mentioned only once and the third always ruled according to the Hillelite opinion. Baba ben Butah was remembered for his extraordinary piety; he was said to have brought a suspended sin offering to the Temple every day of the year except for the day of atonement, to expiate any guilt he might unknowingly have incurred.[3]

---

[1] It is difficult to filter out the words of the so-called schools of Hillel and Shammai, since these titles sometimes represent the opinions of Yohanan's students, Joshua ben Hananiah and Eliezer ben Hyrkanos. Cf. J. N. Epstein, *Mavo*, 59-70; S. Mendelsohn, "Bet Hillel and Bet Shammai," *JE*, III, 115-6; J. H. Weiss, *Dor Dor ve-Dorshav* [Generations and their Exegetes] (Vilna, 1904; 5 vols.; in Hebrew; hereafter – Weiss, *Dor*), I, 167-176; W. Bacher, *Agadot*, I, i, 8-16; Frankel, *Mishnah*, 47-9; Bruell, *Mavo*, 43-49; Schwarz, *Die Controversen der Shammaiten und Hilleliten* (Carlsruh, 1893); Tchernowitz, *Toldot*, IV, 277-340; A. Geiger, *HaMikra ve-Targumav* [Scripture and its translations] (Jerusalem, 1949; translated into Hebrew from A. Geiger, *Urschrift und Übersetzungen der Bible in ihrer Abhängigkeit von der inner Entwicklung des Judentums*, by Y. Barukh; hereafter – Geiger, *Mikra*), pp. 150-1 (on Shammaites); 77, 93, 98, 106, 117 (on Hillel).

[2] TB Eruvin 13b. Cf. alternate readings.

[3] TB Baba Batra 4a.

Yohanan's early education was supposedly in the school of Hillel. This tradition poses chronological difficulty, however, and has, therefore, been rejected by students of the period.[1] It is generally assumed that Hillel died in 10 C.E., because it is said that Hillel, Simon his son, Gamaliel I his grandson, and Simon ben Gamaliel his great grandson, occupied the presidency of the high court for a century before the destruction (that is, from 30 B.C.E. to 70 C.E.).[2] Another source states that Hillel spent forty years as president of the Sanhedrin (in a lifespan of one hundred twenty years), that is, from 30 B.C.E. to 10 C.E.[3] It is argued that Yohanan could not possibly have studied with Hillel, because he would have been too young. If Yohanan died sometime after the destruction in 70 C.E., possibly a decade or more, then he would have been only ten years old when Hillel died, assuming that he lived to the age of eighty. The traditional chronology solved this problem by assuming that Yohanan also lived one hundred twenty years.[4] He could, therefore, have been born at about 45 B.C.E., have spent forty years in business, until 5 B.C.E., studied with Hillel for fifteen years, from 5 B.C.E. to 10 C.E., and continued his studies another twenty-five years, to 35 C.E., and then "sustained all Israel" from 35 C.E. to his death in 75 C.E.[5] Even if one believed that men achieved such longevity, the tradition on Yohanan's education with Hillel states explicitly that he was the youngest of all of Hillel's students, which, at age forty through fifty-five, would suggest that Hillel's school was a kind of old-people's home.

On the other hand, those who deny that Yohanan studied with Hillel would apparently be prepared to grant at the same time the historicity, even to the point of arithmetical precision, of other equally unlikely traditions.[6] They would admit by implication, for example, that both the tradition enumerating the terms of Hillel's dynasty in the Pharisaic presidency, and that which sets out the astonishing life span of Hillel himself, are both entirely historical. The same source which says that Hillel lived one hundred twenty years says that Yohanan ben Zakkai did too, and it is hardly rigorous thinking to admit the one

---

[1] Cf. for example J. Derenbourg, *Essai sur l'histoire et la Geographie de la Palestine* (Paris, 1867; hereafter – Derenbourg, *Histoire*), 276. Compare G. Allon, Toldot, I, 54.

[2] TB Shabbat 15a.

[3] Sifre Deut. 357. Cf. below 36 for parallels.

[4] Sifre Deut. 357.

[5] This is one possible projection of the traditional chronology.

[6] Cf. Derenbourg, *Histoire, loc. cit.*

and deny the other. Assuming, on the contrary, that no one lived one hundred twenty years (although, Josephus related, some of the Essenes "live to a great age, most of them to upwards of a century, in consequence, I imagine, of the simplicity and regularity of their mode of life..."[1]), one may well assume, as we have, that Yohanan ben Zakkai was born about the beginning of the first century C.E. He was certainly a very old man at the time of the revolution, for when he was spirited out of Jerusalem on a bier, the city guards were prepared to believe that he had died a natural death. If Hillel for his part died at about 20 C.E., he might well have taught Yohanan when he was a very very old man, and Yohanan a youth, the two conditions stated explicitly by the tradition (below) on their meeting.

The absolute *terminus ad quem* of Hillel's life appears to be in the twenties of the first century, when his son began to preside over the Pharisaic academy. This much becomes clear from the evidence of the apostle Paul, who stated, "I am a Jew, born at Tarsus... but brought up in this city [Jerusalem] at the feet of Gamaliel..." (Acts 22.3; note also Acts 26.4, Galatians 1.14). If Saul was born about 10 C.E., and went up to Jerusalem as a youth, perhaps about 25 C.E., then Gamaliel must have presided by the middle of the fourth decade of the first century. He was certainly a respected teacher of the law and a member of the Sanhedrin by the year 35 C.E., for when Jesus' followers were persecuted by the priests and Sadducees, they were defended by him (Acts 5.33). If Hillel had been in the Sanhedrin, these traditions would not have hidden that fact. There is no evidence, on the other hand, to suggest that he died two decades earlier, except the tradition that he had a son Simeon; but even if such a son had lived and succeeded his father, he made absolutely no mark whatever on the traditional consciousness, and it may therefore be supposed that he held office for a very short time. Hillel might have lived, therefore, to 20-25 C.E. If Yohanan had entered the academy as a youth, he might well, as the legends tell, have been the youngest of Hillel's students. It is known that students were received at a very early age.[2] One cannot, therefore, say that Yohanan certainly did not study with Hillel. It is at least possible that he did. If so, however, his studies with Hillel could not have lasted for a very long time, and one must recognize that the desire to claim continuity of Pharisaic leadership, from Hillel before the

---

[1] Josephus, *War*, II, 151.
[2] Finkelstein, *Mavo*, p. 112, estimates that the students came to the academy before adolescence. Cf. also Josephus, *Vita*, 2.

destruction, to Yohanan ben Zakkai after it, motivated the ascription of such discipleship.

The tradition reported that Yohanan came to Hillel's school in his mature years:

> "And Moses was one hundred twenty years old" (Deut. 34.7). He was one of four who died at one hundred twenty, and these are they: Moses, and Hillel the Elder, and Rabban Yohanan ben Zakkai, and Rabbi Akiba. Moses was in Egypt forty years, in Midian forty years, and sustained Israel forty years. Hillel the Elder went up from Babylon aged forty years, served as apprentice to the sages forty years, and sustained Israel forty years. Rabban Yohanan ben Zakkai occupied himself in commerce forty years, served as apprentice to the sages forty years, and forty years he sustained Israel. Rabbi Akiba studied Torah forty years, and sustained Israel forty years. There were six pairs whose life span was identical: Rebecca and Kahath, Levi and Amram, Joseph and Joshua, Samuel and Solomon, Moses and Hillel the Elder, Rabban Yohanan ben Zakkai and Rabbi Akiba.[1]

Hillel had eighty disciples, of whom it was recorded,

> Thirty of them were worthy to have the Shekhinah rest upon them as upon Moses our master, but their generation was unworthy of it. Thirty of them were worthy to intercalate the year, and twenty of them were middling. The eldest of them was Jonathan ben Uzziel. The least of them all was Rabban Yohanan ben Zakkai.[2]

A legend was told about Hillel's teaching Yohanan (though some told it of Judah the Prince and *his* student Yohanan, two centuries later). One day two students were seated before Hillel, and one of them was Yohanan. One student asked,

> On what account do you cut grapes in (the condition of Levitical) cleanness, but you do not pick olives in (the condition of Levitical) cleanness?

The other asked,

> Why do you cut grapes in cleanness, but pick olives in uncleanness?

The latter student thus phrased his question indelicately, by using the word "unclean" while Yohanan was sensitive to the nuances of speech. To this Hillel replied,

---

[1] Sifre Deut. 357. Cf. Friedman's notes ad loc. Cf. also Ber. R. 100.24.

[2] ARNa, ch. 14, Schechter ed. p. 29a, Goldin tr. p. 74. Cf. also ARNb, ch. 28, Schechter ed. p. 29a; TB Sukkah 28a; TB Babba Batra 134a; Soferim 16.8 Compare TB Sanhedrin 11a, TP Nedarim 5.6. Cf. below for completion of the tradition.

I believe this one will give instruction in Israel,
and, the tradition concluded,
    Not many days passed before he did indeed teach Torah in Israel.[1]

It was also related that as a student, Yohanan sat before his masters as they judged a capital case, and went to an extraordinary degree to cross-examine the witnesses by whose testimony a man might be put to death. He inquired even about the stalks of the figs under which the murder was allegedly committed,

> The more a judge tests the evidence, the more is he to be praised. Ben Zakkai once tested the evidence even to inquiring about the stalk of fig-trees.

The Talmud concludes that this event took place when Yohanan was still a student, while Jewish courts still allegedly held the right to try capital cases.[2]

As Hillel lay dying, his students gathered at his bedside to take leave of him, but Yohanan did not enter with them.

> Hillel asked, "And where is Yohanan?"
> "There he is, standing outside the door," the students answered.
> "Let him enter, he is worthy," Hillel said.
> When he had entered, Hillel said to the students, "The youngest of you is father of wisdom and father of the future! – and the oldest, among you, how much the more so!" He added, "And concerning all of you Scripture speaks, 'I [Wisdom] walk in the way of righteousness, in the path of justice, endowing with wealth those who love me, and filling their treasuries.' (Prov. 8.21 f.) And concerning you, Yohanan, Scripture says the same,' ...endowing with wealth.'"[3]

---

[1] TB Pesahim 3b. These stories are, of course, all legendary; they represent the only available information on Yohanan's student years, and are therefore included, although they reflect the judgment of considerably later generations on this period in Yohanan's life.

[2] TB Sanhedrin 41a. Compare the Book of Susannah vs. 54. Hoenig, *Sanhedrin* 109, 272 n. 12, dates this event at 66 C.E., when he suggests the Jewish court recovered the power to inflict capital punishment after the first success of the revolutionary armies. The discussion in the Talmud rests on two *beraitot* (traditions), one using the name *ben Zakkai*, and the other, *Rabban Yohanan ben Zakkai*. Granting equal validity to each, the Talmud concludes that the first refers to the event, which took place in Yohanan's youth when he was still merely "ben Zakkai," and the other, to the time of his maturity, when the event was recounted. Allon (*Mehkarim*, I, 273, n. 86) suggests that the first beraita comes from the academy of sages opposed to his authority after the destruction. Cf. chapter eight. Cf. also R. Margoliot, *LeHeker Shemot ve-Kinuyim baTalmud* [On Names and Nicknames in the Talmud] (Jerusalem, 1960, in Hebrew), 10, n. 17; and Finkelstein, *Pharisees*, I, 286. The quotation is Mishnah Sanhedrin 5.2; cf. also Epstein, *Mevo-ot*, 55, 417-418. Cf. also the comment of Rav Sherira Gaon, *Igeret*, ed. B. Lewin (Haifa, 1921).

[3] Cf. TB Sukkah 28a, TB Baba Batra 134a, and n. 37. Compare the midrash of

Thus posterity envisioned how the master's cloak was laid upon the shoulders of the young Yohanan. One assumes, however, that Yohanan remained a student for a considerable time afterwards. He was one of those legendary students who leave behind them incredible stories about their scholarship and diligence. Thus it was told,

> They tell of Rabban Yohanan ben Zakkai that he did not neglect a single Scripture or Mishnah, Gemara [explanation of Mishnah], halakhah [law], agada [legend], supplement [branch of the oral law], or the subtleties of Scripture, or the subtleties of the scribes, or any of the sages' rules of interpretation – not a single thing in the Torah did he neglect, confirming the statement, "That I may cause those that love me to inherit substance, and that I may fill their treasuries."[1]

It was also of him that

> he never in his life engaged in idle conversation, and he never went four cubits without words of Torah and without *tefillin*, either winter or summer, and none ever preceded him into the school house, and he never slept in the school house, either accidentally or intentionally, and he never left anyone in the school house, and none ever found him slumbering there, and none ever opened the door to his students but he himself, and he never made a statement which he had not first heard from his master, and he never said, "The hour has come to arise from our studies," except on the afternoon before Passover and before the day of atonement, and so did Rabbi Eliezer his student after him.[2]

He was quoted as saying,

> If all the heavens were parchment, and all the trees pens, and all the oceans ink, they would not suffice to write down the wisdom which I

Prov. 8.21 in Avot 5.19, Ukzin 3.13, Num. 9.2, Midrash on Psalms 5.2. In Yalkut Shimoni I, 20, the verse is applied to the Garden of Eden, including the third level, at which Yohanan and his students are stationed. In the TB and TP passages, the entire statement beginning "Eighty students..." and ending "endowing with wealth" is actually a unity. I have divided it for my presentation.

[1] ARNa, *loc. cit.*, Goldin tr., *loc. cit.* Cf. notes 37 and 40. TB Sukkah is a late elaboration of the *beraita*. On the curriculum represented here, cf. E. Ebner, *Elementary Education in Abcient Israel during the Tannaitic Period 10-220 C.E.* (New York, 1956), pp. 20-21, 34, and 74-87 on the course of studies. Cf. also W. Bacher, *Agadot*, I, i, 18. On gematria, cf. Javits, *Toldot*, VI, 4. The wearing of Tefillin at all times is also reported of Yohanan in Pesikta Rabbati, ch 22, ed. Friedman, p. 112a, and TP Berahot 2.3. On the various disciplines of education, cf. also S. Krauss, "Etudes de terminologie Talmudique," *Revue des Etudes Juives* (hereafter – REJ), LXVII, 176 f. Krauss suggests that the expression "studied mikra, mishnah, and Talmud" means that he can demonstrate the unity of Talmud, midrash, and the interpretation of Scripture. On the meanings of these terms, cf. especially W. Bacher, *Erkhe Midrash* [Midrashic Terminology] (Tel Aviv, 1923; in Hebrew), s. v., and *Aruk completum*, s.v.

[2] Cf. n. 37 and 40. TB Sukkah 28a, Baba Batra 134a, and ARNa, *loc. cit.*

have learned from my masters, and I took away from them no more than a fly takes from the sea when it bathes, and from whom did he receive Torah? From Hillel and Shammai.

So too his student Eliezer ben Hyrkanos was quoted,

> If all the seas were ink, and all the reeds pens, and all men scribes, they could not write down all the Scripture and Mishnah I studied, nor what I learned from the sages in the academy. Yet I carried away from my teachers no more than does a man who dips his finger in the sea, and I gave away to my disciples no more than a paintbrush takes from the tube.[1]

Sometime after the death of Hillel, it would seem that Yohanan left Jerusalem for Galilee, where he settled in a village called Arav, bringing with him his wife and young son. No source states explicitly when Yohanan ben Zakkai went to Galilee, though several[2] are quite certain that he was there. Indications that the Galilee period was relatively early in his life are as follows: first, he was married and had a young son at that time;[3] if, as was common, he married about the age of twenty, then his son's relative youth would imply that he was in Galilee sometime between ca. 20 C.E. and 40 C.E. Second, he was not well known at this time, for only two cases were brought to him during the entire period of his Galilee sojourn.[4] Third, Hanina ben Dosa, his student in Arav, came to him there to begin his study of Torah; since Hanina lived well before the destruction of Jerusalem, he may have come at an early age; and it would appear that Yohanan did not teach him during his Jerusalem period, since Hanina is omitted from all lists of the Jerusalem circle. Fourth, as we shall see, Yohanan returned to Jerusalem while Gamaliel I was still president of the Pharisees; since the Jerusalem period would certainly seem to have continued uninterruptedly until the destruction, one must date the Galilee period either before ca. 45 C.E. or after 70 C.E. and the period after the destruction seems to have been spent entirely at Yavneh and Beror

---

[1] Cf. ARNa ch. 25, Schechter ed. p. 40a, Goldin tr. p. 109, Also Soferim, 16.8 On the expression, "oceans of ink," cf. Bacher, Agadot, I, i, 19, n. 1, and I. Linn, "If all the sky were parchment," *Publication of the Modern Language Association*, LIII, 951-970. Cf. also TP Berahot 2.3.

[2] Sources on the Galilee period are as follows: TB Shabbat 146a; Mishnah Shabbat 16.7 and 22.3, and TP Shabbat 16.8 and 22.3, and TB Berahot 34b. Also note the ARNa and passages cited below.

[3] TB Berahot 34b. Cited below.

[4] Mishnah 16.7 and 22.3, cf. TP Shabbat 16.8, the statement of Ullah, cited below.

Hayil; furthermore, after the destruction, he was an old man, and unlikely to have had a young son.[1]

Arav, it has been conjectured,[2] is to be identified with Gabara; if so, it was near Sepphoris, and was one of the larger cities in Galilee, suffering destruction at Vespasian's hands in his Galilean campaign of 66 C.E. Tradition said that Yohanan remained in Arav eighteen years.[3] The town, containing a large number of priestly families, was listed in a late source among those providing a "watch" in the Temple service.[4] Apparently Yohanan acted as teacher and magistrate, for two cases of Sabbath law were brought to him, and both he judged severely, though with hesitation. The first was whether on the Sabbath one may cover a scorpion with a dish so that it will not sting anyone, or whether this would be considered an act of hunting (destruction of life), and therefore would be forbidden on the Sabbath. When the case was brought to Yohanan, he stated, "I doubt whether he is not liable to bring a sin-offering for such an act." The decision in the second case was reported in exactly the same words, and one may conjecture that

---

[1] Of course, he might have had a child at a late age, but if so, this would have been a miraculous event for a man in his seventies or eighties, and would likely to have been mentioned in a midrash, perhaps, for example, on Deut. 34.7, but none on that verse at least indicates any such miracle. There was a late memory that he had visited Tiberias as well, cf. TB Shabbat 34a, R. Simeon b. Yohai met an old man who recalled that Yohanan ben Zakkai (referred to as "ben Zakkai") had visited the town. There are other suggestions on the Galilee period, cf. A. Kaminka, *Mehkarim BaTalmud* [Studies in the Talmud] (Tel Aviv, 1950, in Hebrew), 101, who suggests that Yohanan was never in Arav, but that the cases there were reported to him in Yavneh where he gave his opinion. But Kaminka apparently ignores TB Berahot 34b and the statement of Ullah; as well as the apparent recognition of the editor of ARNa, cf. below. Cf. also W. Bacher, "Yohanan ben Zakkai," *JE*, VII, 214, who suggests that Arav was his birthplace; in that case, one would have to assume that he went to Jerusalem to study, and returned there to teach and make a living. This is plausible Cf. also Bruell, Mavo, p. 59; M. Margoliot, *Encyclopedia le-Hokhme HaTalmude ve-Ha-Geonim* [Encyclopedia of Sages of the Talmud and the Gaonim] (Tel Aviv, 1946, 2 vols.; in Hebrew), who identifies the years in Arav with the "forty years in business."

[2] J. Klausner, *Bi Yemei Bayit Sheni* [In the Days of the Second Temple] (Jerusalem, 1954; in Hebrew), 286 f. If Klausner is correct, then the passage in Josephus, *War*, III, 132, is relevant; but there, Professor Smith notes, the reading of *Gabara* is also conjectural.

[3] TP Shabbat 16.8.

[4] Cf. S. Klein, Sefer HaYishuv [Book of the Settlement] (Jerusalem, 1939; in Hebrew), s. v. Arav, pp. 162-163; M. Avi-Yonah, *Geographia Historit shel Eretz Yisrael* [Historical Geography of the Land of Israel] (Tel Aviv, 1951; in Hebrew; henceforth — Avi-Yonah, *Geographia*), 136. Cf. also S. Klein, *Ma-amarim shonim LeHakirat Eretz Yisrael* [Selected Articles on the Study of the Land of Israel] (Vienna, 1924, in Hebrew), 1-29.

the record of both was preserved in a single document, which later was incorporated into the Mishnah.[1] In the third century, Ullah, an Amora in the land of Israel, stated,

> Eighteen years Rabban Yohanan ben Zakkai spent in Arav, and only these two cases came before him, and at the end he said, "O Galilee, Galilee! Thou hatest the Torah! Thine end will be to be besieged!"[2]

Yohanan had one student in the Galilee, Hanina ben Dosa, who remained there after Yohanan returned to Jerusalem. Hanina was renowned for his piety, and celebrated as a faith healer and intercessor. It was told that after praying for the sick, he would say, "This will live, that will die."

> "How do you know?" he was asked.
> "If my prayer is fluent in my mouth, I know that it is received with mercy, and if it is not, I know that it is rejected." When the son of Gamaliel I, was ill he sent two disciples to Hanina to ask his prayers in the boy's behalf. When Hanina saw them, he went to the upper chamber of his house and prayed for mercy. When he came down, he said to the disciples, "Go, for his fever has left him."
> "And are you a prophet?" they asked.
> "I am neither a prophet nor the son of a prophet, but I am accustomed

---

[1] Mishnah Shabbat 16.7 The second case (Mishnah Shabbat 22.3) is as follows: "A man may broach a jar to eat dried figs therefrom, provided that he does not intend to make a utensil of it. He may not pierce the plug of a jar on the Sabbath, so R. Judah, but the sages permit it. They may not pierce the side, and if it was pierced already, a man may not put wax on it on the Sabbath, since he would (need to) smooth it over. R. Judah said, Such a case once came before Rabban Johanan ben Zakkai in Arab, and he said, I doubt whether he is not liable to a sin-offering." Cf. Epstein, *Mavo-ot*, 295, on the joint recension of the incidents. Epstein indicates several such collections. Cf. TB Shabbat 121a, 146a.

[2] TB Shabbat 16.8. On the meaning of "la-asot ba-masikin," the following suggestions are offered: Allon, *Toldot*, I, 37, suggests that the word means *conductores*, tax collectors who seize land. Cf. Sifre Deut. 357 and TP Demai 6; the traditional commentary (TP ad loc.) Korban Adah, explains, "that you will be troubled by brigands"; and Pnei Moshe (ad loc.), "that you will all be olive pickers and not masters of Torah." Jastrow, *Dictionary*, s. v. II, 807, "one who levies contributions, oppressor," citing Tos. Cholot 18.13, Mishnah Baba Kama 10.5, etc. *Aruk Completum*, V, 193, s. v., explains the word by the root "le-hasik," one who steals a field; meaning, thine end is to be at work among the brigands; S. Krauss in the Supplement to the Aruk, IX, 261, explains the word as besieger. J. Levy, *Neuhebraisches und Chadisches Wörterbuch über die Talmudim und Midraschim* (Leipzig, 1883), III, 175-6 s. v., explains the word as "robber," and translates, "Und so wirst du einst unter den Raeubern Beschaeftigungsuchen." S. W. Baron, History, I, 279, follows Levy, "Before long thou wilt make common cause with the tax assessors"; Finkelstein, *Akiba*, p. 62, "Thine end will be seizure by the Romans"; J. Klausner, *Jesus of Nazareth*, 173, n. 103, "Thou wilt in the end beget oppressors." I have followed S. Krauss. On the nature of such prophecies, cf. W. D. Davies, *Paul and Rabbinic Judaism* (London, 1955), 211-3.

to discern thus: if prayer is fluent in my mouth, I know that it is accepted, and if not, I know that it is rejected."

The disciples sat down and wrote a letter, fixing the very hour of the day. When they returned to Jerusalem, Gamaliel said to them, "By the Temple service! You neither subtracted nor added, but it happened at that exact moment his fever broke and he asked us for water to drink."[1]

Hanina was, likewise an ascetic, and one day a "heavenly echo" came forth and announced, "All the world is fed on account of Hanina my son, and Hanina my son suffices on a basket of carobs from week to week."[2] His teaching in the chain of tradition was, "He in whom the spirit of his fellow man takes delight, in him the spirit of the Omnipresent takes delight, and he in whom the spirit of his fellow creatures takes no delight, in him the spirit of the Omnipresent takes no delight."[3] Likewise he taught, "He whose fear of sin takes precedence over his wisdom, his wisdom shall endure, but he whose wisdom takes precedence over his fear of sin, his wisdom shall not endure, as it is said, "The fear of the Lord is the beginning of wisdom" (Psalm 111.10). He used to say, 'He whose works exceed his wisdom, his wisdom shall endure, but he whose wisdom exceeds his works, his wisdom shall not endure, as it is said, 'We shall do and we shall hearken' (Ex. 24.7)."[4] These teachings may well have been influenced by Yohanan, who taught, "If one is wise and fears sin, what is he like? Lo, he is a craftsman with the tools of his craft in his hand. If one is wise and does not fear sin, what is he like? Lo, he is a craftsman without the tools of his craft in his hand. If one fears sin but is not wise what is he like? He is not a craftsman, but the tools of his craft are in his hand."[5] One discerns a difference in the attitude of disciple, for while Hanina said nothing about one who is fearful of sin but is not learned, Yohanan specifically criticized such a man, like Hillel his master, who emphasized that Torah was the prerequisite of piety.

The apparent difference in viewpoints was indicated in their first encounter. Their meeting was recorded as follows:

---

[1] TB Berahot 34b.

[2] TB Taanit 24b.

[3] Avot 3.11.

[4] Avot 3.12.

[5] ARNa ch. 22, Schechter p. 37b, Goldin tr. p. 99 f. This is taught as comment on Hanina's teaching, and would suggest that the editor of ARNa recognized the relationship between Hanina's words and Yohanan's, in placing the latter's teaching as commentary to the former. Note, however, that the editor of ARNb did not connect the two statements; cf. ARNb, Schechter ed. p. 34a.

> When Hanina ben Dosa came to study with Rabban Yohanan ben Zakkai in Arav, it happened that Yohanan's son was deathly sick. He said to him "Hanina, my son, seek mercy for him that he may live." Hanina put his head between his knees, and prayed for mercy, and the boy lived. Rabban Yohanan ben Zakkai said to him, "If ben Zakkai were to throw his head down between his knees all day long, none would pay attention to him." Yohanan's wife then said to him, "And is Hanina greater than you?" "No," he replied, "but he is like a slave before the King, and I am like a prince before the king."[1]

During this period, much of the control of the Roman government passed from elected public officials of the Senatorial class (princes in the eyes of the Palestinians) to favorite freedmen and even slaves of the imperial household. Thus, particularly in later years under Nero, the lives of great public officials were not safe, and any slight offense might lead to their execution; but the favorite slaves of the emperor were given a free hand. Yohanan thus apparently offered a complaint: such is the way of God. He has favorite slaves, but the great ministers of his kingdom are compelled to uphold the most rigorous standards.[2] Such a statement is consistent with the sages' earlier criticism of Honi the Circler,[3] in the time of Simeon b. Shetah (ca. 80 B.C.E.) an earlier miracle worker and rain-maker.

> If it were not that thou art Honi [Onias], I would have pronounced a ban of excommunication against thee! But what shall I do, to thee, thou importunest God and he performeth thy will, like a son that importuneth his father and he performeth his will; and of these Scripture saith, "Let thy father and thy mother be glad, and let her that bare thee rejoice" (Prov. 23.25).

Thus Yohanan gave expression to the tension he felt between himself and the Galilean environment, where Pharisaic sages were few, and fewer still, those who consulted them. He found in the Galilee that none came to seek his learning, and already left behind him a bitter curse, "Galilee, Galilee, thou hatest the Torah!"

---

[1] TB Berahot 34b. This *beraita*, in addition to the juxtaposition in ARNa, are the only indications that Hanina was in fact Yohanan's student; but in addition, one notes that Yohanan did live in Arav (cf. note 44, 47), and that Hanina did too, TP Berahot 4.1.

[2] I am indebted to Professor Smith for this explanation. Note also the comment of Elijah, Gaon of Vilna, ad. loc., one is like the minister before a king when he has attained the highest level in the student of Torah, but like a servant before the king when he has attained the highest level in prayer. Hanina's prayers were, on account of his great piety and facility in worship, more readily answered by God. Cf. also S. Krauss, *Paras Ue-Romi Ba-Talmud U-va Midrashim* [Persia and Rome in Talmud and Midrash] (Jerusalem, 1948; in Hebrew), pp. 119-142.

[3] Mishnah Taanit 3.9.

The Pharisaic sages sought to administer the inner life of Israel in accordance with their understanding of the ancient body of legal and prophetic literature. This prophecy had entailed future consistency: God would not, it was thought, change his mind. He did not need to repeat himself, nor to rehearse the authenticating acts which had originally vindicated his word. Thus the sages did not expect to experience charismatic power. They did not advance a claim to unconditional prophetic authority,[1] as did the contemporary Jesus of Nazareth,[2] or to miraculous abilities, as did Haninah ben Dosa. The sages, and Yohanan ben Zakkai among them, followed another way, between the spontaneous religion of Galilee, which looked for daily miracles, signs, and wonders, and the loyal literalism of the Jerusalem priesthood, which held fast to Scripture's commandments concerning the sacrificial routine. In Galilee Yohanan encountered the wonderful healing gifts of Haninah ben Dosa, and contrasted Haninah's power with his own.[3] From his years in Jerusalem, now beginning, we have a number of stories which indicate how different was his conception of religion from that of the priests who administered the sanctuary.

---

[1] E. Urbach, "Law and Prophecy," Tarbiz, XXIII (1958), 1-25. Also cf. N. N. Glatzer, "A Study of Talmudic Interpretation of Prophecy," *Journal of Religion*, Jan. 1946, 115-137; M. Weber, *Ancient Judaism* (Glencoe, 1952, tr. by H. Gerth and D. Martindale), 385 f. Weber states that a tension between literati and prophets is characteristic "of any stratum of learned men who are ritualistically oriented to a law book as against prophetic charismatics." Weber is wrong in saying (p. 498) that "an esoteric gnosis of aristocratic religious virtuosi could not readily grow on such soil," cf. chapter five.

[2] R. T. Herford, *Christianity in the Talmud* (London, 1903) 352, suggests that Yohanan ben Zakkai had certainly seen and heard Jesus in Jerusalem, and hence passed on to Eliezer ben Hyrkanos teachings about him (Eliezer being accused of the Christian heresy by a Roman magistrate many decades later); it seems possible, also that Yohanan heard something about Jesus during his Galilean years, but there is no ground for such a speculation other than his sojourn there. Cf. also A. Adersheim, *The Life and Times of Jesus the Messiah* (New York, 1910, 2 vols.), I, 451-459, 489-498.

[3] On the Galilee in this period, cf. Baron, *History*, I, 278-9; but Allon, *Toldot*, I, 319 rejects this entire analysis. Cf. p. 29, n. 1. Cf. also Klausner, *Jesus of Nazareth*, 173, 266. Klausner errs in comparing the "miracles" of Yohanan ben Zakkai and his students (cf. chapter five) with those of Jesus (p. 266). The so-called miracles that Klausner cites were not acts of healing, but investigations of esoteric knowledge, in no way comparable to the actual faith healing through prayer which characterized certain Galileans. Cf. also E. Elliott Binns, *Galilean Christianity* (Chicago, 1956), particularly 17-23; R. H. Charles, *Religious Development between the Old and New Testaments* (London, 1948), 157; and Daniel-Rops, *Life and Times*, I, 139-140.

CHAPTER THREE

MIGHTY HAMMER

While it is not entirely certain when Yohanan ben Zakkai returned to Jerusalem, one may conjecture that he arrived during the tenure of Gamaliel I as president of the Pharisaic party, about the year 40 C.E. First, he was active in Jerusalem for a considerable period before the Revolution of 66 C.E., for by 62 C.E., it was alleged, he represented the Pharisees in certain disputes with the Sadducees.[1] Even earlier, however, he was associated with Simeon ben Gamaliel in the leadership of the Pharisaic group; if, as it is commonly assumed, Simeon assumed office about the year 50 C.E.,[2] and if Yohanan's authority was coterminous with Simeon's,[3] then one must conjecture that Yohanan had lived in the city for at least some years to achieve leadership in the Pharisaic community. Second, he certainly exerted some authority during Gamaliel's presidency, since one of his teachings was effectively vitiated by a special enactment of Gamaliel.[4] Third, Yohanan's student Joshua ben Hananiah was born about 30-35 C.E.[5] If he came to Yohan-

---

[1] See below p. 53f. On the position of Yohanan ben Zakkai in the Pharisaic party, see Hugo Mantel, *Studies in the History of the Sanhedrin*. Mantel discusses Yohanan ben Zakkai as "Av Bet Din", p. 104, 117, 123. His extensive discussion on Yohanan ben Zakkai and the title *Nasi* (p. 28-35) summarizes the considerable scholarly discussion on this question. In general, however, Mantel and the scholars he cites assume that all the sources on the life of Yohanan ben Zakkai are of equal and substantial historical value. Thus he assumes that Yohanan actually abrogated the "water of ordeals" and the "eglah ha-arufah" (cf. also p. 291-292, and compare below, p. 61), and assumes that the Pharisees before the destruction of Jerusalem acquired control of both the Priestly Court and the Bet Din Hagadol in the Hewn-stone chamber of the Temple. He assumes also that Yohanan ben Zakkai was in fact a priest (compare below, p. 60). But these assumptions are by no means well grounded. Again, he assumes the literal historicity of the passages on the debates with the Sadducees, which, as we shall note (below p. 49f.) is by no means beyond question. Thus he attempts to solve a problem which the sources are by no means fully adequate to solve. Nonetheless his discussions are extremely suggestive. He proposes that Yohanan ben Zakkai bore the special title *rosh bet din*, which, unfortunately, is nowhere directly ascribed to him in the sources, as Mantel himself notes (p. 34). The title is only implicitly used, but even here, not necessarily as a *terminus technicus* at all, in Mishnah Rosh Hashanah 4.4

[2] Finkelstein, *Akiba*, 298.

[3] Below, p. 41.

[4] Compare Mishnah Ketuvot 13.1 and Gittin 4.3, and discussion below, p. 45.

[5] TB Arakhin 11b. Joshua was a Levite and sang in the Temple choir, an act which indicates he had reached age 30 before the Destruction; and, likely, before the time of Yohanan ben Zakkai's escape from the city in the spring of 68 C.E.

an's academy at the usual age, that is, about thirteen or fourteen, then Yohanan must certainly have been teaching in Jerusalem by the end of the fifth decade of the first century. Finally, one source might possibly date from this period, and if so, it provides evidence that Yohanan and Gamaliel spent some time together during their mature years:

> It happened that the broth was brought for testing to Rabban Yohanan ben Zakkai, and to Rabban Gamaliel two dates and a dipper of water, and they said, "Bring them up to the Sukkah." [It was taught on the incident], not because the law is so [that even random snacks must be eaten in the Sukkah on the festival], but because they wished to be stringent on themselves.[1]

While this Mishnah might refer to Gamaliel II and Yohanan at Yavneh, it has been shown[2] that considerable parts of the Mishnah *Sukkah* antedate the destruction, and it may well be that the above tradition refers to the period before Gamaliel I died.[3] Hence it seems not unlikely that Yohanan returned to Jerusalem during the tenure of Gamaliel I and probably well before his death, which allegedly took place about 50 C.E.; this would suggest that Yohanan had arrived about the year 40 C.E.

In Jerusalem, Yohanan encountered a kind of religion quite different in focus from that of his Galilean student Haninah ben Dosa. It was a

---

(cf. chapter six). Henze he must have been born at 38 C.E. at the very latest, and quite possibly, somewhat earlier. The students in the academies were accepted at the age of adolescence, cf. chapter 2. Compare J. Podro, *The Last Pharisee: The Life and Times of Rabbi Joshua ben Hananyah* (London, 1959), p. 14 and n. 1. Joshua's mother, it is reported, took him to the academy as an infant to hear the sounds of study; but there is no evidence that he actually entered at an unusually early age, nor that he had any other master than Yohanan. Cf. TP Yevamot 1.6. Joshua was proctor of Yohanan's academy when Eliezer ben Hyrkanos arrived.

[1] Mishnah Sukkah 2.5. Cf. also parallels in TB Yoma 79a, TP Sukkah 2.6, TB Sukkah 26b.

[2] Epstein, *Mevoot*, pp. 350-353, shows that chapters four and five of Sukkah date from the time of the Second Commonwealth, and that much other material in the tractate is to be dated before 70 C.E.

[3] Note also that Gamaliel II is not likely to have associated with Yohanan on such intimate terms after the destruction, cf. chapter 8. Also, the third sage cited in this mishnah is Zadok, who also survived the destruction, but was then a very old man. If this is Gamaliel II, then this is one of two sources which juxtapose Gamaliel II; the other, TB Baba Batra 10b, is a very confused text, and, as I shall attempt to demonstrate, requires revision by comparison to the parallel source in Pesikta Rabbati. This is, incidentally, the only place in which it is noted that Yohanan ben Zakkai applied the law more stringently to himself. I should emphasize that this is a very conservative estimate of the latest possible date before the Destruction that Yohanan was in, or might have returned to, the city.

cultic religion administered by the priests of the Temple, and had long held a central place in Israelite faith. Like other peoples in ancient times, Jews believed that all kinds of sacrifice, public and private, propitiated God and achieved forgiveness for sin. There was, indeed, sufficient foundation for such a belief, since the Scriptures had ordained various animal offerings for many spiritual purposes.[1] The priesthood, as loyal to Scriptures as the Pharisaic sages, was internationally famous for its discipline, devotion to the Temple, and the exactness and solemnity with which the Temple service was carried on. The priests were remembered in Pharisaic tradition for their dedication to their task even at the Temple's last hour:

> It says, "Open thy doors O Lebanon, that the fire may consume thy cedars" (Zech. 11.1). This refers to the high priests who were in the Temple, who took their keys in their hands and threw them up to the sky, saying to the Holy One, blessed be He, "Master of the Universe, here are thy keys which thou didst hand over to us, for we have not been trustworthy custodians to do the king's work and to eat of the king's table.[2]

The Pharisees recognized the legitimacy of the cult in Judaism, participated in its ceremonies, mourned at its cessation, and hoped for its restoration. Thus, after the destruction, Joshua ben Hananiah exclaimed,

> Woe unto us, that this, the place where the iniquities of Israel were atoned for, is laid waste.[3]

Likewise, the end of the Temple service was considered by Pharisaic doctrine to be a disaster for the world,

> So long as the Temple service is maintained, the world is a blessing to its inhabitants and the rains come in season... but when the Temple service is not maintained, the world is not a blessing to its inhabitants and rains do not come in season...[4]

The sages, following some of the prophets, thus accepted the sacrificial service, teaching, however, like the prophets, that true repentance must accompany sin- and guilt-offerings,

---

[1] G. F. Moore, *Judaism*, I, 497-506. A summary of biblical sacrifice is given by E. G. Hirsch, "Sacrifice," *JE*, X, 615-623, and of the Talmudic view on the subject by J. Z. Lauterbach, "Talmudic Period," *JE*, X, 625. Cf. also W. D. Davies, *Paul and Rabbinic Judaism*.

[2] ARNa, ch. 4; Schechter ed. 12b; Goldin, p. 37.

[3] ARNa, ch. 4, Schechter, p. 12b; Goldin, p. 34.

[4] *Ibid.*, Goldin, p. 33.

If a man said, I will sin and repent, and sin again and repent, he will be given no chance to repent.[1]

The sages found much to criticize, however, in the secular character of the priesthood. The high priests, depending on political connections for their appointment, did not generally seek to placate public opinion or heed Pharisaic instructions. Since the Pharisees claimed to advance the true interpretation of Scripture concerning even cultic practices, priestly indifference to their pretensions became, as we shall see, a source of considerable irritation. Some priests, moreover, were reputed (in the Pharisaic sources and elsewhere) to be arrogant and heavy-handed in claiming their sacerdotal benefits. Thus Josephus reported,

> Hananiah likewise had servants who were very wicked, who joined themselves to the boldest sort of the people, and went to the threshing floors and took away the tithes that belonged to the priests by violence, and did not refrain from beating such as would not give these tithes to them. So the other high priests acted in the like manner, as did those his servants, without anyone being able to prohibit them, so that some of the priests that were of old wont to be supported from those tithes died for want of food.[2]

A popular song preserved in Pharisaic literature went
> Woe unto me because of the house of Boethus
> Woe unto me because of their clubs!
> Woe unto me because of the house of Hanin
> Woe unto me because of their whisperings!
> Woe unto me because of the house of Kahtros,
> Woe unto me because of their quills.
> Woe unto me because of the house of Ishmael ben Phiabi,
> Woe unto me because of their fists.
> For they are high priests,
> And their sons are treasurers,
> And their sons-in-law are law officers,
> And their slaves beat the folk with sticks.[3]

The Pharisaic teacher, Zadok, was reported to have rebuked the priests for their violence,

---

[1] Mishnah Yoma 8. 8-9.

[2] Josephus, Antiquities XX. 8. 8, XX. 9. 2. Josephus reports these incidents in connection with Ishmael ben Phiabi, whom we shall meet again.

[3] TB Pesahim 57b. Tr. by J. Goldin, "The Talmudic Period," in L. Finkelstein, *The Jews, Their History, Culture, and Religion* (New York, 1949), I, 144.

It once happened that two priests, equal in rank, were running up the Temple ramp to the altar. One got up the ramp before, and in the place of the other. The one behind took a knife and stabbed the first through the heart! Rabbi Zadok stood up on the stairs of the Great Hall, and said, "Oh our brothers, children of Israel, hear! Behold it is written, 'If in the land which the Lord your God gives you to possess, anyone is found slain, lying in the open country, and it is not known who killed him, then your elders and your judges shall come forth, and they shall measure the distance to the cities which are around the corpse, and the elders of the city which is nearest to the slain man shall take a heifer... and all of the elders of that city nearest to the slain man shall wash their hands over the heifer whose neck was broken in the valley, and they shall testify, 'our hands did not shed this blood... Forgive O Lord thy people Israel whom thou hast redeemed, and set not the guilt of innocent blood in the midst of thy people Israel...'" (Deut. 21.1-8). We – for whom shall we bring the heifer? For the city? Or for the Temple court? And all the people moaned and wept.[1]

Shortly before the destruction, Yohanan ben Zakkai was said to have abrogated the rite of breaking the heifer's neck, on account of the growing violence of the time.[2] Reports of cultic corruption ought, however, to be treated with caution; many of the priests and Sadducees were patriots standing in the forefront of the later revolutionary movement, still others counted themselves among the Pharisaic party, and Pharisaic literature itself attests to the loyalty to Scriptural precepts which characterized the administration of the Temple. To think of the leading Sadducees as generally ignorant or corrupt is to be misled by Pharisaic historiography, which preserved its own angry memory of the Sadducean rejection of Pharisaic authority.

The Sadducean rejection of the Pharisaic claim was, indeed, not difficult to comprehend. The sage was not a charismatic figure; he did not enhance his authority through ecstacies, mantic prophecy, or miracle, and even if he did, there is very little ground to assume that the priests, bound by their own traditions of loyalty to the written word of Scripture, would have paid much attention. He was not, on the other hand, a sacerdotal figure, and his authority did not rest on either inherited privilege or acquired sanctity. He could not claim authority by reason of a legitimate place in the cult, and had no function whatever in the Temple service to support his demand to direct and interpret the rites. On the contrary, the sage's only authenticating act was his teaching itself, and, one assumes, his own embodiment of the

---

[1] TB Yoma 23a. Cf. also Mishnah Yoma 2.2.
[2] But cf. below, p. 61.

burden of his message. He would seem to have represented, in retrospect, a third force in religion, opposed to the two primary elements of charisma and traditional routine. As we have seen, Yohanan envied in Hanina ben Dosa a wonderful, spontaneous power he himself did not possess; and, in the Temple, he confronted the inertial force of traditional routine. For the sage, however, charisma was mostly no longer available; charismatic experience had rather been *inherited* in the biblical legacy, and especially in Pentateuchal and prophetic literature. The routine provided by the Temple cult had, likewise, a less central place in his religious life than the routine imposed by the duty to study Scripture. The two dynamics in religion were, as we shall see, united in the experience of Torah, which meant to the sages the act of continuing study and application of Scripture as at once a pneumatic and a disciplining spiritual experience.[1] This was the third way in religion advanced by the sages, as an alternative to Galilee's faith in inherent intimacy with God or Jerusalem's routine of cultic technology.

Before the destruction, the sages apparently had only one opportunity to effect their practical policies through political influence, which came during the reign of Agrippa I (41-44 C.E.), Herod's grandson. Agrippa entered the Pharisaic imagination as a good king; though he seems to have played Greek to the Caesarean Greeks, in Jerusalem at least he presented himself as a loyal Jew and prince of Israel, and observed the commandments as the Pharisees taught him to. On one occasion, he supposedly took part in a public reading of the Scriptures, receiving the scrolls standing, although it was permitted to sit, and reading standing, and therefore won the praise of the sages. When he came to the verse (Deut. 17.15), "Thou mayest not put a foreigner over thee, which is not thy brother," Agrippa, heir of Edomites, burst into tears, but the sages called out to him, "Thou art our brother, thou art our brother." Agrippa may possibly have thought to free the nation from foreign domination, and for this reason he may have cultivated the Pharisaic leaders to win additional popular support. He began to construct a strong wall for the city, and called a meeting of neighboring vassal kings in Tiberias, but the Syrian legate forbade the first and dismissed the second. He died before his plans could be tried, probably of some kind of stroke, and his son, aged seventeen, remained in

---

[1] On study of Torah as a pneumatic experience, cf. chapter five; on study of Torah as a social experience, chapter four. Cf. also Y. Baer, *Yisrael ba-Amim* [Israel among the Nations] (Jerusalem, 1955), pp. 99-120.

retirement.[1] The land returned to the direct authority of the procurators.[2] Under the subsequent authorities, public order apparently
declined, and the sages were reported to have perceived omens of
coming disaster; if so, however, their political impotence prevented
their taking effective remedial action. Thus, for example, Yohanan ben
Zakkai was reported to have witnessed and interpreted the following
omen:

> Forty years before the destruction of the Temple... the doors of the
> sanctuary opened by themselves, until Rabban Yohanan ben Zakkai
> rebuked them saying, "Oh, Temple! Temple! Why do you yourself give
> the alarm? I know about you that you will be destroyed, for Zechariah
> ben Ido has already prophesied concerning thee, 'Open thy doors, O
> Lebanon, that the fire may consume thy cedars.'" (Zechariah 11.1)[3]

Josephus recorded a similar omen, that the massive brass eastern gate
of the Temple's inner court, securely locked by iron-bolts, opened by
itself in the middle of the night, and

> the watchmen of the Temple ran and reported the matter to the cap-
> tain, and he came up and with difficulty succeeded in shutting it.[4]

If Josephus' account is historical, then one would assume that the
story about Yohanan was intended to provide a Pharisaic recension for
the rumored event: a long time before the destruction, the sage was
able to foresee its immanence by correctly interpreting events in the
light of Scripture.[5]

---

[1] On the reign of Agrippa, cf. Josephus, *Antiquities*, 19.6.1, 19.7.3; on the
reading, cf. TB Pesahim 88b, Sotah 7.8, Bikkurim 3.4. Epstein, *Mavo-ot*, 399, says,
however, that this was Agrippa II.

[2] On procuratorial government after Agrippa I, cf. Schuerer, *History*, I, ii,
161-190.

[3] TB Yoma 39b, compare TB Pesahim, 57a. Cf. n. 23.

[4] Josephus, *War*, VI, 294.

[5] The tradition in TP Yoma 6.3. is as follows: "Forty years before the destruction
of the Temple... they would lock the gates of the sanctuary in the evening, and
awake and find them open. Rabban Yohanan ben Zakkai said to it, Temple, Why
do you frighten us? We know of you that your end is to be destroyed, as it is said
(Zech. 11.1), 'Open your doors, O Lebanon, that the fire may devour your cedars.'"
Cf. also A. Buechler, *Types of Palestinian Jewish Piety from 70 B.C.E. to 70 C.E.*
(London, 1922), 258. Note that the identification of Lebanon with the Temple
recurs in Yohanan's conversation with Vespasian, cf. chapter six. The midrash
so created may have offered opportunity to identify Yohanan's prediction with a
still earlier day. That this is a confused tradition is certain, for the same story is told
of Hanina the Suffragan Priest, as follows (ARNb, ch. 7, Schechter ed., p. 11a):
"Forty years before the destruction of the Temple... the men of Jerusalem would
lock the gates, and awake and find them open, as it is said, 'Open thy gates, O
Lebanon...'" While this is closer to the TP version, the confusion of Hanina and

If, whatever their prescience, the Pharisees were unable to prevent the collapse of the social order, they nonetheless continued to evolve their own ideas about the proper conduct of society according to the biblical imperative. They pursued their studies, and attempted when possible and where they were obeyed to apply their insights to public life. As we have noted, they accepted the authority of Gamaliel I, who represented them in the national tribunal.[1] Gamaliel, like Hillel before

---

Yohanan would indicate that it is a late invention, for the purpose suggested in the text. The use of Zechariah son of Iddo in place of Zechariah son of Berechiah son of Iddo (cf. Zech 1.1) is due to the passage in Ezra 5.1, cf. M. D. Cassutto, "The Book of Zechariah," *Encyclopedia Mikrait*, II, col. 924. The Greek *Lives of the Prophets* (C. C. Torrey, ed., *The Lives of the Prophets, Greek Text and Translation*, Philadelphia, 1946), which Torrey dates in the 1st century C.E., makes the same identification, and likewise recognizes the prophet's eschatological focus: "His prophecies, uttered in Jerusalem, had to do with the end of the nations, with Israel, and the temple, with the laziness of prophets and priests, and with a double judgment" (Torrey ed. 44-5). The identification of *Lebanon* with the Temple is made in Sifre Deut. 6 (Friedman ed., p. 66b) as follows: "Lebanon means no other than the Temple, as it is said (Jer. 22.6), You are as Gilead to me, as the summit of Lebanon, yet surely I will make you a desert, an uninhabited city. I will prepare destroyers against you, each with his weapons, and they shall cut down your choicest cedars, and cast them in the fire. And many nations will pass by this city and every man will say to his neighbor, why has the Lord dealt thus with this great city.' And it says (Is. 10.34), Lebanon by a mighty one will fall..." Friedman comments that the verse in Jeremiah is addressed to the house of the king of Judah, and belongs more appropriately in the earlier context of the Sifre passage. However, the *content* of the verse itself (which I have therefore quoted at treater length than the Sifre text) is quite obviously related to the Temple and city. Cf. also Sifre Numbers 134 (Friedman ed. p. 50b), where both Is. 10.34 and Zech. 11.1 are used to prove that the Temple is meant by *Lebanon*. I do not agree with Bacher (*Agadot*, I, i, 19, n. 1) who thinks that the midrash identifying Lebanon with the Temple was created by Yohanan ben Zakkai. I find this unlikely because in the light of Jeremiah 22. 6-7, the usage was the open intent of Jeremiah; and the Sifre Deut. recognized this (Zechariah did also it would seem), even though Friedman did not. It seems most likely, therefore, that Yohanan derived the 'midrash' from the clear sense of Jeremiah, and applied it to the eschatological passages in Zechariah and Isaiah. Cf. also Finkelstein, *Pharisees*, II, 653, n. 68. Hoenig, *Sanhedrin*, 112, regards the incident as a historic event, and dates it at 66 C.E. Cf. also ch. 6, and, for a history of the exegesis on Lebanon, G. Vermes, "The Symbolical Interpretation of Lebanon in the Targums; The Origin and Development of an Exegetical Tradition," *Journal of Theological Studies*, IX, 1. I am grateful to Professor Smith for referring me to Vermes' article.

[1] On the life of Gamaliel, cf. W. Bacher, "Gamaliel I," *JE*, V, 558-560, Bruell, *Mavo*, 50-52; Frankel, *Mishnah*, 59-61. The difficulty in Gamaliel's biography, which we have already faced, is that the sources do not distinguish between him and his grandson, Gamaliel II of Yavneh. Still, the following sources clearly deal with him: on his relations with Agrippa I, TB Pesahim 88b; on his participation in the Temple rites, Mishnah Shekalim 6.1, 3.1,3; on his administration of ritual life, TP Maaser Sheni 5.4 (cf. below); on his suppression of the Aramaic translation of Job, TB Shabbat 115a; on his Takkanot, cf. Gittin 32a, 34b; Rosh Hashanah 23b;

him and Yohanan afterward, issued several legal edicts *(takkanot)* for "the repair of the world," touching matters of family law and calendrical procedure.[1] Gamaliel's authority was apparently accepted by some Jews throughout the land and in the exilic communities, for some of his pastoral letters to other parts of the country and the diaspora are extant. They instruct on the proper fulfilment of tithing regulations, and announce a calendar reform. One of them was as follows:

> It once happened that Rabban Gamaliel was sitting on the stairway of the Temple mount, and Yohanan the scribe was standing before him with three letters prepared. He said to him, "Take one letter and write, To our brothers, man of the lower Galilee, may your peace increase! We beg to inform you that the time of removal has arrived, to remove the tithes from the olive heaps." Take another letter and write, "To our brothers, men of the South may your peace increase! We beg to inform you that the time of removal has arrived, and to separate the tithes from the sheaves of wheat." And take the last letter and write, "To our brothers, Men of the Exile in Babylon, and to our brothers, in Media, and to the rest of the whole Exile of Israel, may your peace increase for ever! We beg to inform you that the pigeons are yet tender, and the lambs weak, and the springtide has not yet come, and the matter seems fit in my eyes and in the eyes of my colleagues, and I have added to this year thirty days.[2]

After the death of Gamaliel I, Simeon ben Gamaliel and Yohanan ben Zakkai continued to send such pastoral letters; the extant record of one of which is as follows:

> Rabbi Joshua reported, Once I went to the Upper Market, to the Refuse Gate in Jerusalem, and I found there Rabban Simeon ben Gamaliel and Rabban Yohanan ben Zakkai, sitting, and two scrolls were open before them, and Yohanan the Scribe was standing before them with pen and ink in his hand, and they said, Write: From Simeon ben Gamaliel and from Yohanan ben Zakkai, to our brothers in the Upper and Lower South, and to Shahlil, and to the Seven Cities of the South, Peace! Let it be known to you that the fourth year has arrived, but still the sacred produce has not been removed. But now, haste and bring five sheaves, for they hinder the Confession; and it is not we who have begun to write to you, but our fathers used to write to your fathers. They said to him, Write a second letter, From Simeon ben Gamaliel and

---

Yevamot 122a; cf. also inter alia, Pesahim 74a, Peah 2.6, 7; Orlah 2.11, 12; Bekorot 38a; Ketuvot 105b, 109a; Moed Katan 27b; Megillah 21a, Sotah 49a, Avodah Zara 11a. Cf. also Buechler, *Das Synhedrion in Jerusalem* (Vienna 1902), 115-131; and Bloch, *Institutionem*, II, ii, 118-202.

[1] Mishnah Gittin 4.2-3, Yevamot 16.7, Rosh Hashanah 2.5.

[2] Cf.. p. 42

from Yohanan ben Zakkai to our brothers in the Upper and Lower Galilee, and to Simonia, and to Oved Bet Hillel, Peace! Let it be known to you that the fourth year has arrived, but still the sacred produce has not been removed. But now, make haste and bring of the olive heaps, for they hinder the Confession; and it is not we who have begun to write to you, but our fathers used to write to your fathers.[1]

---

[1] The letters of Gamaliel are cited in Tos. Sanhedrin 2.2, TB Sanhedrin 11b, TP Sanhedrin 1.2, Maaser Sheni 5.4. The letters of Yohanan ben Zakkai and Simeon ben Gamaliel are preserved in Midrash Tannaim, ed. D. Hoffman (Berlin 1909), pp. 175-6, on Deut. 26.13. A Buechler discusses the matter at great length, cf. *Das Synhedrion*, 131-144; *Studies in Jewish History* (London, 1958), Hebrew section, 1-15. "The letters of Simeon ben Gamaliel the Elder and Rabban Yohanan ben Zakkai on the Removal of the Tithes in the Second Commonwealth." On the commandment to remove old tithes, cf. Deut. 14.28, 26.12; Maaser Sheni 5.8. Buechler dates the letter (p. 14) in 66 C.E., the fourth year in the last seven year cycle (according to the common assumption). It could, nonetheless, have been in 59 C.E. or even in 52 C.E. as well. Simonia was about two hours southwest of Sepphoris, cf. Hoffman *ad. loc.* Oved bet Hillel is not mentioned elsewhere. The "Upper South" may refer to Idumaea, cf. A. Schalit, *Herod*, 412, n. 235. Cf. also A. Kaminka (*Mehkarim*, 106, n. 19), who doubts the authenticity of the letter; cf. also Kaminka, "Rabban Yohanan ben Zakkai and his students," *Zion*, IX, 70. Allon (*Mehkarim*, II, 257, n. 16) doubts the authenticity of the letter of Simeon and Yohanan; he regards the letters of Gamaliel I (Tos. Sanhedrin 2.2, TB Sanhedrin 11a-b) as parallel sources, and says that in them, Yohanan's name is not mentioned; so that it would appear, Allon says, that despite the differences in the subject matter and language which we can distinguish between the above mentioned source and the parallels, only one such event happened, and its repetition was caused by a confusion between Rabban Gamaliel and Rabban Simeon ben Gamaliel (a confusion common in Talmudic literature). Allon adds that Epstein told him that the scribe of Gamaliel the Elder was Nahum the Scribe (Peah 2.6, Nazir 56b), and not Yohanan the Scribe. One must note, first of all, that Nahum the Scribe is *not* explicitly described as Gamaliel's scribe; in the Peah source, he converses with Gamaliel and provides him with an ancient tradition; but there is no evidence that he was actually Gamaliel's scribe. Furthermore, in his own discussion of the source, Epstein (Mavo-ot, 75) does not repeat his alleged doubt on the authenticity of the source. If this is *not* an authentic letter, furthermore, the detail about "we did not begin to write you, but our fathers to your fathers" is counterfeit, and not merely an error in transmission. I am not prepared to assume such a counterfeit, as I can see no motive for it. On the location of Simonia, cf. also Avi Yonah *(Geographia)*, 133; the town is mentioned by Josephus, *Life*, 24. The removal of the tithes that had not been properly disposed of took place at the end of the third year of the septennial cycle, either by means of giving them to the proper recipients, or by destroying them. Cf. *Encyclopedia Talmudit* (Jerusalem, 1947 et seq.), ed. M. Berlin and S. Y. Zevin; hereafter – ETal), IV, 44-46. The maaserot which are liable are those listed in the Confession, cf. Maaser Sheni 5.10-13, and included second tithe, fourth planting, hallah, Maaser Levi, terumah, and Terumat Maaser, poor man's tithe, and the gleanings. Thus the process of Removal is different according to the sanctity involved. It had to be done at the Passover festival, some said before the first night, and some, the last; in any case, the confession had to be recited on the afternoon of the last day of Passover. The practice of sending such pastoral letters is alluded to in the following (Maaser Sheni 5.8): "Rabbi Judah said, Beforetime they used to send to householders in the

Besides his son Simeon, Gamaliel I left a daughter, whose daughter married Yohanan's student Simon ben Natanel the Priest. When he died, it was said, "the honor of Torah ceased, and purity and separateness passed away."[1] Simeon ben Gamaliel also issued special decrees, particularly to improve the position of women. He exhibited great physical skill (he was a juggler), and with "gifts of intelligence and judgment, he could by sheer genius retrieve an unfortunate situation in affairs of state."[2] He led the pro-war faction of the Pharisees during the revolution, and held authority in the first coalition government. It was rumored that he died at the hands of the Romans, but this is by no means certain.[3]

Though Yohanan ben Zakkai spent much of his time with such colleagues as these, he also took up some kind of trade.[4] Many of the sages were poor men, and made their living at skilled and semi-skilled labor such as shoe-making, smithing, and shop-keeping, which permitted free time for their serious concerns. Though the sages had either to work or to starve, the schools were crowded. Yohanan

---

provinces, saying, 'Hasten and duly tithe your produce before the time of removal shall come,' until Rabbi Akiba came and taught that all produce was exempt from removal if its tithing season was not yet come." In the light of this, Buechler suggests that the point of the letters was to urge the people to hasten to bring the fruits into their houses *in order to* render them liable for tithing, cf. *Studies in Jewish History*, p. 7; this would explain the reference to the "five sheaves" and "olive heaps," and cf. the comment of Hoffman, *ad loc*. These letters provide significant evidence that the Pharisaic leaders did exert considerable influence over their followers throughout the country, and in the diaspora communities as well. It would support the assumption that the Romans were not adverse to conciliating the Pharisaic leaders, in order to forestall rebellion in the diaspora communities and among the non-revolted regions in the land, cf. chapter six.

On the letter of R. Simeon b. Gamaliel and Yohanan ben Zakkai, see also H. Mantel, *Studies in the History of the Sanhedrin*, (Cambridge 1961), p. 28-31.

[1] Tosefta Avodah Zarah 3.10., Sotah 9.15.

[2] Josephus, *Life*, 190 f. also 216, 309.

[3] Semahot 8. Cf. also Finkelstein, *Akiba*, 50; Hoenig, *Sanhedrin*, 38 f., 46 f., and Finkelstein, *Perushim*, 22-23. Cf. also Keritot 1.7. He could juggle eight torches at once, Tos. Sukkah 4.4. On his life, cf. Bruell, Mavo, 55-57; Frankel, Mishnah, 65-66; and *inter alia* the following sources: Sotah 49b, Eruvin 61b, Avodah Zara 32a, Sukkah 53a; ARNa ch. 38; Megillat Taanit, last chapter; Avot. 1. 17-8: "Simeon his son said; All my days I have grown up among the wise, and I have found nought of better service than silence; not learning but doing is the chief thing, and who is profuse of words causes sin." As in the case of Gamaliel I, many of his statements may have become confused with those of Simeon ben Gamaliel II, who lived at the middle of the 2nd century. I have not dealt at length with either Gamaliel I or Simon ben Gamaliel, but only touch these elements of their teachings which are important in understanding Yohanan ben Zakkai.

[4] Ch. 1.

conducted one such academy, which had, so far as is known, neither rigid curriculum (after certain fundamentals were mastered), nor even a formally recognized degree of competence (until after the destruction[1]). The academy probably did not have its own building, for the stairway leading to the Temple mount, on the westward side by the Offal Gate, seems to have been the place where he sat and lectured to his students;[2] though some sources[3] imply that he met in some kind of large room. The Temple, like others in the classical world, was a site of public instruction; the Essene master Judah had taught there earlier, as had Jesus of Nazareth. Yohanan did not apparently use the courts of the Temple, but sat in the shadow of the Temple pile, doubtless where he could see it. The Temple was one of the wonders of the ancient world, "He who has not seen Herod's building has never in his life seen a beautiful building,"[4] the saying went, and as the "navel of the universe," provided an appropriate setting for Yohanan's study of Torah.

Yohanan, as a leading Pharisee,[5] came into conflict with the Temple officialdom, and was reported to have criticized the cult and its officers. It was told:

> Simon of Sikhnin, the councilman, supervisor of the water supply, said to Yohanan ben Zakkai, "I am as great as thou." Yohanan replied, Why? Because I, like you, am occupied with the public welfare. Yohanan said to him, "But if someone comes to you for justice or for information,

---

[1] Ch. 7.

[2] On the location of public teaching, cf. Midrash Tannaim, cit. p. 42; also TB Pesahim 26a, TP Avodah Zarah 3.11, compare The Gospel according to St. John, 8.12-20; Josephus, *War*, I, 78. Also, A. Buechler, "Learning and Teaching in the Open Air in Palestine," *JQR*, n. s., IV, 485-6. It was fairly common for the sages to study on the Temple mount. Cf. also Allon, Mehkarim, I, 78-9.

[3] Eliezer ben Hyrkanos' father allegedly heard his son preach in a crowded room, cf. ch. 4.

[4] TP Sukkah 5.1. Cf. also TB Baba Batra 4a, Sukkah 51b. On the layout of the buildings, and conduct of services, cf. Mishnah Middot and Tamid; Josephus, *Antiquities*, XV. 11. 3, Wars 5.5.1 (184 f.). Cf. also A. Parrot, *The Temple of Jerusalem* (London, 1957); and S. Safrai, "The Ritual in the Second Temple" and M. Avi-Yonah, "The Second Temple," in M. Avi-Yonah, ed. *Sefer Yerushalayim* [The Book of Jerusalem] (Jerusalem, 1956), 369-418; also ETal. III, 224-241; J. D. Eisenstein, "Temple, Administration of," "Temple, Plan of Second," and C. A. Barton, "Temple of Herod," *JE*, XII, 81-92.

[5] On the officers of the Pharisaic institution, cf. Finkelstein, *Perushim*, 22-23; *Akiba*, 50; compare Hoenig, *Sanhedrin*, 38 f., 46 f. The problem of the Pharisaic institution, like that of the Sanhedrin, has been discussed by many scholars, and many conflicting theories explain the relevant facts. I have nothing to contribute to the discussion, see p. 33, n. 1.

what will you say to him? Will you say, drink from this cistern, for its waters are pure and cold? Or if a woman comes with a question of ritual uncleanness at her period, will you say to her, dip in this cistern, for its waters purify? [Cistern water cannot purify.] And of this man, Yohanan spoke the verse (Kohelet 4.18), Guard your steps when you go to the house of God. To draw near to listen is better than to offer sacrifice of fools, for they do not know they are doing evil.[1]

Simon's exact title is "council man, digger of trenches, cisterns, and pools." Among the Temple officers, one is listed[2] as a trench digger, and defined elsewhere[3] as a man who knew which rocks were likely to yield water. It seems justifiable, therefore, to identify Simon of Sikhnin, the councilman, with some such Temple authority, particularly in the light of the verse Yohanan quotes against him. Such a "digger of wells, cisterns, and pools in Jerusalem" held an important responsibility; the water supply throughout this period was superb, and withstood the exigencies of siege. Yohanan professed, nonetheless, to regard his own capacities as still more significant; to offer *Torah*, which here comprehends justice and ritual law, is a greater service than pure water, no matter how sophisticated the technology required by sanitation.[4]

The priests contended that they had the right to rule on legal matters as well as Temple rites, and Yohanan opposed their decisions in two known cases. The priestly decisions were handed down by the "sons of the high priests,"[5] in competition, apparently, with the municipal

---

[1] Kohelet Rabbah 4.18.

[2] Mishnah Shekalim 5.1, Nehunyah was the "trench digger." Note also that Nehunya was remembered with favor in the Tannaitic traditions. Apparently filling the same kind of position as Simon of Sikhnin, he was praised by the sages who recalled his administration of his office (cf. TB Baba Kama 50a). Note also his contact with Hanina ben Dosa at this same period, TB Yevamot 121b. Compare also TB Baba Kama 50a and TB Sotah 18b and the parallel, TP Sotah 2.5.

[3] Compare TP Shekalim 5.1, which states explicitly that this officer would dig trenches, wells, and divine for water.

[4] On Sikhnai – Sikhnin, cf. *Aruk*, VI, 53. On the water supply of Jerusalem cf. A. Buechler, "On the Provisioning of Jerusalem in the year 69-70," *Studies*, 98-113. On other disputes between Yohanan ben Zakkai and the priests, cf. A. Geiger, *Mikra*, 75, 95, 98, 100. Sikhnin was northeast of Arav in the Galilee and was a center of priestly settlement, like Arav; cf. M. Avi-Yonah, *Geographia*, 136. Professor Smith suggests that Simon represents the practical, as opposed to Yohanan's theoretical virtue, a classical dispute between Torah and good deeds (cf. Simeon ben Gamaliel's statement in Avot 1.17, n. 30). The editor of Koh. R. clearly understood Yohanan's comment, however, as a criticism of the cultic technocrats.

[5] The "sons of the high priests" constituted a priestly court. Cf. Acts 4.5. Cf. Mishnah Ketuvot 1.5, Schuerer, *History*, II, i, 205 f. The sons of the high priests are mentioned in TB Ketuvot 88b, 105a, 107a, b, Nedarim 33b, and TP Ketuvot 13.1, 2, Nedarim 4.2. Also cf. Mishnah Rosh Hashanah 1.7, Pesahim

courts which judged cases of civil law and commercial transactions.[1]
Yohanan supported the decisions of the municipal justice, in two cases
dealing with women's rights:[2]

90b, Avodah Zarah 36b, Tosefta Sanhedrin 4.7; and Hoenig, *Sanhedrin*, 204, who
suggests that the *Bet Din shel Kohanim* and that of the *Bne Kohanim Gedolim* in the
present mishnah are one and the same. Cf. also Bruell, *Mavo*, 52-3; Frankel, *Mishnah*,
62-3; and Buechler, *Synhedrion*, 114; also Weiss, *Dor*, I, 163, 184; A. Gulak, *Yesode
HaMishpat HaIvri* [Foundations of Hebrew Jurisprudence] (Warsaw, 1913, et.
seq., 4 vols.), IV, 20-21, who regards the priestly court as an institution devoted
solely to the interests of the priesthood. This is not inconsistent with the known
cases, all of which deal with family law, matters of the calendar (very important in
determining the proper offerings), etc. Cf. also Bloch, *Institutionem*, II, ii, 82-91. For
other actual conflicts with the priests, cf. below.

[1] On the municipal courts (judges of civil cases) cf. Mishnah Ketuvot 13.1, TB
Ketuvot 105a, TP Ketuvot 13.1, Nedarim 33 b. According to later reports, there
were several hundred such courts (below.), but the names of only a few of the
judges were known, Nahum the Mede, Admon ben Gidae, and Hanan ben Avis-
halom. These judges were, in fact, related to the Temple, for they were paid from
Temple funds, receiving 99 maneh, or even more if this was insufficient. It is also
recorded that Gamaliel I approved decisions of Admon, cf. Ketuvot 13.3-8, in
opposition to the sages' court. The title was *dayyane gezerot* or *dayyane gezelot*, justices
of ordinances, or justices of larceny. Hoenig, *Sanhedrin*, p. 60 suggests that the
justices might have been experts in such cases only, and that they came under the
authority of the Great Sanhedrin. Cf. also on the municipal courts, Frankel,
Mishnah, 63-65, Bruell, *Mavo*, 53-55. Bruell thinks that these courts were established
after the death of Hillel and Shammai, to provide decisions in the mounting disputes
in matters of law, that is, practical judgments for pressing cases. J. Z. Lauterbach,
Rabbinic Essays (Cincinnati, 1951) 35, n. 15, suggests that these were Sadducean
judges applying a Sadducean code, the *sefer gezerot*. For this reason they were called
in a later beraita (Ket. 105a) and also in the mishnah of the Palestinian Talmud
dayyane gezelot, "for the Pharisees considered their judgments decrees of robbery."
But the context of the mishnah and beraita does not in any was imply a derogatory
judgment of the "decrees of larceny," and one doubts that Yohanan ben Zakkai
would have approved such decrees. Lauterbach would apparently read *dine* in place
of *dayyane*. Cf. also H. Albeck, *Seder Nashim* (Jerusalem, 1954), 356, n. 1, who relates
these courts to those mentioned in Moed Katan 3.3, Ketuvot 1.5, and Rosh
Hashanah 1.7. Cf. also A. Buechler, *Synhedrion*, 111-114, A. Geiger, *Mikra*,
79-80, Gulak, *Yesode*, IV, 21-22 agrees with N. Krochmal's suggestion (*Moreh
Nevukhe HaZeman* [Guide to the Perplexed of this Age], ch. 13, cited in Gulak,
p. 21) that these were neither Pharisaic nor Sadducean courts, but were appointed
by the Romans to judge civil cases, and therefore received the stipend cited by the
Talmud. Such courts would be essential for the administration of commercial law,
damages and torts, and (as cited here) marital relationships. Gulak suggests further
that the reason these decisions were approved by Gamaliel and Yohanan was to
give them force among the Pharisees, who otherwise would not have accepted the
alien jurisdiction. Cf. also Epstein, *Mavo-ot*, 20; Weiss, *Dor*, I, 181-2, who holds
that these courts were appointed to provide practical law, and were established by
the Jewish authorities of the temple. He explains the variant readings in their title
by reference to dialects. Hanan is mentioned in TB Ketuvot 88b, 105a, 107a, b,
108a, 109a, Nedarim 33b, TP Ketuvot 13.1, 2; Nedarim 4.2, Shavuot 7.7.

[2] Finkelstein, *Pharisees*, I, 138-142.

> If a man went beyond the sea, and his wife claimed maintenance, Hanan said, Let her swear [to her claim] at the end of the time, and let her not swear at the beginning.[1]

That is, when the woman comes to claim her marriage-money if her husband died, or if he returns and claims that he left her funds for her own maintenance, she must take an oath that she has not held back any of her husband's property. Hanan ruled that she need not take a presumptive [*propter hoc*] oath, but is required to swear only at the end of the period in question. To this, the "sons of the high priests" said:

> Let her swear when she makes claim for maintenance as well as when she claims what is due her as marriage money.

Yohanan ben Zakkai ruled (possibly for the Pharisaic community):

> Hanan has spoken well. Let her swear only at the end.

In the second case, the same pattern recurred:

> If a man went beyond the sea and another maintained his wife, Hanan said, the second has lost his money. But the sons of the high priests disputed with him, and said, Let him swear on oath how much he has expended, and let him recover it. Rabban Yohanan ben Zakkai said: Hanan has spoken well, he has laid his money on the horn of a gazelle.[2]

The "sons of the high (or important) priests," apparently equivalent to the sages' court and regulating the affairs of those who adhered to their viewpoint, levied twice the normal marriage-money for the daughters of the high priests, communicated with diaspora communities, and tried men charged with the violation on of Temple laws. They also calculated a calendar of their own,[3] employing rules of evidence different from those of the sages.[4] The two groups clearly differed on the position of the wife in relation to her husband's authority, and on the measure of control of the husband's property to be entrusted to the wife.[5] It may well have been that the sages opposed unnecessary oaths,' providing the woman an income with adjuration until the final ac-

---

[1] Ketuvot 13.1.

[2] Ketuvot 13.2.

[3] Cf. Rosh Hashanah 1.7. This provides further testimony that the Pharisees did not, as they later thought they had, govern the Temple cult. The existence of priestly courts which were specifically determining the lunar calendar implies that such courts would have existed to determine many matters of Temple policy. Contrast this with the reported authority of Yohanan in the Temple.

[4] *Ibid.*

[5] Buechler, *Studies*, 156, n. 3.

[6] Finkelstein, *Akiba*, 299-300.

counting. (The circumstance of these decisions provides oblique, but useful information on Yohanan's chronology, for Rabban Gamaliel I later annulled the force of the first decision by making a formal oath unnecessary and substituting an informal vow. Such an ordinance would likely have followed Hanan's decision, which Yohanan approved, for it assumes the necessity of administering a formal oath, rather than an informal undertaking such as a vow, and suggests that Yohanan was, as we have seen, in Jerusalem for some significant part of Gamaliel's reign.)[1]

Yohanan also criticized the upper classes for neglect of "Torah," and warned that children must be kept away from commercial life and brought to the academies, saying

> Keep the children away from the proud, and separate them from the householders, because the householders draw a man far from words of Torah... He used to say, For three [sic] kinds of sins, householders are given over to the Government, because they lend money on interest, because they preserve mortgages which have already been paid, because they promise publicly to give charity, and do not give, and because they remove from themselves the yoke of taxes, and place it on the poor, the needy, and the oppressed, and concerning them it is written, "Cursed is he who will not fulfil the words of this Torah" (Deut. 27.26) – these are the householders.

In this saying, the "proud" clearly refers to the upper classes, and Yohanan was warning against the pernicious influence of business on the education of the youth.[2]

---

[1] This was first pointed out by Weiss, *Dor*, I, 182, who noted that the oath must have been common in Hanan's time, but not after Gamaliel's edict. But Weiss thought that this proved Hanan preceded Gamaliel. I think it more likely that they were almost contemporaries, and that Gamaliel later controverted Hanan's decision by his edict. If this was so, Yohanan's approval of Hanan's opinion came before Gamaliel's edict, and thus while Gamaliel was still in authority. I must admit, however, that it is possible that Yohanan approved Hanan's opinion in the face of Gamaliel's edict.

[2] ARNB, ch. 31, Schechter ed. p. 34a, compare TB Sukkah 29a-b: "For four things the property of householders is given to the Government, because they hold back of indebtedness which have already been paid, and lend at interest, and because they have sufficient authority (Rashi – to prevent sin) and do not prevent it, and because they promise publicly to give to charity and do not give." Note also the teaching of Rav, which included the misapplication of tax obligation. Cf. also Tosefta Sukkah 2.6: "On account of three [sic] things the property of householders in Israel is given to the government, because of those who hold collected bills of indebtedness, and lend on interest, and promise to give publicly to charity and do not give, and who have sufficient (authority to prevent sin?) and do not do so." Cf. also Tractate Derekh Erez Rabbah, ch. 2, cited by Schechter, 34a, n. 11. I have followed Allon's interpretation, cf. *Mehkarim*, I, 313-4. Allon explains *gaon* as

His main antagonists in Jerusalem were not, however, the wealthy men as such, for some leading citizens attended festal gatherings in his academy, and he witnessed the marriage contracts for the richest daughters of the city;[1] nor was he hostile to all members of the priestly classes on account of their sacerdotal privileges, for he counted among his students priests as well as laity. His principal struggle was with the Sadducean party, and in these disputes, he supposedly[2] acted as spokesman for the Pharisees. Each of the extant disputes[3] centered about a petty, sometimes esoteric issue of law, mainly laws on ritual cleanness and uncleanness, and one must be aware of the possibly broader matters at issue which were represented in the relatively narrow terms of argument. Thus, for example, the apparently minor argument on whether Holy Scriptures have the capacity to render the hands unclean or not may have represented the Pharisaic assertion, phrased in ritual and legal terms, that study was equivalent to sacrifice:

> The Sadducees say, We cry out against you, O Pharisees, for you say, The Holy Scriptures render the hands unclean and the books of Homer do not render the hands unclean. Rabban Yohanan ben Zakkai said, "And have we nothing but this against the Pharisees? For lo, they say, the bones of an ass are pure, but the bones of Yohanan the High Priest (John Hyrkanos) are unclean. They said to him, As is our love for them, so is their uncleanness, so that no man may make spoons out of the bones of his father and mother. He said to them, Even so the Holy Scriptures – as is our love for them, so is their uncleanness, whereas the writings of Homer, which are held in no account, do not render the hands unclean.[4]

The issue at hand was whether one had to wash his hands after touching the sacred Scriptures, as the priest had to wash his hands after

---

"world of the householders," and although he rejects Buechler's translation of "the proud" (cf. *Galilean Am HaAretz*, 248) he does not provide philological evidence for his translation, although the parallel supports his interpretation. Note also that Eliezer ben Hyrkanos repeated the same warning, cf. TB Berahot 28a, and cf. Allon, *Mehkarim*, I, 314, n. 9.

[1] The richest men in the city heard Eliezer's inaugural lecture, cf. ch. 4. Yohanan witnessed for a wealthy family, cf. TB Ketuvot 66b, and parallels, cited in ch. 7.

[2] I shall discuss the stylized form of the traditions below, and other difficulties in the historical evaluation of the disputes.

[3] Sources provided below.

[4] Mishnah Yadaim 4.6, cf. Tosefta Yadaim 2.9. Compare also TB Shabbat 4a. On the meaning of *sifre Homeros*, cf. S. Lieberman, *Hellenism in Jewish Palestine*, 106. Cf. also Buechler, *Priester und Cultus*, 25, for discussion of the general direction of the disputes with the Sadducean priests. Cf. also D. Daube, "Three Notes Having to Do with Johanan ben Zaccai," *Journal of Theological Studies*, n. s., XI, part 1, 1960, p. 53–56.

priestly rites. The Sadducees ruled in the Temple, and so even the Pharisaic rule was that the Scroll of the Sanctuary does not defile the hands, but outside the Sanctuary, the Pharisaic rule on the uncleanness of Scriptures applied in their circles. Some have thought that thus the sage and his students at the academy asserted, their service of God through study of Torah merited the same sacred devotion as that of the priest in the Temple. This idea found expression in possibly later literature as follows:

> Whoever busies himself in Torah needs neither burnt-offering nor sin offering.
> Whoever busies himself in Torah – it is as if he offered a burnt-offering.[1]

A second argument in a minor detail of the law of cleanness likewise may have concealed a more important principle. In order to understand the dispute at hand, one must have in mind how troublesome the laws of purity were for the Jerusalem tradesman and worker, who prepared wine and grain for use in the sacrificial service. In order to keep the wares fit for the Temple, the worker had to remain in a state of purity. Furthermore, many Jerusalemite workers ate second tithe, which was brought from round about to be consumed in Jerusalem, and they had to remain pure for that purpose. (On the other hand, the rural populace rarely obeyed such laws, while the priests, who spent considerable time in the Temple, found it easy to avoid ritual contamination.) Thus the lower and middle classes bore the burden of the purity laws. The Pharisees, legislating in their behalf, tried to ease this burden. One of their most important enactments was to declare that when a man had bathed after becoming unclean from a major impurity, he remained unclean until evening (in accordance with Scripture), *but* not in the original degree of impurity. His degree of impurity was diminished so that he himself would not impart impurity to household utensils, thus being able to go about his work; he was only barred from the Temple. This was the *tevul-yom*, a man who has bathed from impurity but had

---

[1] Finkelstein, *Pharisees*, I, 279–280. The rule on the Temple scroll is in Kelim 15.6, cited by Finkelstein. Cf. also H. Albeck, *Seder Taharot* (Tel Aviv, 1958), 608, n. 6. Yohanan supposedly ridiculed the Sadducees. In this case, the reason he gives, like those below, is not necessarily the serious halakhic principle at issue at all. Albeck notes that the decree of uncleanness of Scriptures will prevent them from being mishandled, or handled at random, which is clear also from Yohanan's words. Cf. also A. Geiger, *Mikra*; Buechler, *Synhedrion*, 142. Teachings on equvalence of study and sacrifice are in TB Menahot 110a.

not yet finished out the day of Levitical uncleanness.[1] The Pharisaic legislation, however, was rejected by the Sadducean party, who wished to maintain the full stringency of the laws of uncleanness for the entire period, and would not recognize that the bathing had diminished it in the slightest.

One occasion (apart from the paschal sacrifice) provided an opportunity to advance this viewpoint in action, at a sacrificial ceremony which took place outside the sanctuary. The burning of the red heifer to create purification ashes took place not in the sanctuary, but on the Mount of Olives. The ceremony would not require absolute purity, and if the Sadducean priests observed their more stringent ruling, they would thereby manifest their rejection of the Pharisaic ruling. Later Pharisaic tradition had evidently no reliable information on the sacrifice of the cows, but it preserved various, mutually contradictory, stories about high priests forced to conform to the Pharisaic viewpoint, and even crediting Yohanan ben Zakkai with having defiled one in the midst of the ceremonies to prevent his completing them in purity. One considers, nonetheless, the stories as they were handed down. First, the Pharisees related that the ceremony took place only seven times in the entire history of the Second Commonwealth:

> Who had prepared them? Moses prepared the first, Ezra prepared the second, and five were prepared after Ezra, so Rabbi Meir. But the sages say, Seven since Ezra. And who prepared them? Simon the Just and Yohanan the High Priest prepared two each, and Elyehoenai the son of Hakkof (Caiaphas) and Hanamel the Egyptian, and Ishmael the son of Phiabi prepared one each.

The Mount of Olives contained a place of immersion, and the high priest was rendered unclean:

> because of the Sadducees, that they should not be able to say, It must be performed only by one on whom the sun has set. They laid their hands upon him and said, My Lord high priest, immerse thyself this once. He went down, immersed himself, came up, dried himself...[2]

Then, as a *tevul-yom*, the high priest supposedly slaughtered the cow and burned its ashes.

---

[1] This is the interpretation of L. Finkelstein, *Pharisees*, I, 121 f., esp. 125–128. Cf. also Buechler, *Priester und Cultus*, 57, *Synedrion*, 107, 140, 142. Compare, G. Allon, "The Boundaries of the Laws of Ritual Cleanness," *Mehkarim*, I, 148–177, particularly 176-177.

[2] Cf. Mishnah Parah 3.5, 7, 8.

The following account included Yohanan ben Zakkai:

> It once happened that a certain Sadducee waited out the night of his uncleanness and came to burn the red heifer. Rabban Yohanan ben Zakkai heard of the matter, and placed his two hands on him, rendering him unclean again, and said to him, My lord high priest, how fitting it is for you to be high priest! Now go, immerse. The men went and immersed, and came back. When he came up, he slit his ear (thereby rendre ing him unfit for the priestly service),and the priest said to Yohanan, Ben Zakkai – when I have time to deal with you... If you have time, he replied. Three days did not pass by before they buried him, and his father came to Yohanan and said, My son has time.[1]

Since the traditions deal here with Yohanan ben Zakkai and an unnamed high priest, and since Ishmael ben Phiabi was a contemporary, it has been thought that Yohanan's encounter was with him, but this is manifestly impossible, for it was also recorded[2] that Ishmael ben Phiabi did accept the sages' ruling; one could scarcely harmonize such a tradition with his sudden death on Yohanan's account. Furthermore, Ishmael was remembered with high regard, "When Rabbi [sic] Ishmael ben Phiabi died, the splendor of the priesthood ceased."[3] If the incident did not happen with Ishmael, however, it is difficult to explain, for no other high priest is known to have officiated, or attempted to officiate at the heifer ceremony during Yohanan's lifetime; Hanamel having been high priest under Herod.[4] Since the sources so clearly conflict[5] one must conclude that the editors of the Mishnah and Tosefta had no reliable information on the subject. It seems certain,

---

[1] Tosefta Para 3.8.

[2] Tosefta Para 3.6. On the laying on of hands and slitting the ear, cf. D. Daube, "Three Notes Having to Do with Johanan be Zaccai," *Journal of Theological Studies*, n. s., XI, part 1, 1960, p. 56-62.

[3] Mishnah Sotah 9.15

[4] Cf. S. Mendelsohn, "Hanameel the Egyptian," *JE*, VI, 203.

[5] One cannot harmonize the list of high priests who burned the cow with the events recorded in Tos. 3.6, 8. Note also the manner in which the sages allegedly treated the high priest, cf. Yoma 1.3,5. On Ishmael b. Phiabi, cf. Schuerer, *History*, II, i, 200, Josephus, *Antiquities*, 20, 8, 8, 11; Derenbourg, *Essai*, 232-5, who bypasses the burning of the cow. M. Kayserling, Ishmael ben Phabi II (*JE*, VI, 650-651) states, "Ishmael at first followed the Sadducean method of burning the sacrificial red heifer, but finally authorized the procedure according to the Pharisaic teaching," apparently on the basis of Tos. Parah 3.6. If so, he is not the high priest whom Yohanan was said to have blemished; and if not, why was he remembered with some affection. It is conceivable that the incident did not happen with Ishmael ben Phiabi at all, but in that case the Mishnah knows of no high priest during Yohanan's lifetime who executed the rite. But compare Buechler, *Synhedrion*, 141, who thinks it may have been Joseph Kabi or Anan b. Anan, or Jesus b. Damnai. Cf. *Studies*, 38; *Priester und Cultus*, 57, where he settles on Anan. But there is no proof.

however, that the Pharisaic position, which Yohanan was said to have advanced even with violence, favored the interest of the urban populace, who would have found it difficult to cope with the laws of purity if they, defiled almost daily from some source of contamination, could render unclean by a slight touch every object around them. (The Pharisaic rule also encouraged the custom of bathing in a ritual pool each morning, a measure that contributed to hygienic purity in the crowded city.[1])

Three other disputes, recorded in the *Fasting-Scroll*,[2] resulted in victory for Yohanan ben Zakkai, and were supposedly commemorated by "days on which one is not permitted to fast... or to mourn." The stories are preserved in highly stylized form, and this, together with the dubiety of commemorating Yohanan's victories with festival celebration, casts doubt on the historicity of the account. It is clear, however, that these were matters at issue between the parties, and that later generations, recalling Yohanan's leadership, might well have ascribed to him the "incident" which epitomized the dispute. Broadly interpreted, the disputes concerned religious doctrine, national economic policy, and priestly privilege.

The first was, specifically, a debate on the proper date for Pentecost. The Scrolls stated:

> From the eighth thereof (Nisan) until the close of the festival of Passover, a holiday was declared, during which it was forbidden to mourn... The Boethesians said that Pentecost follows the Sabbath. Rabban Yohanan ben Zakkai dealt with them, saying, Idiots, how do you know? None among them, however, could find an answer, except for one old man who mumbled and stumbled, and said, Moses our master loved Israel, and he knew that Pentecost lasted for one day. He went, therefore, and arranged to have it fall after the Sabbath so that Israel could have two days of rejoicing. Yohanan recited this verse to him, "It is eleven days' journey from Horeb by way of Mount Seir to Kadesh Barnea [The gateway to the Land of Israel]" (Deut. 1.2). Now if Moses our master loved Israel, why did he detain them in the wilderness forty years? He answered, Rabbi, with this do you dismiss me? He said, Idiot! Let not the complete Torah of ours [That is, both oral and written Torah] be like the idle chatter of yours! One Scripture says (Lev. 23.15) You will count fifty days [between Passover and Pentecost]

---

[1] This is not to suggest that hygiene was the primary motive.

[2] Cf. H. Lichtenstein, "Die Fastenrolle," HUCA VIII-IX, 275 f. and A. Neubauer, *Medieval Jewish Chronicles* (Oxford, 1887, reprinted New York, 1959), II, 3 f.; and S, Zeitlin, *Megillat Taanit as a Source for Jewish Chronology* (Philadelphia, 1922). Two of the three stories are paralleled by beraitot, cf. TB Menahot, 65a, TB Baba Batra 115b.

and another Scripture says (Lev. 23.16) – Seven full weeks there will be [between the two festivals]. Now how is this possible? One Scripture refers to a [Passover] festival that happens to fall on the Sabbath, and the other to a festival that falls in the middle of the week.[1]

But Pentecost does not necessarily have to fall on a Sunday. The point at issue[2] was the interpretation of conflicting Scriptures, for Pentecost, alone of all festivals, is not given a definite date in Scripture. It is merely stated that the holiday should be celebrated fifty days after the offering of the *omer* which is "on the morrow after the *Sabbath*" of Passover. The Sadducees interpreted *Sabbath* literally, and the Pharisees said the *Sabbath* may also connote *festival day*.[3] Thus the Sadducees said that the *omer* was to be offered annually on the first Sunday after Passover, and that therefore Pentecost will always come on the seventh Sunday after Passover, while the Pharisees disagreed, and held that the *omer* is offered the day after the first day of Passover, that is, on the sixteenth day of Nisan, and Pentecost would always then fall on the sixth day of Sivan. The underlying question, Finkelstein suggests,[4] was what meaning would attach to Pentecost. The Pharisees apparently insisted that Pentecost should have a fixed date, perhaps because they held that it commemorated the giving of the Torah on Mount Sinai, which occurred the fiftieth day after the Exodus, while the Sadducees denied both that the festival had any historical allusion, and that the date of revelation was known. It may have troubled the Pharisaic scholars that revelation was not marked by any festival, and they may have been disturbed by the comparative irrelevance to the city-dweller of the holiday of the first fruits (Pentecost's ancient significance). Hence they may have suggested the association of Pentecost with Sinaitic revelation and insisted on a fixed date, and if so,

---

[1] Lichtenstein, 276 f. Parallel in TB Menahot 65a. I have followed the text of the TB. Cf. also Zeitlin, 72.

[2] Finkelstein, *Pharisees*, I, 115 f. Cf. also Buechler, Synhedrion, 142-3. The three stories in the *scholion* of Megillat Taanit, which preserve these disputes, are discussed by Lichtenstein also.

[3] H. Schauss, *The Jewish Festivals from their Beginnings to Our Own Day* (Cincinnati, 1938), 87-88. Also Y. Vainstein, *Cycle of the Jewish Year* (Jerusalem, 1953), 133.

[4] Cf. n. 2. Examples of such Pharisaic midrash on the holiday include the following, TB Shabbat 86b, Yoma 4b, Taanit 28b, Avoda Zara 3a, and note also Pesikta Zutrata, ch. Emor, "And thou shalt proclaim on that very day – that is the fiftieth day, the day that Israel stood before Mount Sinai to receive the Torah, for our fathers received the Torah on the fiftieth day after they went forth from Egypt. He gave them the day of the first fruits at the end of the fifty days of the festival of unleavened bread, as Israel was called the first fruit (Hosea 9.10)." Thus the two themes were skillfully woven together in later years.

the dispute between Yohanan and the Sadducees (or Boethesians[1]) may well have represented conflict over both exegesis and doctrine.[2]

The second conflict concerned national economic policy, specifically, how to divide a legacy without subdividing it beyond the point of economic efficiency.[3] Biblical law had recognized male issue as primary heir, and permitted daughters to inherit only where there were no sons (Num. 27.8). It was also assumed that grandsons took precedence over daughters. The question arose whether this rule also applied to the prior rights of the son's daughter over the progenitor's own daughter: if the son died while his father was alive, who would inherit? His daughter or his sister? It would appear that little might be gained by favoring the granddaughter and disinheriting the daughter, and indeed, the Sadducees maintained that the property ought to be divided. The Pharisees held that the granddaughter inherited all of her father's property. (Since both potential heirs were female, the issue was not women's rights.) The question was whether to divide inherited property between heirs, and the Pharisees, generally men of smaller means, opposed any rule that would increase the number of potential heirs to their limited estates; the Sadducees, generally larger landowners, could well bestow equal rights on the daughter and granddaughter.

This dispute was preserved as follows:

> On the twenty fourth day in it [Av[4]], we returned to our law... for the Sadducees said, Let the daughter inherit with the granddaughter. Rabban Yohanan ben Zakkai busied himself with them. Idiots, he said, how do you know? Not one of them could answer, except for one old man who mumbled and stumbled, and said, "Just as the daughter of his son, who comes from the power of his son, inherits him, so his own daughter, who comes from his own power, is it not logical that she should inherit him?" He replied, concerning you this verse is written, "And these are the sons of Seir the Horite, the inhabitants of the land, Lotan, Shobal, Zibeon, Anah (Gen. 36.20) and another verse reads, "He is Anah who found the hot springs in the wilderness as he pastured the asses of Zibeon his father... This proves that Zibeon came upon his mother and fathered Anah from her!" He said to him, Rabbi, with this do you dismiss me? He answered, Idiot! Do not make our complete Torah to be like your idle chatter! Why does the daughter of the son ever

---

[1] In these sources, the Boethesians are identified with the Sadducees.

[2] What is at issue may be simply a question of exegesis (cf. the argument of Sonne, cited above), but Finkelstein's extended interpretation makes considerable sense, and I have therefore cited both his sociological analysis and the narrower exegetical analysis, which is, of course, well known.

[3] Finkelstein, *Pharisees*, I, 138 f.

[4] TB reads Tevet. Except for the date, I follow the TB text.

inherit? Because her power is strong in the place of her brothers [That is, she inherits in place of her deceased father along with her uncles, his brothers], but will you say of his own daughter that she should inherit, seeing that her power of inheritance is weak where she has brothers? And he vanquished them, and that day they made a holiday.[1]

The third case reveals the alleged efforts of Yohanan to limit priestly rights to consume certain parts of the sacred offerings. The priests claimed the right to consume meal offerings, but the Pharisees opposed this claim, regarding it as extravagant:

On the twenty-seventh day of Heshvan, they began again to bring the offerings of fine flour upon the altar, on account of the Sadducees, who said, one may eat the meal-offering which accompanies the animal sacrifice. Rabban Yohanan ben Zakkai said to them, How do you know? None among them could answer with proof from the Torah except for one old man who mumbled against him, saying, Because Moses loved Aaron. He said, Let him not eat the meat alone, but let him eat meal and meat together like a man who says to his friend, here is some meat, here are some delicacies to go along with it. Concerning him Rabban Yohanan ben Zakkai read the following Scripture: Then they came to Elim, where there were twelve springs of water and seventy palm trees, and they encamped there by the water (Ex. 15.27). He said to him, and what has one thing to do with the other? He answered, Idiot, do not let our whole Torah be like your idle chatter! Has it not already been said (Lev. 23.18), And you shall present with the bread seven lambs a year old, with their cereal offering and their drink offering and the offering by fire, a pleasant odor to the Lord.[2]

---

[1] TB Baba Batra 115b. Rashi explains that the use of verses in Genesis is to indicate equality in matters of inheritance of grandchildren with sons. Cf. Finkelstein, *Pharisees*, II, 669, n. 66, and comments he cites there. One notes also that the Sadducees here employ the device of the argument *ad majorem* (kal ve-homer), but that Yohanan shows the wakness of their argument by destroying the kal ve-homer internally. Cf. also Finkelstein, in *Harvard Theological Review*, XXIII, 255 f. For another explanation of the use of the Genesis verses, cf. S. Abramson, ed., *Baba Batra* (Jerusalem, 1958), 136, who explains as follows: Zibeon and Anah were brothers, and Anah was also the son of Zibeon, thus he was both brother and son, and he is among "the dwellers in the land," that is, he inherited the land of Seir his grandfather: thus the grandson inherited as the son, and just as the daughter does not inherit with the son, and in this the Sadducees agreed, so she does not inherit with the granddaughter. Abrahamson cites an alternative explanation: Anah was a *mamzer* (illegitimate according to Jewish law), and a mamzer does not inherit even according to the Sadducees; and even though he came "of his father's power"; so too the daughter, who comes from his power, likewise cannot inherit with the granddaughter." That is, Yohanan provides a precedent in which the fact of one's birth does not necessarily entail rights of inheritance.

[2] Lichtenstein, 338. No parallel in Talmudic sources. Zeitlin places this holiday in Maccabean times; cf. also Lichtenstein, 298, and compare Mishnah Menahot 6.2; Albeck, *Seder Kodashim* (Tel Aviv, 1956), 364, n. 2; Josephus, *Antiquities*, III, 9, 4.

That is to say, just as the burnt-offering is completely dedicated, so too are the meal and drink offerings.[1]

These stories present striking examples of traditions repeated in one consistent form. Whether Yohanan taught these doctrines, or whether he was the putative "ancient authority" for them, the representation of the sole Sadducean spokesman as a stumbling old man is either deliberate misrepresentation, or represents a popular conception of the Sadducees at a time long after 70, when the party had almost died out and was represented chiefly by a few very old men.

For their part, the Sadducees and priests did not leave records of their opinions of Yohanan and his colleagues, but one is certain from his legacy that they ignored his viewpoint. Thus Yohanan and his associates claimed to determine who may or may not marry a priest, for families of impure lineage were denied that right. Yohanan's viewpoint was that certain families excluded by the more strict rules of the priests were, in fact, permitted to marry into the priesthood. The priests rejected the Pharisaic leniencies, and avoided marriage to such families. In despair, Yohanan was reported to have prohibited calling court sessions on such questions, and so Gamaliel II reported in Yavneh after the destruction:

> Rabbi Joshua and Rabbi Judah ben Bathyra [the former was Yoha-nan's student] testified that the widow of one who belonged to an *Isah* family [a family suspected of having doubtful stock] was eligible for marriage with a priest, and that the members of such a family were qualified to bear testimony about which of themselves is clean or unclean [in lineage], and which must be put away, and which may be brought

---

Albeck explains the reference to the verse in Exodus: even though Moses loved all Israel, still he provided them with only dates and water. Then he brought proof to controvert their claim that the "offering of the Lord" does not refer also to the meal offering, citing the Scriptures quoted. Cf. Albeck's discussion of the particular meal offerings at issue here.

[1] Finkelstein, *Pharisees*, II, 640. In each case, Yohanan's challenge is the same: how do you know? He demands proof from Scripture and/or reason, and in each case, rejects all proposed proofs, and shows them either irrelevant (possibly quoting equally irrelevant Scriptures by way of ridicule; as in the third case, in which the connection between the wells at Elim and the issue at hand is hardly clear, for all the ingenuity of the commentators), or immaterial. In two cases, Hillelite principles of exegesis are employed, and in each, the Sadducees offer an interpretation of Scripture that is based on common sense reasoning. Moses loved Israel, or he loved Aaron, and therefore made the law so-and-so, and in each case, Yohanan refuses to entertain such an argument. Yet as we shall see, he himself produced exegeses based on common sense when he expounded certain biblical commandments, finding either their reasonable, or their allegorical significance. Cf. ch. 5.

near. Rabban Gamaliel said, We should accept your testimony, but what shall we do? For Rabban Yohanan ben Zakkai decreed that courts may not be called into session concerning this matter. The priests would listen to you in what concerns putting away, but not in what concerns bringing near [to marry into the priesthood].[1]

Another such case in which the priests refused to accept the sages' judgment involved one of Yohanan's students:

> Rabbi Yosi the Priest and Rabbi Zechariah son of the Butcher testified concerning a young girl that was left as a pledge in Ashkelon, and the members of her family kept her far from them [that is, the eligible bachelors refused to marry her], although she had witnesses that testified that she had not been closeted with any man, and thereby been defiled. The sages said to them, If you believe that she was left as a pledge, believe also that she had not... been defiled, but if you do not believe that she had not gone aside and been defiled, do not believe that she has been left as a pledge.[2]

Yohanan felt bitterness against the priests who took such strict measures to preserve their family purity, and said that Elijah the prophet, who would come to herald the messiah and to solve all kinds of insoluble problems,[3] would concern himself first and foremost with righting the wrongs committed by the priests. Joshua reported:

---

[1] Eduyot 8.3. TB Ketuvot 14a, 26b. The *Isah* family was marked by the suspicion of *halalut*, that is, having as an ancestor one who was born of amarriage between a priest and a forbidden mate, such as a divorced woman. Cf. Tos. Kiddushin 5.3. The Isah is prohibited to the priesthood, and cf. also TB Ketuvot 14a, TP Ketuvot 1.9. Compare the opinion of Hisda, Kiddushin 75a, the widow of an Isah-husband is prohibited to the priesthood, but compare TP *ad loc.* Cf. also Tos. Eduyot 3.2, which indicates that the court after Joshua accepted his testimony. Cf. also *Aruk*, s.v. Isah.

[2] Cf. Eduyot 8.2, TB Ketuvot 26b. On the meaning of the expression *to bring near, to drive away*, cf. M. D. Gross, *Ozar HaAgada* [Treasury of the Agada] (Jerusalem, 1955), III, 1, 126-1, 130. Cf. also Schalit, *Hordos* [King Herod, the Man and His Work], 493, n. 3; Schuerer, *History*, II, i, 207 f. on the priesthood as a distinct order; also Buechler, Studies, 90-98 and expecially, 96.

[3] Compare Malachi 4.5 f. On Elijah, cf. *inter alia*, L. Ginzberg, "Elijah," *JE*, V, 121 f., M. Friedman, ed., Seder Eliahu Rabbah (Jerusalem, 1960), 2 f., J. Klausner *The Messianic Idea in Israel*, tr. W. F. Stinespring (New York, 1955), 451-7, esp. 453, n. 9; A. Buechler, *Studies*, 69, "The point at issue was the recognition or the denial of the purity of two priestly families, and the dictatorial ben Zion, who excluded one of them, must have been a priest." For further copious discussion of Jewish traditions on Elijah, cf. L. Ginzberg, *Legends of the Jews*, tr. H. Szold (Philadelphia, 1946), IV, 202 f., and B. Cohen, *Index to the Legends of the Jews by Louis Ginzberg* (Philadelphia, 1946), 133-135. Cf. also E. Margoliot, *Eliahu Ha Navi be Sifrut Yisrael* [The Prophet Elijah in Jewish Literature] (Jerusalem, 1960), esp. p. 35, 79, 157.

I have received as a tradition from Rabban Yohanan ben Zakkai, who heard it from his master, and his master from his, as a law given to Moses on Sinai, that Elijah will not come to declare clean or unclean, to remove afar or bring near, but only to remove afar those that have been brought near by violence, and to bring near those that were removed far away by violence...[1]

Another way in which the priests ignored the sages' rules was by refusing to pay the *shekel* to the Temple. Yohanan interpreted Scripture (Ex. 30.13) to mean that the priests were included in the commandment to support the Temple: "Each who is numbered in the census shall give this: half a shekel according to the shekel of the sanctuary...," meaning, all twelve tribes. But, it was taught,

> They did not exact pledges from the priests in the interests of peace. Rabbi Judah said, Ben Bukri testified at Yavneh that if a priest paid the shekel, he did no sin. Rabban Yohanan ben Zakkai answered, Not so, but if a priest did *not* pay the shekel, he committed sin, but the priests used to expound this scripture to their advantage, "And every meal offering of the priest shall be wholly burnt, it shall not be eaten" (Lev. 6.23). Since the *omer* and the two loaves and the showbread are ours, how can they be eaten [if we have contributed to their cost].[2]

That is to say, since these meal offerings were brought as charges on the Temple funds, the priests could not contribute, for if they did, the offerings would have to be burned ("every meal offering of the priest shall be wholly burned"), and this would be contrary to Scripture itself. The Pharisees had no monopoly on clever exegetes.

---

[1] Eduyot 8.7. Cf. also Tos. Eduyot 3.4, TP Yevamot 8.3, and Margoliot, *Eliahu*, 157, n. 9. I follow the interpretation of Buechler, *Studies*, p. 69, "Perhaps this case is referred to in part in the observation of R. Johanan b. Zakkai in M. Edyuy. viii. 3, where he says that it is useless to make decisions about persons wit plemishes, as the priests listen to the authorities only when such persons are to be rejected, not when they are to be admitted..."

[2] Mishnah Shekalim 1.3, 4. Cf. TP Shekalim 1.3. Rabbi Beraiah provide the explanation which I bring for Yohanan's exegesis. The TP and commentaries ad loc. suggest that Yohanan would reply to the priests, the offering of the individual priest must indeed be burned up completely, but not that brought by the whole community of Israel. For the existence of a contemporary priestly tradition of exegesis, cf. Epstein, *Mavo-ot*, 342, 429, 513. Note also that in the earlier dispute of Megillat Taanit and Mishnah Menahot 6.2, the priests are conceded the two loaves and showbread, and on this they base their argument, rather than on the disputed meal offering. Cf. Albeck, *Seder Kodashim*, 364. Cf. also Albeck, *Seder Moed*, 458. Compare TB Menahot 21b, 46b, and Arekhim 4a. I have followed Maimonides' commentary to the mishnah ad loc.: Ben Bukri says that the priests do not sin if they do give the shekel, and Yohanan, that they must give the shekel. This beraita (TB Menahot and Mishnah Shekalim) is the only extant reference to ben Bukri.

Some have surmised that Yohanan ben Zakkai himself was a priest, but the evidence of this is rather scanty, and even if he were, he never participated in the cult, never on this account mitigated his opposition to the priesthood's excessive claims, and never received from the priests any enhanced respect on account of his alleged ancestry.[1]

No less than the Temple authorities, Sadducees, and priests, Yohanan and his colleagues were concerned with the welfare of the city. It was reported of Yohanan that he prayed and fasted for rain, as local authorities among the Pharisees had done for generations. It was said that once, when he looked forward to rain, he observed the rules of fasting which applied to community authorities, refraining from having his hair cut. Finally he said to his barber,

> Stand up before the Temple and say, My master is grieved because he wants to have his hair cut and must not do so – and immediately, the rains came.[2]

As an authority in the city, Yohanan was supposed to have used his power to annul ancient rites in the Temple on the pretext that troubled times rendered them no longer applicable. Later Pharisaic tradition represented him as abrogating the rite of the heifer (sacrificed as in the case to which Zadok referred, where the murderer was unknown), and the rite of the waters of cursing, applied to determine whether a woman suspected of infidelity was guilty or not:

---

[1] Some of the sages were priests, such as Tarfon, Yosi the Priest (Yohanan's student), and others were Levites, such as Joshua ben Hananiah. This conflict was not, therefore, an absolutely cleancut caste-struggle. The question of Yohanan's own priesthood is raised by Rashi, cf. TB Shabbat 34a, s. v. *Tor-muse Terumah*, based on the passages in Tos. Para and Sifra (chapter four) in which Yohanan tells his students concerning the rite of burning the red heifer, "A deed which I did with my own hands…" Compare the Tosafot in Menahot 21b, s. v. *Shehakohanim*, who reject this interpretation, saying that the expression means that the act was done according to his direction (a viewpoint consistent with certain traditions, cf. above). Cf. among the modern historians, Buechler, *Synhedrion*, 141, n. 126, *Priester und Cultus*, 18, n. 2; Allon, *Mehkarim*, I, 158, who is prepared to admit that both Eliezer ben Hyrkanos and Yohanan were priests, and for that reason ordered their disciples to clear the house of contaminable vessels before they died, as they ate even profane foods in purity; but Allon in *Toldot*, I, 56, says that from the source in question, one cannot bring proof at all, and the incidents of conflict with the priests suggest to Allon that Yohanan ben Zakkai was not. Cf. also the comments of Horowitz, in Sifre Hukat, 183, p. 151. My own judgment is that the language in question, which includes the statement, "some say it was Hillel," is insufficient to prove that Yohanan was a priest, and in the light of the Tosafot explanation of the one possible proof, the evidence to the contrary is overwhelming.

[2] TP Taanit 3.13. On the rules governing the fast of community leaders for rain, cf. Mishnah Taanit 1.4, 5, 6, 7. I have followed the commentary in TP ad loc. of Korban HaEdah, in the absence of philological assistance.

When the adulterers increased, the waters of cursing ended [and Rabban Yohanan ben Zakkai ended them, as it is said (Hosea 4.14), "I will not visit upon your daughters when they go awhoring..."][1]

However, a second more reliable[2] tradition was that Yohanan ben Zakkai merely reported the cessation of these rites, probably because they fell into desuetude. After the destruction of Jerusalem, Yohanan began the ultimately successful work of making the Pharisaic court into the national tribunal. It is, however, anachronistic to exaggerate his role as "critic" of the Temple rites.

Yohanan, moreover, taught his students that the purification ceremonies had no *ex opere operato* efficacy, but provided merely an additional means to fulfil the will of God as it had been revealed to Moses. Thus a pagan said to him (perhaps after someone burned a red heifer in the 60's, if, indeed, anyone did):

> These deeds which you do look to me like hocus pocus. You bring a heifer and burn it, and crush it, and take its ashes, and if one of you is defiled by a dead corpse, you sprinkle him on the third and seventh day

---

[1] Sotah 9.9. Cf. TB Sotah 47b, TP Sotah 9.9, Tosefta Sotah 14.12, and Midrash HaGadol on Num. 5.11. Cf. Bruell, *Mavo*, 57; Derenbourg, *Essai*, 278, n. 2; Finkelstein, *Akiba*, 50; Lauterbach, *Essays*, 143-4, n. 50; Buechler, *Studies*, 82. Mishnah Sotah 9.9. reads: "When murders became many, the rite of breaking the heifer's neck ceased... When adulterers became many, the bitter water ceased, and R. Yohanan ben Zakkai brought it to an end..." Tosefta Sotah 14.1.-2 reads:

14.1: "Rabban Yohanan ben Zakkai says, When murderers multiplied, the rite of breaking the heifer's neck ceased, because, the rite of breaking the heifer's neck is only efficacious in a case of doubt (whether murder has been committed), and now, murders are committed openly."

14.2: "When adulterers increased, the waters ceased, for one administers the waters only in the case of doubt."

And compare the form of the TB beraita.

[2] Epstein, *Mavo-ot*, 41-42 points out that Yohanan probably did not abrogate the waters (etc.) but only *reported* (or, even contemporaneously, recorded) their abrogation. He suggest that the Mishnah Sotah 2.3 is Yohanan's, taught without citing him by name. Note also that Helene gave a golden table for use in this rite (Yoma 3.10, Tos. Sotah 2.1) thus any abrogation must have come quite close to the destruction. Epstein (p. 400) further regards the tradition that Yohanan actually abrogated the waters as very late, by comparison to the clause dealing with the heifer. He explains that 'ceased' means that the rites in question were no longer practiced. Cf. also Hoenig, 110 f. Note, Sotah 9.9, "When murders became many, the rite of breaking the heifer's neck ceased. When Eleazar b. Dinai came, and he was also called Tehinah b. Parishah, they changed his name to Son of the Murderer." Tos. Sotah 14 credits the abrogation to Yohanan. Cf. also Sotah 47b. Compare Kaminka, *Mehkarim*, 106. On Eleazar, cf. Albeck, Seder Nashim, 392 n. 9. On the name Tehinah cf. I Chron. 4.12, Koh. Rab. 9.7, Aruk s. v., II, 113, Derenbourg, 279, n. 3. Epstein (41-42) notes again that this was testimony on the abrogation of the rite, and not the actual legal abrogation; certainly it could not have preceded the incident with Zadok, Yoma 2.2, Tos Yoma 1.12, and above.

of his uncleanness, and say to him, you are purified. He answered, Has a
wandering spririt ever entered into you? No. But have you ever seen a
man into whom a wandering spirit ever entered? Yes. And what did
you do for him? You put smoking roots under him, and threw water
over him, and the spirit flees. He said, Listen then with your ears to
what your mouth speaks! This is a spirit of uncleanness, as we learn in
Zechariah (13.2)... and also I shall cause the spirit of uncleanness to
pass away from the earth. You sprinkle on him waters of purification
and it flees. After the man left, the disciples said to Yohanan, Master,
this man you have driven off with a broken reed. What will you reply?
He answered, By your lives! It is not the corpse that renders a man
unclean, nor the waters which purify, but the Holy One said, A statute
have I enacted,   an ordinance have I ordained, and you are not
permitted to transgress my commandment, as it is said, This is the
ordinance of the Torah.[1]

If this report be true, neither Yohanan nor his students believed that
an unclean spirit truly caused substantial uncleanness, nor that the
sprinkling of the heifer's ashes and water purified; yet they carried out
these ceremonies, and possibly disputed with the officiating priests
who did not follow their instructions precisely. In the end, however,
they offered only one rationale for such ceremonies: to do them was a
part of God's will.

The whole will of God for man, however, was, in Yohanan's
opinion, to be found in the Torah, and Yohanan offered study of it as
an alternative, perhaps as effective as the cultic rite, to achieve the
service of God.[2] Indeed, after many generations, the destruction of
the Temple and the burning of the "academy" of Yohanan ben Zakkai
were mourned with equal lamentation:

> Rabbi Joshua ben Levi said, "And he burned the house of God"
> (II Kings 25.9) – this is the Temple. "And the house of the king" – this
> is the palace of Zedekiah. "And all the houses of Jerusalem" – these are
> the four hundred and eighty synagogues that were in Jerusalem, as
> Rabbi Pinhas said in the name of Rabbi Hoshaiah, Four hundred eighty
> synagogues were in Jerusalem, and each one had its school house and

---

[1] Numbers Rabbah 19.4. Cf. Tanhuma, ed. S. Buber, Hukat, 26. Cf. also Bacher,
Agadot, I, i, 29, n. 6; and Sifra on Lev. 18.4, TB Yoma 67b. This attitude is expressed
more fully by Eleazar ben Azariah, cf. Sifra Kedoshim at the end; S. Buber, ed.,
Pesikta de Rav Kahana 40a; and Pesikta Rabbat , ch. 14; Yalkut on Hukat ad loc.
On wandering spirit, cf. Aruk, s. v. tazaz. Bacher says that the reason provided for
the students would not have been intelligible to the pagan, and that therefore
Yohanan provided a more rationalistic explanation; but compare W. D. Davies,
Paul, 262.
[2] Cf. p. 50, n. 1.

academy, the school house for Scripture, and the academy for mishnah, and all of them Vespasian sent up in flames. "And every great house he burned in flames" – this refers to the academy of Rabban Yohanan ben Zakkai, for there they would rehearse the great deeds of the Holy One, blessed be he.[1]

---

[1] TP Megillah 3.1. Cf. Pesikta Rabbati ch. 14, ed. Friedman 65 b, which adds "for there they would acknowledge the greatness of the Holy One, blessed be He." Compare the midrash of this verse in TB Megillah 27a.

CHAPTER FOUR

FATHER OF WISDOM

At Jerusalem Yohanan ben Zakkai assembled a circle of students to whom he taught Torah. With their master, the students constituted a social group founded on the study of biblical literature, and, where possible, on its application to the present condition of Israel. They brought to Scripture questions which touched on moral, legal, ethical, and ritual matters. Through study of Scripture, they sought to find guidance on the conduct of daily affairs, beliving that in commonplace actions, the crucial and consequential issues of life were decided. Indeed, the very act of study represented both content and form in Yohanan's religious doctrine. He spent most of his life in study, and through such study, he taught how to live:

> If thou hast wrought much in the study of Torah, do not claim merit for thyself, for to this end wast thou created.[1]

If Yohanan thought that the very purpose of existence was to study Torah, one understands why he taught that study of Torah may even preserve life:

> It was told that a certain family in Jerusalem used to lose its male issue at the age of eighteen. They came and told Rabban Yohanan ben Zakkai. He said to them, Perhaps you are of the descendants of Eli, of whom it is written, Behold the days are coming when I will cut off your strength and the strength of your father's house, so that there will not be an old man in your house (I Samuel 3.31). Go and study Torah, and live. They went, studied Torah, and lived, and called their family by the name of Rabbi Yohanan ben Zakkai in his honor.[2]

Yohanan was probably interpreting Scripture, for it is said, "Therefore I swear to the house of Eli that the iniquity of Eli's house shall not be expiated by sacrifice or offering forever" (Samuel 3.14). Sacrifice and offerings would not save the priestly family, but study of Torah would.

Study of Torah provided an alternate focus for religious life to either cultic ritual or charismatic action. The priests thought to do God's will through the Temple rites, the ecstatics by prayer and meditation, and

---

[1] Avot 1.15. Cf. ARNa, ch. 14, Schechter ed. p. 29a; Goldin tr. p. 74.
[2] TB Rosh Hashanah 18a. My explanation is based on Rava's, *ad loc.*

Yohanan and the other sages, by memorizing, interpreting (or, sometimes, misinterpreting), and applying ancient texts. These texts were believed to contain the secret to the inner structure of reality; through them, one came to an understanding of the whole of existence, and therefore, to an apprehension of the divine will in creation. Torah made manifest the universal design and plan for existence:

> "The Lord made me as the beginning of his way, the first of his works of old. I was set up from everlasting, from the beginning or even the earth was made,... when he marked out the foundations of the earth, then I was beside him, like a master workman; I was daily his delight, rejoicing before him always." (Prov. 8.22-30 *pass.*) The Torah says, "I was God's instrument. According to the custom of the world, when a mortal king builds a palace, he does not build it by his own skill, but with the skill of an architect. And that architect does not build it out of his own head, but employs plans and diagrams in order to know how to arrange the chambers and wicket doors. So too did the Holy One, blessed be He, He looked into the Torah and created the world.[1]

The idea of Torah rested on the notion that the world presented an order and regularity which man might uncover through the study of revelation, the source of insight into the cosmos. In studying Torah, therefore, a man studied the divine architect's plan for life itself, and achieved the possibility to penetrate into life's meaning. Study of Torah may have been an act of intellect, but when Yohanan taught that it was to this end that man was created, he manifested more than an intellectual dedication to the exposition of ancient revelation. He proposed, rather, what was a religious program: if God was trancendant, his word was immanent, and the sage and disciple should serve him through study of that word.

This program was not, of course, Yohanan's invention. The ideal of Torah was held, for example, by Ben Sira, three centuries earlier. For Ben Sira, however, the achievement of "Wisdom" depended on the leisure and means to support study. It is instructive to note therefore how this ideal had become transformed in the intervening centuries from that of the upper-class intellectual to that of the generally poorer sage:

[1] Bereshit Rabbah 1.1. Cf. E. Goodenough, *By Light, Light, The Mystic Gospel of Hellenistic Judaism* (New Haven, 1935), 72-74; H. A. Wolfson, *Philo* (Cambridge, 1948), I, 242-3, 268; N. N. Glatzer, *Hillel The Elder: The Emergence of Classical Judaism* (New York, 1956), 51–53; also my article, "Does Torah Mean Law?", *Journal of the Central Conference of American Rabbis*, October, 1959, 42-45; Ebner, *Elementary Education* 19-20. This conception of Torah/Wisdom was not unique to Hellenistic Judaism.

The wisdom of the scribe depends on the opportunity of leisure,
And he who has little business may become wise (Ben Sira 39.1-5).[1]

Ben Sira promised that the sage, a kind of *magus* in his view, would
have a great career, appear before rulers, travel far and wide:

He will serve among great men and appear before rulers
He will travel through the lands of foreign nations
For he tests the good and the evil among men (Ben Sira 39, 4-5).[2]

While some of the sages, particularly Gamaliel I, Simeon ben Gamaliel, and Josephus (who claimed to adhere to the Pharisaic party) did
pursue public careers, and, Yohanan himself served among the great
men of Jerusalem, for the most part the sages did not find public
careers open to them, and did not travel abroad. They were mostly
poor, and appeared before rulers only when the tax-farmer hailed them
into court. Yohanan himself did, however, see the fulfilment of one of
Ben Sira's promises:

If he lives long, he will leave a name greater than a thousand, But
if he goes to rest, it is enough for him (Ben Sira 39.11).[3]

If the sage merited long life, he could hope to leave a lasting monu-
ment, but if he died before his time, he could at least say, "Enough,
I have had my portion in Torah."[4] Thus when Yohanan's son died,
he was comforted to know that his son had done the labor which he
had been made to do; if so, it was enough for Yohanan:

When Rabban Yohanan ben Zakkai's son died, his disciples came to
comfort him. Rabbi Eliezer entered, sat down before him, and said to
him, Master by thy leave, may I say something to thee? Speak, he replied.
Rabbi Eliezer said to him, Adam had a son who died, yet he allowed
himself to be comforted concerning him. And how do we know that

---

[1] Yohanan considered pursuit of wealth a hindrance to pursuit of Torah.

[2] Professor Smith suggests the comparison to the *magus*. Cf. S. Schechter, "A
Glimpse of Social Life of the Jews in the Age of Jesus Son of Sirach," *Studies in
Judaism: Second Series* (Philadelphia, 1908); 55-101; W. O. E. Oesterley, *The Books
of the Apocrypha, their Origin, Teaching, and Contents* (London, 1915), 326; C. C.
Torrey, *The Apocryphal Literature* (New Haven, 1956), 95; R. Preiffer, *History of
New Testament Times with an Introduction to the Apocrypha* (New York, 1945), 361,
"No one can become a scribe without leisure." In later times, some of the sages
did travel far and wide in the service of the Palestinian Patriarchate.

[3] M. Segal, *Sefer Ben Sira HaShalem* (Jerusalem, 1959), 252. Segal's Hebrew text
reads:
    If he will stand (endure), he will be more blessed than a thousand And if he rests,
he will suffice (to leave) for himself a name.

[4] Segal comments (260), that if the scribe-sage lives long, he will leave a great
name after death, and if he dies young, he will suffice with a good name.

he allowed himself to be comforted concerning him? For it is said And "Adam knew his wife again" (Gen. 4.25). Thou too, be thou comforted. Rabbi Yohanan said to him, Is it not enough that I grieve over my own, that thou remindest me of the grief of Adam? Rabbi Joshua entered and said to him, Master, by thy leave, may I say something to thee? Speak, he replied. Rabbi Joshua said, Job had sons and daughters, all of whom died on one day, and he allowed himself to be comforted concerning them. Thou too, be thou comforted. And how do we know that Job was comforted? For it is said, The Lord gave and the Lord hath taken away, blessed be the name of the Lord (Job 1.21). Rabban Yohanan said to him, Is it not enough that I grieve over my own, that thou remindest me of the grief of Job? Rabbi Yosi entered and sat down before him. He said to him, Master, by thy leave, may I say something to thee? Speak, he replied. Aaron had two grown sons, he said, both of whom died in one day, yet he allowed himself to be comforted for them, as it is said, "And Aaron held his peace" (Lev. 10.3) – and silence is no other than consolation. Thou too, be thou comforted therefore. Rabban Yohanan said to him, Is it not enough that I grieve over my own, that thou remindest me of the grief of Aaron? Rabbi Simeon entered and said to him, Master, by thy leave, may I say something to thee? Speak, he replied. Rabbi Simeon said, King David had a son who died, yet he allowed himself to be comforted. Thou too, therefore, be thou comforted. And how do we know that David was comforted? For it is said, And David comforted Beth Sheba his wife, and went in unto her, and lay with her, and she bore a son, and called his name Solomon (II Samuel 12.24). Thou too master, be thou comforted. He replied, Is it not enough that I grieve over my own son, that thou remindest me of the grief of King David? Then Rabbi Eleazar ben Arakh entered. As soon as Rabban Yohanan saw him, he said to his servant, Take my clothing and follow me to the bath house, for he is a great man, and I shall be unable to resist him. [Yohanan realized that Eleazar would succeed in consoling him, and therefore he prepared to go to the bath house, a luxury normally forbidden to a mourner.] Rabbi Eliezer entered, sat down before him, and said to him, I shall tell thee a parable. To what may this be likened? To a man with whom the king deposited some object. Every single day the man would weep and cry out, saying, Woe unto me? When shall I be quit of this trust in peace? Thou too, Master – thou hadst a son, he studied Torah, prophets, the holy writings, he studied mishnah, halakhah, agada, and he departed from the world without sin. And thou shouldst be comforted when thou hast returned thy trust unimpaired. Rabban Yohanan said to him, Rabbi Eleazar my son, thou hast comforted me the way men should give comfort.[1]

---

[1] ARNa, ch. 14, Schechter ed. p. 29b, 30a; Goldin tr. p. 76f. Cf. also the story of Meir's children, Midrash Mishle ch. 31. I have not included the concluding paragraph in ARNa ch. 14, beginning, "And when they left him," concerning Eleazar ben Arakh's departure from the other disciples, because Schechter is of the opinion that Eleazar left the others after the death of Yohanan ben Zakkai. I have, therefore,

When Yohanan's son was sick, he was revived by Haninah's miracle; when he died, Yohanan found comfort in his own conviction that his son had done that for which he had been created.

Study of Torah yielded more than moral and religious benefit. It created a community, bringing student and teacher together; sitting, walking, traveling by the way, the sages speculated together on momentous matters. This fellowship of interested men represented another kind of polity in the urban, anomic situation. Like the Pharisaic fellowship (havurah), the Nazarene community in Jerusalem, and the monastery at Quran, it entailed a social commitment: among these men and in their society, the spiritual life will be lived. Such a social group was not unique, for the pagan world had long witnessed the formation of societies for the communal study of religious and intellectual problems.[1] Speculative problems, studied by Academic and Peripatetic masters and their disciples, had however long ago given way to the deepening concern for moral issues. Ancient metaphysical perplexities were left behind, for, with the end of the corporate life of ancient cities, ancestral laws and institutions lost their cloak of almost divine authority, and the moral supports of society became the focus of men's concern. Indeed, the individual was thrown upon his own resources, and the great problems of philosophy centered upon how to achieve autonomy of character.[2] Not only in the land of Israel, but throughout the world men had been uprooted from their ancient foundations.[3] The sensitive among them experienced profound

cited that story in chapter nine. Schechter cites TB Shabbat 147b (Eleazar forgets his learning in Emmaus), and Kohelet Rabba ch. 7. Compare, however, the opinion of Allon, who thinks that Eleazar left Yohanan because he disagreed with his pacifist policy. The two reasonable possibilities are that Eleazar left Yohanan outside of Jerusalem after the escape, or after his death; but I do not see any sense in his having left him after his son died. It is possible that the similarity of language between ARNa ch. 14, "When the son of Rabban Yohanan ben Zakkai died..." and TB Bearhot 28b, "When Rabban Yohanan ben Zakkai fell ill..." led to the misplacement of the detail on Eleazar's leaving. In any case, it seems illogical that the disciple whom Yohanan praises so highly would leave him after his be eavement. On the detail about going to the bath house, cf. Goldin, 192: n. 19; compare II Samuel 12.20, in which David terminated mourning for his son by bathing and putting on his clothes.

[1] Cf. also I. Levi, *La Légende de Pythagore de Grèce en Palestine* (Paris, 1927); M. Hadas, *Hellenistic Culture* (New York, 1960), 194, 308 n. 20-23, 25; H. A. Wolfson, *Philosophy of the Church Fathers* (Cambridge, 1956), 1-3. I think that the major particularity of the sages' society was their concern not for sacramental meals but for study of Torah.

[2] S. Dill, *Roman Society from Nero to Marcus Aurelius* (New York, 1957), 200 f. Cf. also Hadas, *Culture*, 245.

[3] Parallels between Stoic and Pharisaic teachings have been studied by A.

alienation from their past, and from their contemporaries in the present. Submerged into the masses of men in the metropolitan cities, they lacked adequate expression for their individuality. Those who were able to find new expression for their own souls, such as the sages of Israel and of the nations, had to speak to a new social setting, and provide their disciples with a new corporate society to explore the implications of ancient wisdom for daily affairs. The academy was thus both a school for life and, at the same time, the setting for individual living and for the expression of the private person's individuality. Opportunities for such self-expression were no longer easily available in the common life of the city; the end of the corporate community of the ancient city, in which each man had his place and his hour, created undifferentiated masses, and from such masses came men seeking for themselves a means of individual and social expression.

In Rome, such uprooted men found for themselves a kind of spiritual or moral master who would impart the "art of life." Such a moral director was qualified by his profound knowledge of the pathology of the soul, and offered private counsel, much as the analyst does today, for the particular needs of his spiritual patient. He encouraged his charge to "make full confession of the diseases of his soul," trained him in moral self-examination, and tried to help him find the way to right living in a world gone wrong.[1] The goal was to produce the *sapiens*, who was

> the man who sees in the light of Eternal Reason the true proportions of things, whose affections have been trained to obey the higher law, whose will has hardened into an unswerving conformity to it in all the difficulties of conduct, and the true philosopher is no longer the cold, detached student of intellectual problems far removed from the struggles and miseries of human life. He has become the *generes humani paedagogus*, the schoolmaster to bring men to the Ideal Man...[2]

Kaminka, "Les Rapports entre le rabbinisme et la philosophie stoicienne," *REJ*, LXXXI (1926), pp. 233-252. Cf. also Bergmann (no first name given), "Die Stoische Philosophie und die juedische Froemmigkeit," *Hermann Cohen Festschrift* (Berlin, 1912), 145-166. Bergmann notes the parallel between Seneca's, "One ought not to say, I have lost a son, but rather, I have given back a son" to Yohanan's bereavement and Eleazar's comfort. Cf. especially pp. 163-165, the contrast between rabbinic and philosophical learning. Cf. also Josephus, *Life*, 2, where he says that the Pharisees "have points of resemblance to that which the Greeks call the Stoic school." The major points of resemblance seem to be, first, the creation of an "academic" society, and second, the focus on moral concerns. Professor Judah Goldin's study of this question in reference to Yohanan ben Zakkai's academy will be printed in the H. A. Wolfson "festschrift" in the near future. [Sec non vidi].

[1] Dill, 293.
[2] *Ibid.*, 299.

There could be no more congruent description of the task assumed
by Yohanan ben Zakkai and his colleagues, but, in characteristically
Jewish fashion, he found "eternal reason" in the Torah, looked for the
"higher law" in ancient revelation, and would bring men not to the
ideal man, but closer to the Father in Heaven. If Seneca, who was
Yohanan's contemporary, thought to root character in a faith in the
rational law of conduct, Yohanan saw the foundation of all natural
law in the Torah. Both would have agreed, however, that freedom is
achieved through conformity to the higher part of being, the vision
of which provides universal laws for particular actions. Both thus tried
to make a place where men might once again matter.

Since Yohanan's conception of the good life was to learn a sacred
text and its interpretation, the form of the good society which he
created for his disciples was the academy; his sole credential as master
was his learning; and his main function was to teach. His main peda-
gogical technique was the hoary method of catechism. He would ask
questions and hear answers; he would be asked questions and provide
answers. On occasion, he gave a wrong answer, which was interpreted
as an effort to keep his students alert. He was asked,

> In what garments is the heifer prepared? He said, in golden garments.
> The students replied, but have you not taught us, master, in white
> garments? He answered, If I have forgotten what I saw with my own
> eyes and did with my own hands, how much the more what I taught!
> Why did he go to such an extent? In order to keep the students alert.
> And there are those who say, this was Hillel the Elder, but that he could
> not say, what my own hands did.[1]

On a second occasion, he tried to make his nephew's misfortune
yield a spiritual truth, that philanthropy must be done for its own sake.
It was reported as follows:

> Rabbi Judah son of Rabbi Shalom preached as follows: In the same
> way as a man's earnings are determined for him from New Year, so his
> losses are determined for him from New Year. If he finds merit, then
> "deal out thy bread upon the poor" but if not, then he will "bring the
> poor that are outcast to his house." A case in point is that of the nephews
> of Rabban Yohanan ben Zakkai. He saw in a dream that they were to
> lose seven hundred dinars in that year. He accordingly forced them to
> give money for charity, until only seventeen dinars were left of the seven

---

[1] Sifre Numbers 123 (Friedman ed. p. 41a). Compare Tosefta Para 4.7. Another
such incident is reported in Tos. Oholot 16.8. Joshua is reported to have commented, "He who learns and does not review is like a man who sows and does not harvest,
and a person who studies Torah and forgets is like a woman who bears and buries..."

hundred. On the eve of the day of Atonement, the Government sent and seized them. Rabban Yohanan ben Zakkai said to them, Do not fear (that you will lose any more). You had seventeen dinars, and these they have taken. They said to him, How did you know that this was going to happen? He replied, I saw it in a dream. And why did you not tell us, they asked. Because, he said, I wanted you to perform the religious precept without ulterior motive.[1]

As we have seen, Yohanan ben Zakkai had five disciples in his circle in Jerusalem. For each he had a name:

Eliezer ben Hyrcanus he called "plastered cistern" which loses not a drop, pitch-coated flask, which keeps its wine. Joshua ben Hananiah he called three fold cord not quickly broken. Yosi the Priest he called "the generation's saint." Simeon ben Nathanel he called "oasis in the desert which holds onto its water." And Eleazar ben Arakh he called "overflowing stream and ever-flowing stream whose waters ever flow and overflow" – confirming the statement, "Let thy springs be dispersed abroad, and courses of water in the streets" (Prov. 5.16).

For one, he had very special praise:

He used to say, "If all the sages of Israel were in one scale of the balance, and Rabbi Eliezer ben Hyrcanus were in the other scale, he would outweigh them all. Abba Shaul says in his name, If all the sages of Israel were in one scale of the balance, and even if Rabbi Eliezer ben Hyrcanus were with them, and Rabbi Eleazar ben Arakh were in the other scale, he would outweigh them all.[2]

---

[1] TB Baba Batra 10a. (Trans. by M. Simon, *The Babylonian Talmud: Soder Nezikin*, London, 1952, III, 41-8).

[2] ARNa ch. 14, ed. Schechter p. 29a, Tr. Goldin 74 f. Avot 2.8 f. Cf. Finkelstein, *Mavo*, 38-44. The antiquity of these sayings (Probably the oldest record of Yohanan ben Zakkai) is proven by the high praise recorded for Eleazar ben Arakh. Since he was isolated from the rabbis at Yavneh, one must assume that this collection of *logia* was edited before his reputation for learning was lost, and, therefore, during Eleazar's lifetime, if not during Yohanan's. Cf. Finkelstein, *Mavo*, 60-61. The "three fold cord" may refer to Joshua's learning, piety, and wisdom (Kohelet 4.12). Indeed, in the light of this praise, one may understand Joshua's recommendation of the good companion, for the verse continues, "If two lie together, they are warm, but how can one be warm alone?" And though a man might prevail against one who is alone, two will withstand him. A three fold cord is not quickly broken." Cf. also A. Kaminka, "Stoic Parallels," 238, who cites Seneca's *damnorum omnium maximum est, si amicum perdidisse*. Finkelstein comments (44) that a good heart is better than a good impulse, because the impulse is dependent on the goodness of the heart. Cf. also Hoenig, *Sanhedrin*, 176-8. The praise of Joshua's mother in Avot 2.8 may refer to her bringing him as an infant to hear the words of Torah, TP Yevamot 1.6. Note especially the variant reading of Abba Shaul in ARNb, ed. ed. Schechter, p. 30a, "Abba Shaul said in the name of Rabbi Akiba, who said in his (Yohanan's) name,..." Finkelstein notes that the dispute on the place of Eliezer and Eleazar among the next generation indicates the antiquity of the source. Cf. also

Much like the philosophical director in Seneca's Rome, Yohanan would discourse with his students on basic questions facing moral man. Yohanan phrased his questions in universal terms. He sought an ethic applicable to all men and in all places. Yohanan asked "what is the good way of life," and "what is the evil way of life," always phrasing his moral inquiries in universal terms. In each case, he demanded observation of life as it was lived, telling his disciples to go out and see the world for themselves. Thus it was reported that he told them:

> Go out and see which is the good way to which a man should cleave, so that through it he may enter the world to come.

The students returned with their conclusions:

> Rabbi Eliezer came in and said, a good eye (that is liberality).
> Rabbi Joshua came in and said, A good companion.
> Rabbi Yosi came in and said, A good neighbor, a good impulse and a good wife.
> Rabbi Simeon came in and said, Foresight.
> Rabbi Eleazar came in and said, Good-heartedness toward heaven, and goodheartedness toward the commandments, and goodheartedness toward the commandments, and goodheartedness toward mankind.
> Rabban Yohanan said to them, I prefer the words of Rabbi Eleazar ben Arakh to your words, for in his words, your words are included.

Again, he instructed the students:

> Go out and see which is the evil way which a man should shun, so that he may enter the world to come.

The students again returned:

> Rabbi Eliezer came in and said, An evil eye (that is, avarice).
> Rabbi Joshua came in and said, An evil companion.

Albeck, *Seder Nezikin* (Tel Aviv, 1953), 495. If, as seems likely, Abba Shaul's statement was made at Yavneh, it would certainly not support Allon's hypothesis (n. 8) that Eleazar left Yohanan before his death. Two other possibilities are, first, that the denigration of *Eliezer* in Eleazar's favor represents the later opposition to Eliezer, after his excommunication; second, the saying of Abba Shaul might be based on an earlier opinion of Yohanan, before Eleazar left him and the praise of Eliezer might be Yohanan's reaction to Eleazar's disloyalty. Allon might certainly argue so. If, however, the clause, "and even if Rabbi Eliezer... were with them" is Abba Shaul's and not an interpolation, and there is no reason to doubt this, then it seems likely to me that the statement of Abba Shaul comes *after* the original praise for Eliezer; thus contradicting Allon. Cf. also the comments, *ad loc.* of Bertinoro, who suggests that the greater praise for Eleazar was on account of his superior acumen (certainly the plain sense of the text). The extant sources do not indicate this, but only Eleazar's great capacity for mystical speculation.

Rabbi Yosi came in and said, An evil neighbor, and evil impulse, and an evil wife.

Rabbi Simeon came in and said, Borrowing and not repaying, for he that borrows is as one who borrows from God, as it is said The wicked borroweth and payeth not, but the righteous dealeth graciously and giveth (Ps. 37.21).

Rabbi Eleazar came in and said, Meanheartedness toward heaven and meanheartedness toward the commandments, and meanheartedness toward mankind.

To this Yohanan replied:

I prefer the words of Rabbi Eleazar to your words, for in his words, your words are included.[1]

Thus a circle of students came together with Yohanan ben Zakkai for the study of moral questions. How did they happen to meet? At least two of them began their education with him, starting from the most elementary duties of religious life. One of these, Simeon ben Natanel, was apparently an ignorant man at the beginning, coming in his mature years from an unlettered family, and therefore Yohanan called him an "oasis in the desert."[2] The coming of the second, Eliezer ben Hyrkanus, was also at a mature age. It happened this way, according to one recension:

What were the beginnings of Rabbi Eliezer ben Hyrcanus? He was twenty-two years old, and had not yet studied Torah. One time he resolved, I will go and study Torah with Rabbi Yohanan ben Zakkai. His father Hyrcanus said to him, Not a taste of food shalt thou get before thou hast plowed the entire field. He rose early in the morning, plowed the entire field, and then departed for Jerusalem. It is told that the day was the evening of the Sabbath, and some say he went for the Sabbath meal to his father-in-law's, but some say, he tasted nothing from six hours before the eve of the Sabbath until six hours after the departure of the Sabbath. As he was walking along the road, he saw a stone. He picked it up and put it into his mouth. Some say, it was cattle dung. He went to spend the night at a hostel. Then he went and appeared before Rabban Yohanan ben Zakkai in Jerusalem, until a bad breath rose from his mouth. Said Rabban Yohanan ben Zakkai to him,

---

[1] ARNa ch. 14, ed. Schechter p. 29a, Goldin 75f. For the expression "go forth and see," cf. TB Berahot 19a. Compare also the statement of Judah the Prince, Avot 2.1, "Which is the right course that a man should choose for himself? That which he feels to be honorable to himself and which also brings him honor from mankind."

[2] Finkelstein, *Mavo*, 43-44; and appendix III, 243-244. Tos. Avodah Zara 3.10. But compare the opinion of L. Ginzberg, *Perushim veHiddushim BaYerushalmi*, III, 334, cited by Finkelstein, 243.

Eliezer my son, hast thou eaten at all today? Silence. Rabban Yohanan
ben Zakkai asked him again. Silence again. Rabban Yohanan ben
Zakkai sent for the owners of his hostel and asked them, Did Eliezer
have anything to eat at your place? We thought, they replied, he was
very likely eating with you. He said, And I thought he was very likely
eating with you. He said, And I thought he was very likely eating with
you. You and I, between us, left Rabbi Eliezer to perish. Thereupon
Rabban Yohanan said to him, Even as a bad breath rose from thy
mouth, so shall fame of thee travel for thy mastery of the Torah. When
Hyrcanus his father heard of him, that he was studying Torah with
Rabban Yohanan ben Zakkai, he declared, I shall go and ban my son
Eliezer from my possessions. It is told, that day Rabban Yohanan ben
Zakkai sat expounding in Jerusalem, and all the great ones of Israel sat
before him. When he heard that Hyrcanus was coming, he appointed
guards and said to them, if Hyrcanus comes, do not let him sit down.
When Hyrcanus arrived, and they would not let him sit down, he pushed
on ahead until he reached the place near Ben Sisi HaKeset, Nakdimon
ben Gurion, and Ben Kalba Sabua. He sat down among them [leading
citizens in Jerusalem] and trembled. It is told, On that day, Rabban
Yohanan ben Zakkai fixed his gaze upon Rabbi Eliezer and said to him,
Deliver the exposition. I am unable to speak, Rabbi Eliezer pleaded.
Rabban Yohanan pressed him to do it, and the disciples pressed him
to do it, so he arose and delivered a discourse upon things which no ear
had ever before heard. As the words came from his mouth, Rabban
Yohanan ben Zakkai rose to his feet, and kissed him upon the head and
exclaimed, Rabbi Eliezer, master, thou hast taught me the truth. Before
the time had come to recess, Hyrkanus his father rose to his feet and
declared, My masters, I came here only in order to ban my son Eliezer
from my possessions. Now all my possessions shall be given to Eliezer
my son, and all his brothers are herewith disinherited, and have naught
of them.[1]

A second source adds that R. Eliezer replied:

He said to him, If I were to seek from the Omnipresent silver and gold
he, would have enough to give me, as it is said, Mine are the silver and gold
(Haggai 2.8), and if I wanted land, he could give me, as it is said (Psalm
24.1) The earth is the Lord's, and the fulness thereof. I sought only,
that I might find merit in Torah, as it is said (Ps. 119.118), Thou dost
spurn all who go astray from thy statutes, yea, their cunning is in vain,
all the wicked of the earth does thou count as dross; therefore I loveth

---

[1] ARNa ch. 6, Schechter, p. 15b f., Goldin, 43 f. ARNB, ch. 13, Schechter, p.
15b-16a. Parallels are in Yalkut Shimoni on Gen. p. 72; Gen. R. ch. 41.1, Pirke de
Rabbi Eliezer, chs. 1-2. The apparent interpolation about his father-in-law (who
was Simeon ben Gamaliel I, cf. TB Nedarim 20a and below) is very difficult to
understand. According to the beginning paragraphs in PRE, he was unmarried
when he came to Jerusalem; and it is unlikely that he was married to the daughter
of the Pharisaic leader *before* he had studied at the academy at all.

thy testimonies, my flesh trembles for fear of thee, and I am in awe of
thy judgments.[1]

---

[1] This paragraph is added from Pirke de Rabbi Eliezer, ch. 2. Trans. G. Friedlander (London, 1916), 8. The PRE account provides variant details, as follows
(omitting the details common to both recensions):
His father had many ploughmen who were ploughing arable ground, while he
was ploughing a stony plot. He sat down and wept. His father said to him, My son
why do you weep? Are you perhaps distressed because you plough a stony plot?
Now behold you will plough with us in the arable ground. He sat down and wept.
His father said to him, but why do you weep? Are you perhaps distressed because
you plough the arable land? He replied to him, No. Hyrkanus said to him, Why do
you weep? He answered, I weep only because I desire to learn Torah. Hyrkanus
said to him, Behold you are twenty eight years old, yet you want to study Torah?
But go, take a wife and have sons, and take them to the schoolhouse... He arose
and went up to Jerusalem, to Rabban Yohanan ben Zakkai, and sat down and wept.
Yohanan said to him, Why do you weep? He answered, Because I wish to learn
Torah. He said to him, whose son are you, but he did not tell him. He asked him,
Have you never learned to read the Shema or the Prayer, or the grace after meals?
He replied to him, No. He arose and taught him the three prayers. Again he sat down
and wept. Yohanan said to him, My son, why do you weep? He replied, Because
I desire to learn Torah [and not merely prayers]. He then taught him two rules every
day of the week, and on the Sabbath he repeated them and learned them. He kept a
fast for eight days without tasting anything until the odor of his mouth attracted
the attention of Rabban Yohanan ben Zakkai, who directed him to withdraw from
his presence. He sat down and wept. Said Yohanan to him, Why do you weep?
He answered, Because you made me withdraw from your presence just as a man
makes his fellow withdraw when he has leprosy. Yohanan said to him, My son,
just as the odor of thy mouth has ascended before me, so may the savor of the statutes
of the Torah ascend from your mouth to heaven. He said to him, My son, whose son
are you? He replied, I am the son of Hyrkanus. Yohanan answered, And are you
not the son of one of the great men of the world, and you did not tell me? By thy
life, today you will eat with me. Eliezer answered, I have already eaten with my host.
Yohanan asked, Who is your host. He replied, Joshua ben Hananiah and Yosi the
priest. Yohanan sent to inquire of his hosts, saying to them, did Eliezer eat with
you today? They answered, No, moreover has he not fasted during eight days
without tasting any food? Joshua and Yosi went and told Yohanan, during the last
eight days he has not partaken any food... The sons of Hyrkanus said to their
father, Go up to Jerusalem and ban your son Eliezer from your possessions... At
the banquet Yohanan fixed his gaze on Eliezer, saying to him, Tell us some words
of Torah. Eliezer answered him saying, Master, I will tell you a parable, to what is
the matter likened? To a well which cannot yield more water than the amount which
it has drawn (from the earth). Likewise I am unable to speak words of Torah more
than I have received from thee. [Note that Yohanan actually praised Eliezer as a
plastered cistern which loses not a drop.] Yohanan said to him, I will also tell you
a parable. To what is the matter likened? To a fountain which bubbles and sends
forth water in greater quantity than it receives. So too, you are able to speak words
of Torah more than Moses received at Sinai. Yohanan continued, Lest you should
feel ashamed on my account behold I will arise and go away from you. Yohanan
then arose and went outside. Then Eliezer sat down and expounded. His face shone
like the light of the sun and his radiance beamed like that of Moses, so that no one
knew whether it was day or night. He came from behind him, and kissed him on the
head, saying "Happy are you, O Abraham, Isaac, and Jacob, that such as this has

Eliezer kept the promises of his youth, and became one of the great masters of the next generation. He married the sister of Gamaliel II. A loyal and devoted disciple of Yohanan, he escaped with him from Jerusalem and accompanied him to Yavneh. After Yohanan died, Eliezer left for Lud (Lydda) where he conducted his own court and academy. He was devoted to tradition, and deeply conservative in his judicial philosophy. He was finally excommunicated for his stubbornness in holding to ancient traditions, and died in retirement, after a melancholy old age. When he died, the words of Yohanan ben Zakkai lingered on his lips.[1] He left three sayings:

> Let the honor of thy fellow be as dear to thee as thine own.
> Be not easily angered.
> Repent one day before thy death.
> Let thy honor of thy fellow be as dear to thee as thine own: how so?
> This teaches that even as one looks out for his own honor, so should he look out for the honor of his fellow. And even as no man wishes that his own honor be made light of, so should he wish that the honor of his fellow shall not be made light of.

Eliezer's disciples asked him:

> Does a man then know on what day he will die, that he should know when to repent?

He replied,

> All the more so: let him repent today lest he die on the morrow. Let him repent on the morrow, lest he die the day after, and thus all his days will be spent in repentance.

His unhappy years of excommunication probably were reflected in the warning:

> Keep warm at the fire of the sages, but beware of their glowing coals

---

come forth from your loins!" Hyrkanus his father said, To whom does Rabban Yohanan ben Zakkai speak thus? The people answered, To Eliezer your son. He said to them, He ought not to have spoken in that manner, but thus, "Happy am I, because he has come forth from my loins." While Rabbi Eliezer was sitting and expounding, his father was standing upon his feet. When he saw his father standing on his feet, he said to him, My father, be seated, for I cannot speak words of Torah when you are standing on your feet. Hyrkanus replied to him, My son, it was not for this reason that I came, but to disinherit thee...

Note that the above is close to the text of ARNb, ch. 13, Schechter 17a, n. 39, and p. 16a, n. 55.

[1] Cf. ch. 9; TB Nedarim, 20a; Baba Meziah 59b, TP Moed Katan 1. The parallel teachings of R. Yohanan b. Zakkai are cited in Ch. 6.

lest thou be scorched, for their bite is the bite of the jackal, and their sting the sting of a scorpion. Moreover, all their words are like coals of fire.[1]

In later years, Eliezer's chief rival in the academy at Yavneh was Joshua ben Hananiah, Yohanan's earlier student at Jerusalem and prefect of his school. He left three sayings as well:

> Avarice, an evil impulse, and hatred of mankind put a man out of the world. What is to be understood by avarice? This teaches that even as a man looks out for his own home, so should he look out for the home of his fellow, and even as no man wishes that his own wife and children be held in ill-repute, so should no man wish that his fellow's wife and children be held in ill repute. There was once a certain man who begrudged his companion his learning, and his life was cut short and he passed away.[2]

Joshua went on missions as representative of the sages' *curia*, a function he carried out after the destruction as well. Thus it was told:

> There was once a certain man of Bet Ramah who cultivated a saintly manner. Rabban Yohanan ben Zakkai sent a disciple [Joshua] to examine him. The disciple went and found him taking oil and putting it on a pot range, and taking it from the pot range and pouring it into a porridge of beans. What are you doing? the disciple asked him. I am an important priest, he replied, and I eat heave offering in a state of purity. The disciple asked, Is this range unclean or clean? Said the priest, Have we then anything in the Torah about a range being unclean? On the contrary, the Torah speaks only of an oven being unclean, as it is said "Whatsoever is in it shall be unclean" (Lev. 11.33). Said the disciple to him, Even as the Torah speaks of an oven being unclean, so the Torah speaks of a range being unclean, as it is said, "Whether oven or range for pots, it shall be broken in pieces, they are unclean" (Lev. 11.35). The disciple continued, If this is how you have been conducting yourself, you have never in your life eaten clean heave offerings.[3]

The third student, Eleazar ben Arakh, said:

---

[1] Avot 2.10, Bereshit R. 52, Pesikta Rabbati 9b. For a brief discussion of Joshua's and Eliezer's later careers, cf. chapter nine. Cf. also B. Z. Bokser, *Pharisaic Judaism in Transition* (New York, 1935).

[2] Avot 2.16. ARNa ch. 16, Schechter p. 31b, Goldin 82.

[3] ARNa ch. 12, Schechter 28b; Goldin 71. ARNb, ch. 27, Schechter 28b specifies that it was Joshua; cf. Schechter *ad loc*. n. 26. Also Midrash HaGAdol, cited by Schechter in ARNa 18b, n. 77. Heave offering must be prepared and eaten in purity, cf. Num. 18.8, Deut. 18.4. In ARNb, it is clear that this happened after the destruction. Cf. also Buechler, *Priester und Cultus*, 21.

Be diligent in the study of Torah, and know how to answer an unbeliever.

Let not one word of the Torah escape thee.

Know in whose presence thou art toiling, and who is the author of the covenant with thee.[1]

Eleazar distinguished himself in mystical speculation, which he probably learned from Yohanan ben Zakkai.[2] After Yohanan died, he went to Emmaus, a mountain town which enjoyed a healthy climate, rather than to Yavneh, where his fellow students settled, and later lamented,

> Settle in a place where the Torah is studied, and think not that it will seek thee, for only thy colleagues will perpetuate it in thy possession, and rely not on thine own understanding.[3]

He left almost no legal doctrines which were preserved, having been out of touch with the main discussions of his mature years. He was a distinguished student who never kept the promise of his youth. He left the saying,

> I am not a prophet nor the son of a prophet, but my teachers have taught me the ancient truth that every counsel enhancing the glory of God leads to good results.[4]

The fourth member of the circle was Yosi the Priest, surnamed "the pious." He said:

> Let thy fellow's property be as dear to thee as thine own, make thy self fit for the study of Torah, for it will not be thine by inheritance, and let all thine actions be for the sake of heaven.[5]

Also involved in mystical speculation, he left very few teachings, and only one of a moral nature:

---

[1] Avot 2.19, ARNa ch. 17, Schechter 33b, Goldin 90.

[2] Cf. chapter five.

[3] ARNa ch. 17, cited above; Kohelet Raba 7.7, cf. also TB Shabbat 147b, Avot 4.14.

[4] Midrash Tehillim 1.3. See trans. W. G. Braude, The Midrash on Psalms (New Haven, 1959) ad loc.

[5] ARNa ch. 17, Schechter 33a, Goldin 87. The commentary of ARNa is as follows: "Let thy fellow's property be as dear to thee as thine own: How so? This teaches that even as one has regard for his own property, so should he have regard for his fellow's property; and even as no man wishes that his own property be held in ill repute, so should he wish that his fellow's property shall not be hald in ill repute." Note the parallel comments on the teachings of Eliezer ben Hyrkanus in this connection, ARNa, ch. 15, Goldin 78; and of Joshua ben Hananiah, ARNa ch. 16, Goldin 82. Cf. also Avot. 2.17.

Beluriah the convert asked Rabban Gamaliel, It is written in your Torah, "Who will not show favor" (Deut. 10.17), and it is written "May God show you favor" (Num. 6.26). Rabbi Yosi the Priest engaged her. He said to her, I shall tell you a parable, to what is the matter compared? To a man who lent his fellow a coin, and arranged the time for repayment before the king, and the borrower swore to him by the life of the king. When the time came, he did not repay him. He came to appease the king, and the king replied, My claim is forgiven to you, but go and appease your fellow. Here also, Scripture speaks of sins between man and God, and there, between man and man.[1]

The fifth member of the circle, Simeon ben Natanel, said:

Be prompt in reciting the Shema and the Prayer. When thou prayest, do not make thy prayer a chattering, but a supplication before the Holy One, blessed be He, for it is said, "For he is a God compassionate and gracious, longsuffering and abundant in mercy, and repenteth him of the evil" (Joel 2.13); and be not wicked in thine own sight.[2]

The five disciples[3] of Yohanan ben Zakkai reflected the main concerns of their academy. They sought to find ways to receive the divine words ("Qualify thyself for the study of Torah, since the knowledge of it is not an inheritance of thine..."), to apply them to commonplace matters ("Let thy friends honor be as dear to thee as thine own..."), as well as to the broader issues of morality ("Repent one day before thy death...") and to abstract from them fundamental principles for the conduct of the good life ("A good heart"). Strikingly, Eliezer, Joshua, and Yosi all repeat the reciprocal rule of good conduct laid down in Leviticus 19.18, "Thou shalt love thy neighbor as thyself,"

---

[1] ARNa ch. 17, Schechter 33b, Goldin 90. Also Jonah 4.2. Goldin comments 194, n. 13 that the verse in the text does not correspond exactly either to Joel 2.13 or to Jonah 4.2, and the copyist may have quoted from memory.

[2] Avot 2.18.

[3] For further references to Eliezer and Joshua, cf. chapter nine. Other references to the main disciples are as follows: Eleazar ben Arakh: TB Shabbat 147b, Eruvin 13b, Hagigah 14a, b, Hullin 106a; TP Demai 7.7, Hallah 3.1, Hagigah 2.1, Yevamot 2.1, 3.4, 4.7, 6.4; Nedarim 10.6, Kiddushin 1.1; also Mishnah Demai 7.7, Tos. Terumot 5. Tos Nedarim 6: "Rabbi Eliezer said to Rabbi Akiba, It is unfortunate for you, for if you were in the days of Rabbi Eleazar ben Arakh, he would have answered you,..." Thus Eleazar died before Eliezer. Yosi the Priest: TB Shabbat 19a, Taanit 13a, b; Hagigah 14b; Rosh Hashanah 15b, 17b; Ketuvot 26b, 27a; TP Ketuvot 2.9; Mishnah Eduyot 8.2; Simeon ben Natanel: TB Mishnah Avot only; TP Hagigah 2.1, Tos. Avodah Zara 3.1. Cf. also Bacher, *Agadot*, I, i, 50-53; Bruell, *Mavo* 87-8; Frankel, *Mishnah*, 94-95; A. Hyman, *Toldot Tannaim ve-Amoraim* (London, 1920, three vols.) s. v.; S. Mendelsohn, "Eleazar ben Arak," *JE*, V, 96-97; I. Broyde, "Jose HaKohen," *JE*, VII, 243-4; J. Z. Lauterbach, "Simeon b. Nethaneel," *JE*, XI, 356.

phrasing the law in more specific terms (honor, property, reputation).
Thus they tried to bring the word to bear on day-to-day issues of life,
and to create a society capable of accepting and embodying the divine
imperative.

CHAPTER FIVE

THE SPLENDOR OF WISDOM

For Yohanan ben Zakkai, who said man was made to study Torah, Scriptural exegesis provided a creative experience. The act of biblical study was a religious duty, for Scripture was regarded as the revealed word of the Creator. A generation earlier, Hillel had taught that an ignorant man cannot be pious, and that the increase of Torah led to the increase of life;[1] a generation later Tarfon taught, If thou hast studied much Torah, much reward will be given you.[2] A century later, Rabbi Jacob taught, if a man is walking by the way and studying, and breaks off to say, How lovely is that tree, How fine is that virgin land, he is guilty, according to Scripture, as if he had forfeited his life.[3] *Torah* led to wisdom, understanding, good manners, and fear of God;[4] it was the source of virtue in this world, and merit for the world to come; it was held, by those who studied it, to be a greater honor than priesthood or royalty,[5] and a sage even of illegitimate origin was supposed to take precedence over a high priest who was ignorant of Torah.[6] Study of Torah represented the religious program of the Pharisaic sages, and they multiplied their praise of its merits.

Although the act of study in the academies produced a social entity and an ethics, the true focus of the sages' concern lay beyond Torah's social consequences. Benefits for the moral life were only a fortunate byproduct of a deeper and less tangible concern for the word itself. Torah should be studied for its own sake. Reward for study came from the act of study itself, not necessarily for the discoveries of the sage; and one certainly ought not to look for base reward, as Rabbi Meir taught in the second century,

> Whoever labors in the Torah for its own sake merits many things, and not only so, but the whole world is indebted to him. He is called friend, beloved, a lover of the Omnipresent, a lover of mankind. It clothes him in meekness and reverence, and prepares him to be righteous and pious, upright and faithful, and keeps him away from sin, and brings him

---

[1] Avot 2.6, 8.
[2] *Ibid.*, 2.21.
[3] *Ibid.*, 3.9.
[4] *Ibid.*, 3.21.
[5] *Ibid.*, 6.6.
[6] Horayot 3.8.

near to virtue, and through him men enjoy counsel and sound knowledge understanding and strength, as it is said, "Counsel is mine, and sound knowledge; I am understanding, I have strength (Prov. 8.14); and it gives him sovereignty, and dominion, and discerning judgment; to him are the secrets of the Torah revealed, and he is made like a never-failing fountain that never fails, and like a self-replenishing river; he becomes modest, long-suffering, forgiving of insults; and it magnifies him above all deed.[1]

In Yohanan's age Sacred Scripture was thought to contain many more levels of meaning than the static and one-dimensional printed text yields to men today. The Psalmist said, "Once did God speak, but two things have I heard" (Ps. 62.11).[2] The sages assumed that the Torah, in both its written recension and the oral traditions believed to have been given along with it, was the indivisible, exhaustive account of the event of revelation at Sinai. If it revealed some truth, it encompassed all truth; hence it was the sages' task to draw out of the given text the widest possible range of insight. Every word was thought to have many modulations of meaning, each awaiting the inquiring sage to unfold its special message for a particular moment in time. The Pharisaic sages, and Yohanan ben Zakkai among them, proposed to draw out that message for their time.

Yohanan lived between two revolutions in Scriptural hermeneutics. The first was that effected by Hillel, who, as we have noted, opened the way to Scriptural interpretation according to the well-known principles of linguistic analogy, inference, association, and deduction.[3] The second came in the next generation, with the application of the hermeneutic method devised by Nahum of Gimzo and carried forward by Akiba ben Joseph, who expounded grammatical parts and other

---

[1] Avot 6.1.

[2] This is the rabbinic interpretation of the verse. The RSV reads, "Once has God spoken, twice have I heard this: that power belongs to God, and that to thee O Lord belongs steadfast love." Cf. TB Sanhedrin 34b, Berahot 22a, Shabbat 88b, Sukkah 52b, Taanit 4a, 7a, Hagigah 27a, Kiddushin 30b; TP Nedarim 3.2, Shavuot 3.8, Mekilta Beshalakh 15.11, Sifre Num. 26, Deut. 12, 15. Cf. also I. Heineman, *Darkhe HaAgadah* [The Ways of the Agadah] (Jerusalem, 1954), who discusses the philological and historiographical creativity of the sages, and examines the fundamental critical methodology of midrash.

[3] Cf. also D. Daube, "Rabbinic Methods of Interpretation and Hellenistic Rhetoric," HUCA XXXI, 239 f. Daube notes (p. 257), "The true explanation [of parallels in rhetorical method between Cicero, Hillel, and Philo] lies in the common Hellenistic background." All of Hillel's principles of interpretation do not appear in the extant midrash of Yohanan ben Zakkai. Of the seven, the most common in Yohanan's exegesis are the *kal vehomer* (inference a minori ad majus), and deduction from context, that is to say, those principles which which devolved upon the *content* of Scripture, rather than its form.

structural elements of the language of Scripture with little or no regard for the actual meaning. Because of neglecting the meaning, this method provided new opportunities to advance textual pretexts for the many kinds of innovation and interpretation that had taken root unnoticed and unintended in the course of generations. According to Nahum and Akiba, every word and letter of Scripture had significance; even the accusative particle *et* must be explained wherever it is found. Some sages were aware of the revolution in hermeneutics which this method implied. Earlier interpretation focused on the meaning, intention, and content of verses, while after Akiba, the form and manner of expression were considered legitimate sources of interpretation.[1]

Yohanan held ancient traditions, and had the capacity to use both Hillel's norms and his own good sense in the interpretation of Scripture. He did not always have the means to discover a Scriptural basis for the traditions he held. Akiba, coming after him, found Scriptural pretexts for Yohanan's traditions:

> That same day [on which Gamaliel II was deposed in favor of Eleazar ben Azariah], Rabbi Akiba expounded, "And every earthen vessel whereinto any of them falleth, whatsoever is in it conveys uncleanness" (Lev. 11.22). It does not say *is unclean* (Kal), but *shall render unclean* (Pi'el), so that it makes other things unclean. This teaches that a loaf suffering second-grade uncleanness renders another unclean in the third grade. Rabbi Joshua said, Who will take away the dust from off thine eyes, O Rabban Yohanan ben Zakkai! – for thou didst say that another generation would declare the third loaf clean, for there is no verse in the Torah to prove that it is unclean, and now does not thy disciple

---

[1] If Yohanan had had knowledge of Akiba's methods, his exegesis would likely not have rested so heavily on the content of verses. The method of Akiba and Nahum is described by Finkelstein, *Akiba*, 89, and 308-312, "The difference between the schools [of Akiba and Ishmael, who did not accept the new method] is clearly reflected in their disagreement in the interpretation of Exodus 20.22. The Mekilta of Rabbi Ishmael explains the verse as follows, 'Thus thou shalt say to the children of Israel – in the language in which I speak to thee, in the holy language.' It is obvious from this statement that the School of Ishmael believed that the only limitation which God imposed on Moses' words was that they should be in Hebrew. The school of Akiba, however, as represented in the Mekilta of Rabbi Simeon (20.22) maintains that the verses required Moses to speak to the children of Israel in the precise words which he received from God... He was required to speak 'in the holy language, and in this sense, and in this order, and with these divisions, and in these sections...'" Cf. also H. Strack, *Introduction to the Talmud and Midrash* (New York, 1959), 96. The principles were 1. Ribbui, the particules of 'af, gam, et, indicate an inclusion or amplication; 2. mi'ut, the three particles of ak, rak, min, point to a limitation, exclusion, or diminution; 3. Ribbui-ahar ribbui, when two of the particles named are joined, 4. mi'ut ahar miut, when two limiting or excluding principles are joined. Cf. also W. Bacher, Agadot, I, ii, 24-80; for a rabbinic reaction, cf. TB Menahot 29b.

Akiba bring a verse from the Torah to prove that it is unclean! For it
is written, Whatsoever is in it shall render unclean.[1]

Thus although Yohanan read the same Scripture as Akiba, he lacked
the technique to expound it with the philological and grammatical
ingenuity of Nahum and Akiba.

If by comparison to Akiba, Yohanan's use of Scripture was limited,
he nonetheless expressed his views on the ways by which man ought
to serve God through his exegesis. He used parables, homilies; he
carried on theological speculation in biblical terms, but, mainly, he
interpreted the literal sense of Scripture. He did not however retain
the plain meaning of a verse, if the plain sense seemed incongruous.
This was a common practice at this time. For example, the apostle Paul
expounded the commandment, "You shall not muzzle an ox when it
is treading out the grain" (Deut. 25.4) to mean that he might properly
receive wages. He asked, "Is it for oxen that God is concerned? Does
he not speak entirely for our sake?" (I Corinthians 9.9). At times,
Yohanan likewise attached to Scripture a meaning that seemed to him
more appropriate and relevant than the plain sense:

> "Let your garments be always white, and let not oil be lacking on
> your head" (Kohelet 9.8). Rabban Yohanan ben Zakkai said, If Scripture
> speaks of white garments, how many white garments do the pagans
> have! And if Scripture speaks of good oil, how much good oil do the
> pagans have! But Scripture speaks only of the performance of the
> commandments, and good deeds, and the study of Torah.[2]

An apparent continuation of the same homily is as follows:

> Said Rabban Yohanan ben Zakkai, It is like the king who invited his
> servants to the banquet and did not name the exact time. The wise
> among them came and sat at the door of the palace, saying, Does the

---

[1] Mishnah Sotah 5.2. Cf. tr. H. Danby, p. 298, with slight changes. For degrees
of uncleanness in foods, cf. Mishnah Taharot ch. 1, and 2.3. Cf. parallels in Sifra
Shemini 7.12, TB Sotah 27b, Hullin 33b, Pesahim 18a; TP Sotah 5.2, Tos. Sotah
5.13. Cf. also Albeck, *Seder Nashim*, 384. Compare the reaction of Eliezer ben
Hyrkanus, who was living at Lud at that time, and approved another midrash given
on that day, Mishnah Yadaim 4.3. Cf. also Epstein, *Mevo-ot*, 81, 375, 310, 424. For
another view of Yohanan's difficulty in the matter, cf. the commentary to the
mishnah of Yom Tov Lipman Heller, *ad. loc.* Cf. also TB Sotah 29a-b, for discussion
of Rav on why, if Yohanan had no proof, he nonetheless held that the third loaf
was unclean. Rav answers by suggesting a *kal ve-homer*. Yohanan had no proof
from Scripture, but only one based on reason. On his understanding of the Mishnah
I have based my interpretation that Yohanan did not have the methodology later
devised by Akiba, but only that provided earlier by Hillel. But cf. the discussion of
the kal ve-homer in TB Sotah 29b.

[2] Kohelet Rabbah 9.8.

king's palace lack for anything? But the fools went about their business, saying, Was there ever a banquet without a set hour? All of a sudden, the king summoned them to his presence. The wise ones appeared all dressed and cleaned up for the occasion; while the fools appeared in their dirt. The king rejoiced to see the wise ones, and was angered at the appearance of the fools, and said, Those who have dressed themselves for the banquet, let them sit and eat and drink, while the ones who are unprepared may stand by and look at them.[1]

White garments were the regular garb of the freeman, and especially on festivals. Anointing was a sign of prosperity and happiness. Yohanan argued that if Kohelet said, the purpose of life is the good things of this

---

[1] TB Shabbat 153a. The parable is brought as a comment to the vs. here, but without the homily of Yohanan known to the editor of Koh. R. Rather it is brought apparently by Eliezer, in his discussion with his students, or, more likely, by the editor of the Talmud, because of its relevance to Koh. 9.8. Thus the TB Shabbat passage is built as follows:
1. Rabbi Eliezer says, "Repent one day before thy death..."
2. and even Solomon said, "Let your garments..."
3. Said Rabban Tohanan ben Zakkai, "It is to be likened..." Compare ARNb, ch. 29, Schechter 31b:
   1. Repent one day before your death.
   2. It happened that Rabbi Eliezer ben Hyrkanus was saying to his disciples, Repent one day...
   3. They said to him, Does a man know (etc.)
   4. He answered, Every day...
   5. And this is the meaning of the matter, "Let your garments..." Compare also Midrash Tanhuma, ed. Buber, II, Ahare 35a. The Tanhuma is apparently a reformulation of Yohanan's midrash after the Destruction, in a more philological style:

   "The Holy one, blessed be he, foresaw that the Temple was destined to be destroyed, and he said, while the Temple is standing and you offer sacrifices in it, it will make atonement for you; but when the Temple is not standing, what will make atonement for you? Occupy yourselves in matters of Torah for they are compared to sacrifices, and they will atone for you..."

The midrash continues, comparing the matters of Torah to various sacrifices, wine, bread, and oil:

   They offer oil on the altar, as it is said, "Meal mixed in oil" (Lev. 2.5), and Torah is compared to oil, as it is said, "At all times let thy clothes be white and oil on thy head."

In only one place, to my knowledge, is this verse interpreted to apply to study of Torah (etc.), and that is Koh. R. 9.8. Hence I conclude that the midrash reformulates Yohanan's teaching. This would seem to be a statement of Yohanan's interpretation of the verse, in the idiom of the later hermeneutic. Compare also the late formulation of the Yalkut Shimoni, II, 979, where Eliezer's treatment of the verse as in ARNb ch. 29 is repeated. But Schechter (ad loc n. 35) is of the opinion that the citation of Koh. 9.8 in ARNb is a late addition. Note that ARNa ch. 15, Schechter 31b omits the vs. However, its use in TB Shabbat 153a would suggest that Eliezer learned the midrash on Koh. 9.8 from Yohanan; on this I base my interpretation.

world, the gentiles have a better lot than Israel. This is unthinkable. Therefore, one must face the precariousness of life by preparing for death and the good world to come. Such preparation was devotion to Torah, commandments, and good deeds, which represent a trilogy of religious concerns. Torah meant study of God's word, commandments, the doing of God's word, and good deeds, the service of the creator through service of his creatures who were made in his image. By these three practices, a man might keep himself ready for death.[1] Yohanan's student, Eliezer ben Hyrkanus, taught his students the same lesson:

> Rabbi Eliezer ben Hyrkanus said to his disciples, Repent one day before your death. They said to him, And does a man know when he will die, that he should repent? He said to them, Every day a man should say, today I will repent, lest I die tomorrow. Thus all his days will be spent in penitence, and this is the explanation of the matter, "At all times let thy clothes be white..."[2]

Thus Yohanan formulated his program for religion through innocent exegesis, reading into Scriptural phrases categories of religious expression more appropriate, in his mind, than those implied by the plain meaning of Scripture.[3]

Yohanan's attention to the moral appropriateness of Scripture led him to exposit its literal sense by analogy to contemporary legal procedure, or to past events, or to the common consensus on ethical behavior. The particular form of his analogical exegesis, known as *homer*,[4] has been compared to the allegorical method of

---

[1] On the religious program of Torah, commandments, and good deeds, cf. M. Kadushin, *Organic Thinking. A Study in Rabbinic Thought* (New York, 1938), 17, 69, 95, 113-14. Cf. also Ebner, *Education*, 25. Philo offers a trilogy of the good things of the mind, cf. *The Migration of Abraham*, 1. 105 (Colson Tr. IV, 193).

[2] ARNa ch. 15, Schechter p. 31b; TB Shabbat 153a. Cf. n. 13.

[3] Note the parallel to Yohanan's parable, Luke 14.15-24, Matthew 22.1-14. Cf. also A. Edersheim, *The Life and Times of Jesus the Messiah* (New York, 1910), II, 425-6.

[4] The meaning of the word is not known. Yohanan's midrash is mostly described as *kemin homer*, that is, in the *manner* of *homer*; but, as we shall see below, in some instances, the distinction is not made at all. The method is discussed by the following:

W. Bacher, *Erkhe Midrash* (Tel Aviv, 1923), s. v., 42-43. Following Rashi, Bacher explains the expression by reference to the Aramaic *humra* (cf. TB Sotah 15a, Kiddushin 22b). *Humra* – a bundle of spices or a pearl, that is, some kind of ornament; the meaning would be "a pleasant thing to which the statement (of Scripture) is comparable in that it has special value; or that the Scripture is to be connected to an allegorical explanation through the deeper "reason" that is hidden in it, according to the symbolical message that can be discovered in the verse. M.

Philo.[1] His known exegeses, however, do not reveal allegorization

---

Jastrow, *Dictionary*, s. v., I, 436, explains homer as "bead, little ball; jewel, clasp, seal." *Kemin homer* would mean "like a jewel," that is, a precious ethical principle. The *dorshe hamurot* were, according to Jastrow, "symbolizing interpreters."

A. Kohut, *Aruk*, III, 218, derives the word from homer, through the root *hamir*, to change. Thus the *dorshe hamurot* would be those who expound through analogy, cf. TB Hullin 134b. Kohut also cites the etymology based on "pearl." I have followed his explanation.

Cf. also: Weiss, *Dor*, I, 204; Bruell, *Mavo*, 58; Y. Heinemann, *Altjuedische Allegoristik* (Breslau, 1936), 66f.; *Darkhe HaAgadah*, 137 f.; *Philons griechische und juedische Bildung* (Breslau, 1932), 421, n. 3; L. Ginzberg, *On Jewish Law and Lore* (Philadelphia, 1955), 134. J. Perles, "Etudes Talmudiques," *REJ* III, 109 f. A. Feldman, *Parables and Similes of the Rabbis* (Cambridge, 1924), 3-4, n. 1 I. Levi, in *REJ* LX, 14 f. Levi supposes that there was a whole school of agadists before Hillel and Shammai who employed such a principle. D. Neumark, *Maybaum Festschrift* (Berlin, 1914), p. 179 f.; Bacher, *Agadot*, I, i, 24-25; L. Ginzberg, *Allegorical Interpretation*, JE I, 403-411; H. A. Wolfson, *Philo*, 91-2, n. 29-34; *Philosophy of the Church Fathers* (Cambridge, 1956), p. 24 f. Also, cf. J. Hamburger, *Real Encyclopedie*, II, 52 s. v. allegorie; Weiss, in REJ III, 276 f., J. D. Eisenstein *Ozar Yisrael*, s. v. *dorshe reshumot*.

[1] J. Z. Lauterbach, "The Ancient Jewish Allegorists in Talmud and Midrash," *JQR*, n. s. I, 291 f. Cf. p. 328, "*Kemin Homer* means 'in the style and method of the *dorshe hamurot*, those who interpreted Scripture in an allegorical way, taking the words not in their literal meaning, but as signs and symbols.'" But the known examples of Yohanan's midrash in this manner do not reveal his ignoring the literal meaning of Scripture, but rather, his interpreting *that* meaning homiletically. Consider, for example, the one significant parallel to Philo:

> "Yohanan says, Why was the ear most fitting of all limbs (to be bored, (cf. Ex. 22.6)? Because it heard on Mount Sinai, 'Unto me are the children of Israel slaves' (Lev. 24.55)... Let the ear come and be bored, for it has not observed what it heard." [Tos. Baba Kama, 7.5, cf. parallels below.]

Philo explains the verse allegorically:

> "... whoever dares to say that anything is his own will thereby has registered himself a slave in perpetuity, even as the man who says, I have come to love my master, my wife, and my children, I decline to go away free. It is well that he has acknowledged himself a slave, for how can the man be other than a slave who says, Mine is the master, even mind, that is, its own master and absolute Lord; mine also is sense-perception, a means of judging material forms... But let him not only give evidence against himself, let him be condemned also by God and submit to slavery eternal and inexorable, when God brings his ear to be pierced, in order that it may not admit words of virtue, and gives him to be slave forever to mind and to sense, bad and pitiless masters." Cf. *Allegorical Interpretation*, III, 198; Colson, I, 435.

Philo comments elsewhere on the matter also:

> "But if you leave yourself forever unschooled and untaught, you will be eternally enslaved to hard mistresses, vain fancies, lusts, pleasures... For if, says Moses, the servant should answer and say, I have come to love my master, my wife, and my children, I will not go out free, he shall be brought to the tribunal of God, and with God as judge, shall have his request ratified, having first had his ear bored with an awl, that he may not receive the divine message of the freedom of the soul. For lofty words like these of having

at all, but rather homiletical moralizing. Others in his time, particularly Gamaliel II and Eleazar of Modin, utilized the same analogical method,[1] but it became mostly obsolete when the new hermeneutic focused attention on the form of Scripture as much as on its content, and by the end of the third century, the method ceased to be employed.[2] Many examples of the analogical technique remain, five of which were collected as follows:

> Five matters did Rabban Yohanan ben Zakkai expound in the manner of *homer*:[3]
> 1. On what account did Israel go into exile to Babylon rather than to any other land? Because Abraham's family came from there. To what is the matter comparable? To a woman who was unfaithful to her husband. Where does he send her? Back to her father's house.
> 2. Of the first tablets it is said, "And the tablets were the work of God" (Ex. 32.16), but of the second, "The tablets were the work of Moses" (Ex. 34.1). To what is the matter comparable? To a king of flesh and

---

come to love the mind and thinking of his master and benefactor are worthy of a reasoning disqualified and rejected as it were from the sacred arena... And so too when he speaks of his exceeding affection for outward sense and his belief that she is his own possession... So to with the children of these two, the children of mind... the children of sense. He who seeks intimacy with these can have had no perception, can not even have dreamt of freedom..." *On the Cherubim*, 72 (Colson II, 53). Cf. also *Who is the heir*, 1. 186, Colson IV, 377.

Philo's interpretation is allegory, that is, "interpretation of a text in terms of something else, irrespective of what that something else is," cf. Wolfson, *Philo*, I, 92-3. Here the slave is no longer a slave, and the subservience no longer to a real master; but Scripture speaks for Philo to a completely different matter. For Yohanan, on the other hand, the slave is literally a slave; he has not done away with the plain sense of Scripture, but rather has tried to interpret it. I do not see, therefore, that this is allegory in the precise meaning of the term. Beside Wolfson, the relationship between Philo and rabbinic Judaism is discussed by Y. Baer, *Yisrael ba-Amim*, 81-98; A. Kaminka, "Hillel's Life and Work," *JQR*, n.s. XXX, 107 f. Cf. especially, Wolfson, *Church Fathers*, 31 f., "Rabbinic midrash is not exactly Philonic allegory..."

[1] Cf. Bacher, *Agadot*, I, i, 23-25; TB Sotah 15a, etc.

[2] Lauterbach's contention is (p. 509) that the method of the *dorshe hamurot* was abandoned because it diminished the literal importance of Scripture and the necessity of carrying out Scriptural commandments. Cf. Neumark's criticism of this view. Lauterbach states, "Thus the tendency of the dorshe hamurot led to the neglecting, if not the abrogating, of the practical observance of the law and it was this tendency that brought them into disfavor with the teachers of the traditional law, so that but few of their interpretations have been preserved." But I doubt that Yohanan ben Zakkai, Gamaliel II, Eleazar of Modin, and the other sages were ever suspected of neglecting the Scriptural commandments because they had uncovered their "spiritual" significance! The sages did not abandon the letter of the law, as they understood it, in favor of its spirit.

[3] Tosefta Baba Kama 7.3-7.

blood who betrothed a woman. He brings the scribe, the pen and ink, the parchment, and the witness. If she is disloyal to him, she brings everything. It is enough for her if the king will give his signature.

3. Behold it says, "When a ruler sins, doing unwittingly any one of the things which the Lord God has commanded not to be done... he shall bring as his offering a goat... it is a sin offering" (Lev. 4.22). Happy is the generation whose prince brings a sin-offering for his unwitting sin!

4. And it says, "Then his master shall bring him to the door or the doorpost, and his master shall bore his ear through with an awl, and he shall serve him for life" (Ex. 22.6). Why was the ear the most fitting of all the limbs? Because it heard on Mount Sinai, "Unto me are the children of Israel slaves, they are my slaves" (Lev. 24.55), and broke from itself the yoke of heaven and accepted upon itself the yoke of flesh and blood, therefore Scripture said, Let the ear come and be bored, for it has not observed what it heard. Another matter, it did not wish to be subservient to its master, let it come and be subjugated to his children.[1]

5. And it says, "An altar of stones – thou shalt not raise upon them iron...," Now why was iron declared unfit of all metals? Because the sword is made from it. The sword is a means of punishment, and the altar, a means of atonement. Keep away that which signifies punishment from that which brings atonement. And behold, just as stones, which neither see, nor hear, nor speak, on account of their bringing atonement between Israel and their Father in Heaven, Scripture said, Do not raise upon them iron, sons of Torah, who themselves are atonement for the world, how much more so that none of the destroyers should touch them.

The following paragraph is also presented in the same collection:

And behold it says, Perfect stones you should build the altar of the Lord your God (Deut. 27.6) – Stones which make perfect [the relationship] between Israel and their Father in Heaven, the Omnipresent said, should be perfect before me, Sons of Torah, who make peace in the world, how much the more so that they should be perfect in the sight of the Omnipresent.

Other such analogues, not, however, identified as being "in the manner of the *homer*" include the following:

If a man steals surreptitiously, he pays double; if he slew or sold (the sheep or ox), he pays four or five fold; but the robber (who takes openly) pays double in either case. His disciples asked Rabban Yohanan ben Zakkai, What led the Torah to be more stringent on the thief than on the robber? He said to them, the robber (who broke in by daylight) equated the honor of the slave to that of his master; the thief (who came

---

[1] My translation follows the alternate reading, cf. Zukermandel, p. 358, n. 10.

by night) rendered honor to the slave over the master. It is as if the thief made the eye above as if it does not see, and the ear as if it did not hear, as it says, "Woe to those who hide deep from their Lord their counsel, whose deeds are in the dark, and who say, who sees us, who knows us? You turn things upside down! (Is. 29.15). And it says, And they say, The Lord does not see, the God of Jacob does not perceive' (Ps. 94.7), and it says, "The city is full of injustice, for they say, the Lord has forsaken the land, and the Lord does not see." (Ez. 9.9).[1]

Five oxen for an ox, and four sheep for a sheep (Ex. 22.1). Rabban Yohanan ben Zakkai said, The Omnipresent had respect for the honor of his creatures. For an ox, which goes on its own feet, he shall pay five; for a lamb, which he had to carry on his shoulder, he pays four.[2]

Each who is numbered in the census shall give this: half a shekel according to the shekel of the sanctuary (the shekel is twenty gerahs)... (Ex. 30.13). Rabbi Joshua son of Rabbi Nehemiah in the name of Rabban Yohanan ben Zakkai said, "Because they transgressed the Ten Words, each must give ten gerah."[3]

For after only seven days more I will cause it to rain upon the earth forty days and forty nights (Gen. 7.4)... Said Rabban Yohanan ben Zakkai, They destroyed the face, which was given to them on the fortieth day, [the time it takes to form the child in the womb], therefore it will rain forty days and forty nights to destroy the face of the earth.[4]

Thus the *homer* method was to take the literal sense of Scripture, and to suggest analogies to it in legal procedure, or past events, or morally appropriate parallels.[5] Israel was sent back to Babylon as an unfaithful wife is returned to her father's house in disgrace. The second tablets

---

[1] Tos. Baba Kama 7.1-2. This provides the introduction to the five exegeses cited above, and is, apparently, a *homer*-exegesis.

[2] TB Baba Kama 79b. Cf. Mekilta Nezikin 12. Compare the opinion of Rabbi Meir, TB Baba Kama 79b. Compare also the opinion of the Targum ad loc., which explains that the ox has likely performed useful labor for the thief, and the sheep not, and therefore the greater fine for the ox; Rabbi Meir likewise emphasized the aspect of work, and not the honor of the thief.

[3] TP Shekalim 2.3. Cf. Pesikta Rabbati 19b. The statement apparently answers the question, why was the half-shekel used? Because it has the weight of ten gerahs. And why this? Exodus 30.13. W. Nowack, "Shekel," *JE*, XI, 257-8.

[4] Bereshit Rabbah 44.25. For the explanation of "40 days," cf. Rashi, Yevamot 69b, the creation of the child in the womb takes forty days.

[5] Cf. also Mishnat Rabbi Eliezer (ed. Enelow, p. 333), in which Yohanan provides an analogy for the meal-offering of the suspected adulteress, "Since her deed was the deed of cattle, her offering is the food of cattle." But in the Mishnah-Sotah 2.1, this is brought in the name of Rabban Gamaliel. Cf. also Epstein, Mavo, ot, 402-3, who suggests that this is Gamaliel I, and that Yohanan preserved his tradition. More complete recensions of the above exegeses were preserved, several

Continued note from p. 90.

in the form of "His students asked Rabban Yohanan ben Zakkai..." Parallels include the following:

On the tablets:
"The students of Rabban Yohanan ben Zakkai asked him, on what account were the first tablets the work of heaven, and the second, the work of man? He said to them, To what is the matter comparable? to a king who married a woman, and brought the paper, and the scribe, and the ink of his own, and brought her home. He caught her playing with a certain one of his slaves, was angered, and divorced her. A friend of hers came to him and said, My Lord, do you not know from whence you took her? Was it not among the slaves that she was brought up? And since she was brought up among slaves, she shows no pride among them. He said to him, And what do you propose? That I take her back? Bring paper and a scribe of your own, and I shall sign the document. So Moses said to the Holy One blessed be he when Israel came to that deed. He said to him, Do you not know from which country you took them? From Egypt, a place of idolatry. The Holy One said to him, and what do you want, that I be appeased to them? Bring the tablets of your own, and behold my handwriting I shall inscribe on *your* tablets." [Deut. R. Ekev 3.17; cf. also Yalkut Shimoni I, 397].

In this recension, the king apparently takes the unfaithful wife back, and is therefore a closer parallel to the biblical event. On the ruler who brings a sacrifice, TB Horayot 10b, TP Horayot 3.2; Sifra Hova 5.1. On boring the ear: TB Kiddushin 22a, TP Kiddushin 1.2, Mekilta Mishpatim 2. Cf. also Pesikta Rabbati ch. 21, Friedman ed. 110b:

"The ear which heard on Mount Sinai, I am the Lord, and took upon itself the yoke of the sovereignty of flesh and blood... the ear which heard before Mount Sinai, thou shalt have no other gods... and this one went and acquired himself a master... therefore the ear should come and be bored..."

This story is also reported as a conversation with his students, cf. TP Kiddushin 1.2, "His pupils asked of Rabban Yohanan ben Zakkai, why should the slave's ear be punished above his other members? He said to them, the ear that heard on Mount Sinai, thou shalt have no other gods but me..." In Kiddushin 22b, it is presented as follows:

"Rabban Yohanan ben Zakkai used to expound this Scripture *kemin homer*, Why was the ear set apart of all the limbs in the body? Said the Holy One blessed be he..."

It is followed by a similar midrash of R. Simeon son of R. Judah,

"And R. Simeon son of Rabbi used to expound this verse *kemin homer*, Why were the door and door post set apart from all the vessels of the House? Said the Holy One blessed be he..."

Cf. also Mekilta Mishpatim 2 (Lauterbach ed. III, 16),

"And what is the reason that of all the organs the ear alone is to be bored? Rabban Yohanan ben Zakkai interpreted it *kemin homer*: His ear had heard the commandment, Thou shalt not steal (Ex. 20.13), and yet he went and stole, therefore it alone of all the organs shall be pierced through."

Cf. also Yalkut Shimoni I, 317, 318, 999.
On the altar-stones:

were provided by Moses, as a divorced wife provides the materials for the contract of remarriage.[1] The ruler brings an offering for unwitting sin, would that our rulers were so scrupulous! The ear is to be bored as a sign of voluntary slavery, because hearing the Torah should prevent

---

Cf. also Mekilta Bahodosh 11; Sifra Kiddushin 10.8; Semahot 8.17; Mekilta de Rabbi Ishmael, Epstein-Melamed ed., p. 157, 1. 29. Cf. Middot 3.4, where a parallel idea appears:

> "The stones of the Ramp and the stones of the altar were alike taken from the valley of Beth Keren, where they were quaried from below virgin soil, and brought from thence as whole stones upon which no iron had been lifted up. For iron renders invalid even by a touch, and by a blemish in every respect... They did not plaster them with an iron trowel lest it should touch and render them invalid; for iron was created to shorten man's days, while the altar was created to lengthen man's days; what shortens may not rightly be lifted up against what lengthens."

The Mekilta reads (Lauterbach II, 290):

> "For if thou lift up thy sword upon it... In this connection, R. Simon ben Eleazar used to say, The altar is made to prolong the years of man, and iron is made to shorten the years of man. It is not right for that which shortens life to be lifted up against that which prolongs life. Rabban Yohanan ben Zakkai says, Behold it says, thou shalt build... of whole stones (Deut. 27.6). They are to be stones that establish peace. Now by using the method of kal vahomer you reason, The stones for the altar do not see nor hear nor speak. Yet because they serve to establish peace between Israel and their Father in heaven the Holy one blessed be he said Thou shalt lift up no iron tool upon them, How much the more then should he who establishes peace between man and his fellow man, between husband and wife, between city and city, between nation and nation, between family and family, between government and government, be protected so that no harm should come to him."

On the robber and the thief: cf. Mekilta Nezikin 15; Midrash HaGadol, Mishpatim, *ad loc.*

On the penalties for sheep and oxen: cf. Mekilta Nezikin 12. For other examples of such exegesis, cf. below, ch. six. One recalls Yohanan's alleged disputes with the Sadducees, for they attempted to argue from this type of hermeneutic: why must Pentecost follow the Sabbath? Because Moses our master wished to give Israel two days of rejoicing. Why does the priest eat the meal offering? Because Moses our master loved Aaron his brother. In these instances, Yohanan was supposed to have rejected such exegesis out of hand, yet here he is seen to have used the same kind of exegetical principle. Likewise, he gave the reason that Scripture renders the hands unclean: to make certain men do not profane the Scrolls. It is evident that Yohanan did not reject the Sadducean arguments on account of faulty method (if, indeed, the arguments are accurately represented in extant sources); he seems rather to have rejected their claim to authentic traditions, and would therefore have rejected any proof they proposed.

[1] The document in question is not apparently a divorce certificate *(get)*, but a new marriage-contract *(ketuvah)*, and, therefore, the analogy to the new tablets made by Moses is quite precise. [But cf. p. 91 n. 5.] Normally an unfaithful wife must be divorced, and may not remarry her cuckold-husband. Cf. Mishnah Sotah 5.1; also D. W. Amram, "Adultery," *JE*, I, 216-218.

it. Iron is not to touch the altar, because iron is the material of war. Just as perfect stones ('avanim shelemot) were used on the altars, so should the sages be perfect in the sight of God. The Torah's penalties are guaged by religious and moral values. Two of the exegeses, the one concerning the ruler ('asher, 'ashre) and the other concerning the altar (shalem shalom) are plays on words. These are all, therefore, moral homilies, not allegories in any sense, and are meant to elucidate the common sense morality of Scripture.[1]

Yohanan commented on the plain meaning of Scripture:

---

[1] Cf. Semahot 8.17, ed. M. Higger, 165 f., in which anonymous exegesis of the *Dorshe Hamurot* may well be Yohanan's. If so, the distinction between the sages who expounded in the *manner* of the *homer*, and those who were expounders of *hamurot*, proposed by Lauterbach, simply cannot be drawn. Yet Lauterbach himself recognized the similarity between the Semahot midrash and Yohanan's. The passage is as follows:

> "The *dorshe hamurot* used to say:
> 1. You shall surely destroy all the places where the nations whom thou shall dispossess served their gods, upon the high mountains and upon the hills, and under every green tree; you shall tear down their altars, and dash to pieces their pillars (Deut. 12.2–3). How did the wood and stones sin? But on account of them there came upon man confusion, and therefore Scripture said, 'You shall destroy their altars.' And behold it is a deduction: if in the case of stone and wood, which have neither merit nor demerit, neither good nor evil, because on their account confusion comes upon man, Scripture said to destroy their altars, a man who causes others to sin, and turns them from the way of life to the way of death, how much more so will he suffer."

The antonymic relationship to the midrash on the stones of the altar is obvious; Yohanan does comment on the same verse, cf. ARNb ch. 31, Schechter 33b and ch. 6, and the editor of Yalkut Shimoni brought this midrash and that of Yohanan contiguously, cf. Yalkut I, 724, thus recognizing their relationship.

> "2. And so too, if a woman approaches any beast and lies with it, you shall kill the woman and the beast, they shall be put to death, their blood is upon them (Lev. 20.16). If the woman sinned, what sin did the beast commit? But because there came upon man confusion on its account, Scripture said to kill the beast, that the bull should not go into the market place and people say, See, there is the cow on whose account so-and-so was put to death. And behold, it is a matter of deduction: if in the case of the beast, who has neither merit nor demerit, because on its account man was brought to confusion, Scripture said to stone it, a man who causes his fellow to sin, and leads him from the way of life to the way of sin, how much the more so (will he suffer)."

This case is brought anonymously in Mishnah Sanhedrin 1.4, and Tos. Sanhedrin 3.2. Compare the teaching of Yohanan, which is not quite congruent:

> "Antigones the Prince asked Rabban Yohanan ben Zakkai, The ox will be stoned, and also its master will die. Why? He said to him, The accomplice of a thief is like a thief. And when he went out, the students asked, Master,

Wo is us, that Scripture weighs against us light sins as heavy sins. "Then I will draw near to you for judgment. I will be a swift witness against the sorcerers, against the adulterers, against those who swear falsely, against those who oppress the hireling in his wages... against those who thrust aside the sojourner (Malachi 3.5). Woe is us for the day of judgment, woe is us for the day of rebuke. The Scripture juxtaposed those who swear falsely to all the most severe transgressions. Therefore the Holy one blessed be He warned not to swear falsely.[1]

_____

this one you pushed away with a reed, but to us what will you reply? He said to them, It is written, the ox will be stoned and also its master will die – the death of the ox is to be like the death of the master..."

Cf. T.P. Sanhedrin 1.2, and compare Yalkut I, 724.

"3. And likewise it says, An altar of stones, thou shalt not raise upon them iron (Deut. 27.5), and in another place it says (Ex. 20.25), And if you make me an altar of stone, you shall not build it of hewn stones, for if you wield your tool upon it, you profane it; and why is iron specified to be unfit for the altar from among all kinds of metal? Because from it the sword is made, and the sword is a sign of curse, and the altar, of blessing. One sets aside something which is a sign of curse on account of something which is a sign of blessing, and behold, it is a matter of deduction. If in the case of stones, which neither see, nor hear, nor speak, nor eat, nor drink, on account of their bringing peace between Israel and their father in heaven, Scripture said, thou shalt not raise upon them iron, sons of Torah, who are an atonement for the world, how much the more so that the demons should not touch them."

As we have seen, this is a midrash explicitly assigned to Yohanan elsewhere.

"4. And likewise it says (Deut. 27.6) You shall build an altar of whole stones – stones which bring wholeness to the world; and behold, it is a matter of deduction: just as stones, which neither see nor hear nor speak nor eat nor drink, because they bring peace between Israel and their father in heaven, the Holy One blessed be he said that they shall be whole before me, sons of Torah who are an atonement for the world, how much the more so should they be whole before the Holy One blessed be he."

It seems clear that Semahot brings two midrashim by Yohanan himself, a third which is strikingly close to known midrashim of Yohanan, and a fourth on a verse with which he himself was concerned. I think this brings into question Lauterbach's contention that those who were _dorshe hamurot_ intended to abrogate the law once they discovered what it symbolized. Since the _dorshe hamurot_ obviously included Yohanan ben Zakkai himself, and since there is no evidence whatever that Yohanan favored the "spirit" in exclusion of the "letter" of the law, I think Lauterbach's contention stands refuted.

[1] TB Hagigah 5a, Tanhuma Shoftim 7. As in the sources in Koh. R. and TB Shabbat, I have combined two midrashim which appear independently, since they are apparently interdependent. The Hagigah source reads, "Rabban Yohanan, when he would reach this verse, he would weep, 'And I shall bring you near to judgment...' – a slave whose master brings him near to judgment, and hastens to testify against him, does he have any hope?... Rabban Yohanan ben Zakkai said, Woe unto us that Scripture weighed against us light sins as heavy sins." One must note that

He also elucidated many difficult passages for his students. He thus expounded verses which posed particular difficulty to later critics:

> "And out of the ground, the Lord God formed every beast of the field" (Gen. 2.19). Rabban Yohanan ben Zakkai was asked, Since it is already written (Gen. 1.24), "Let the earth bring forth the living creature," what is taught by the verse, "And out of the ground the Lord God formed..."? He replied, The earlier verse refers to creation, while this treats of gathering them together (in order to name them) as you read, "When thou shalt mass" (wayyizer – zur) against a city (Deut. 20.19), that is, the Lord God assembled the beasts of the field which were created from the ground.[1]

He tried also to answer obvious questions that Scripture might pose:

> And the eyes of both of them were opened (Gen. 3.7) – Then were they blind? Rabbi Yudan in the name of Rabban Yohanan ben Zakkai, and Rabbi Berekiah in the name of Rabbi Akiba, explained it by comparing them to a villager who was passing a glass-workers shop, and just when a basketful of goblets and cut-glassware was in front of him, he swung his staff around and broke them. Then the owner arose and seized him, and cried, I know that I cannot obtain redress from you, but come, and I shall show you how much valuable stuff you have destroyed. Thus he opened their eyes, and showed them how many generations they had destroyed.[2]

In the course of such homilies, he may have used Scripture to convey his own comments on affairs of the day. Thus early in his career, he taught concerning the verse (Prov. 14.34), "Righteousness exalteth a nation, but the kindness of the peoples is sin," that just as the sin-offering makes atonement for Israel, so charity makes atonement for the heathen. After the destruction of Jerusalem, he accepted a strongly xenophobic interpretation of the same verse.[3] His exclamation, "Happy is the generation whose ruler brings an offering on his unwitting sin" may have expressed his distress with the procuratorial government (to say nothing of the Zealots). Likewise, his discussion of the altar as source of peace and not of war would have been especially relevant in the debate on the "loyal sacrifices" in the summer of 66 C.E., when the question was whether to continue sacrificing in the name of the emperor

---

perjury is hardly a light pecadillo, and this is a curious attitude. Cf. Rashi's comment *ad loc.*

[1] Ber. Rabbah 17.4.
[2] Ber. Rabbah 19.6.
[3] TB Baba Batra 10a. Cf. ch. 7.

or not.[1] His counsel of patience at the start of the war also may have found expression in Scriptural exegesis.[2]

Through the study of Scripture, men also carried on theological discussion. An issue which troubled the sages was, What is the proper motive from which to serve God? Should man serve him through love ("Thou shalt love the Lord thy God with all thy heart, with all thy soul, and with all thy might," Deut. 4.6), or through fear and awe ("My covenant with him was a covenant of life and peace, and I gave them to him, that he might fear, and he feared me, he stood in awe of my name," Malachi 2.5). It had been said earlier, "Be not like servants who minister to their master in expectation of receiving a reward, but be like servants who minister to their master in no expectation of receiving a reward."[3] But what motive ought to induce selfless service? In this dispute, Yohanan may well have expressed his opinion not in abstract terms but in a comment on a Scriptural figure. He said that Job had served God on account of fear, as it is written,"The man was perfect and upright, and one that feared God and eschewed evil" (Job 1.1, 27.5):

> On that same day (that Rabban Gamaliel II was deposed), Rabbi Joshua ben Hyrcanus expounded, Job served the Holy One, blessed be He, only from love, as it is written "Though he slay me, yet will I wait for him." Thus far the matter rests in doubt, whether it means, "I will wait for him," or "I will not wait," but Scripture says explicitly, "Till I die I will not put away mine integrity from before me," teaching that he acted from love. Rabbi Joshua ben Hananiah said, "Oh who will remove the dust from between thine eyes, Rabban Yohanan ben Zakkai – for all thy days thou didst expound that Job served the Holy One, blessed be He, only from fear, and has not Joshua, thy disciple's disciple, now taught us that he acted from love."[4]

The sages contrasted the service of the patriarchs, which was out of love, with that of the upright gentile, Job, who served out of fear, and praised the "Pharisee for love" over the "Pharisee from fear."[5] Thus

---

[1] This is the suggestion of C. Roth in an unpublished MSS., "The Pharisees in the Revolution of 66 C.E." which he lent me. Cf. Sifra Hova 5.1, Horayot 10b.

[2] Cf. ARNb ch. 31, Schechter, p. 33b; and ch. 6.

[3] Avot 1.2.

[4] Sotah 5.5.

[5] On the Pharisee from fear and love, cf. ARNb, ch. 46, Schechter, 62b. The discussion on the patriarchs and Job is in TB Sotah 31a. On rabbinic ideas about Job, cf. L. Ginzberg, *Legends*, V, 381-399. On the parallel dispute in Alexandria, cf. Wolfson, *Philo*, II, 286-7, 296; cf. also G. F. Moore, *Judaism*, II, 99; Buechler, *Sin and Atonement*, 122-148. Note also that Yohanan holds up as a virtue the service of God through love, cf. Mekilta to Ex. 19.6, "Because thou didst not serve the Lord thy God with love, therefore shalt thou serve thine enemy with hatred...," compare Deut. 28.46, "with joyfulness and with gladness" for Yohanan becomes simply

Yohanan apparently expressed his view that God should be served for love, by preaching that the upright heathen, Job, served from fear, but the true motive for a Jew is love.

The study of Scripture revealed something about Yohanan's intellectual life. He appeared as a vigorous partisan leader, calling his opponents idiots, using Scripture as a means to express a wide range of opinion on religious, social, and ethical questions, and possibly on political issues as well. All this represented the outer man, the open and partly recoverable part of Yohanan's life. Within his Scriptural exegesis, however, particularly in his use of prophetic symbolism, one may discover a trace of his inner life.[1] With his disciples, he speculated on the visions of the heavenly chariot which Ezekiel recorded. One cannot hope to uncover what this speculation meant to Yohanan and his disciples, but only to suggest tentatively the relevance of its external imagery. It was recorded:

Our rabbis taught, Once Rabban Yohanan ben Zakkai was riding on an ass, when going on a journey, and Rabbi Eleazar ben Arakh was driving the ass behind. Rabbi Eleazar said to him, Master, teach me a chapter of the work of the chariot. He answered him, Have I not taught you thus, Nor may the work of the chariot be taught in the presence of one, unless he is a sage and understands of his own knowledge? Rabbi Eleazar then said to him, Master, permit me to say before thee something which thou hast taught me. He answered, Say on! Forthwith, Rabban Yohanan ben Zakkai dismounted from the ass, wrapped himself up in his cloak, and sat upon a stone beneath an olive tree. Said Rabbi Eleazar to him, Master, wherefore did you dismount from the ass? He answered, Is it proper that while you are expounding the work of the chariot, and the Divine Presence is with us and the ministering angels accompany us, that I should ride upon an ass? Forthwith Rabbi Eleazar ben Arakh began his exposition of the work of the chariot, and fire came down from heaven and encompassed all the trees of the field, whereupon they all began to utter song. (And what was the song they uttered? Praise the Lord from the earth ye seamonsters and all deeps, fire and hail, snow and frost, stormy wind fulfilling his command, mountains and all hills, fruit trees and all cedars! [Ps. 148.7 9]) An angel then answered from the fire and said, This is the very work of the chariot. Thereupon Rabban Yohanan ben Zakkai rose and kissed him on his head and said, Blessed be the Lord, God of Israel, who hath given a son to Abraham our father

---

"with love." Cf. TB Baba Batra 16a for the same argument with Joshua and Eliezer as disputants. For Joshua's view, cf. also Tos. Sotah 6.1. Note also Joshua's use of Job in comforting Yohanan, ch. 4. On the Pharisee out of fear like Job, and out of love like Abraham, cf. also Sotah 22b, and TP Berahot 9. Cf. also Buechler, 139, who thinks that this view of Job arose at Yohanan's academy.

[1] Cf. M. Kadushin, *The Rabbinic Mind* (New York, 1952), on the "experience of God," 201-222.

who knoweth to speculate upon and to investigate and to expound the work of the chariot. There are some who preach well but do not perform well; others perform well but do not expound well, but you expound and perform well. Happy art thou O Abraham our father that Rabbi Eleazar ben Arakh hath come forth from thy loins. Now when these things were told to Rabbi Joshua, he and Rabbi Yosi the Priest were going on a journey. They said, Let us also expound the work of the chariot, so Rabbi Joshua began an exposition. Now that day was the summer solstice, but nonetheless, the heavens became overcast with clouds, and a kind of rainbow appeared in the cloud, and ministering angels assembled and came to listen like people who come to watch the entertainments of bridegroom and bride. Thereupon Rabbi Yosi the Priest went and told what had happened before Rabban Yohanan ben Zakkai, and he said, Happy are you, and happy is she that bore you. Happy are my eyes that have seen thus. Moreover in my dream, I and you were reclining on Mount Sinai when a heavenly echo was sent to us saying, Ascend hither, ascend hither! Here are great banqueting chambers and fine dining couches prepared for you, you and your disciples, and your disciples' disciples are designated for the third class.[1]

Other evidence of the transmission of an esoteric doctrine includes the following:

Rabbi Yudan bar Pazzi in the name of Rabbi Yosi bar Yudan: Three lectured their Torah before their master, Rabbi Joshua before Rabban Yohanan ben Zakkai, Rabbi Akiba before Rabbi Joshua, and Rabbi Hananiah ben Hakinai before Rabbi Akiba. Thenceforth their knowledge is impure.[2]

It is taught, Rabban Yohanan ben Zakkai said, What answer did the heavenly voice give to that wicked man (the king of Babylon in Is. 14.14) when he said, "I will ascend to heaven, above the stars of God, I will set my throne on high, I will sit in the mount of assembly in the far

---

[1] TB Hagigah 14b. Compare parallels in Mekilta de Rabbi Simeon bar Yohai, Epstein-Melamed ed. 158 l. 9 f., TP Hagigah 2.1, Tos. Hagigah 2.1-2. Cf. also Ber. R. 37, 2-4; Esther R. 1.1. The Mekilta parallel presents the following variant details: Yohanan does not descend from the ass until he sees fire playing round about; after the "happy art thou, Abraham..." phrase, it adds, he used to say, If all the sages of Israel were in one side of the balance, etc. Variants in the TP Hagigah 2.1 include the following: he descended from the ass and said, "It is not proper that I should hear the Glory of God and ride upon an ass. They went and sat under a tree, and fire descended and surrounded them round about..." The song of the trees was Ps. 96. Yohanan uttered the following blessing: Blessed is the Lord God of Abraham, Isaac, and Jacob, who gave to Abraham our Father a son, wise and knowing how to expound the Glory of Our father in Heaven..." It was Rabbi Yosi the Priest and Simeon ben Nataneel who heard and emulated Eleazar's example. The voice spoke to them, saying, Behold a place is ready for you...

[2] TP Hagigah 2.1, cf. Tos. Hagigah 2.2, TB Berahot 61b.

north, I will ascend above the heights of the clouds, I will make myself like the most high"? A heavenly voice went forth and said, "O wicked man son of a wicked man, grandson of Nimrod the wicked who stirred the whole world to rebellion against me by his rule! How many are the years of man. Seventy, for it is said, The days of our years are three score years and ten... (Ps. 90.10). But the distance from the earth to the firmament is a journey of five hundred years, and the thickness of the firmament is a journey of five hundred years, and likewise the distance between one firmament and the other. And above them (the seven heavens) are the holy living creatures. The feet of the living creatures are equal to all of them together (fifteen, that is, seven heavens and eight interspaces, times 500 years). The legs of the living creatures are equal to all of them. The knees of the living creatures are equal to all of them. The bodies of the living creatures are equal to all of them. The necks of the living creatures are equal to all of them. The heads of the living creatures are equal to all of them. The horns of the living creatures are equal to all of them. Above them is the throne of glory. The feet of the throne of glory are equal to all of them. The throne of glory is equal to all of them. The king, the living and eternal God, high and exalted, dwelleth above them. Yet thou didst say, I will ascend above the heights of the clouds, I will be like the most high! Nay, but thou shalt be brought down to the nether world, to the uttermost parts of the pit (Is. 14.15).[1]

Since the content of such esoteric speculation was kept secret in Yohanan's day,[2] all one can say with certainty is that there *were* mystical elements in Yohanan's thought. Several salient characteristics will, however, suggest what these speculations may have meant to him.[3]

---

[1] TB Hagigah 13a, cf. TB Pesahim 94a-b, Bereshit R. 25, Eruvin 53a. Note also TB Sukkah 32b, Rabbi Joshua ben Levi said, and some say that it was taught by Rabba bar Meri in the name of Rabban Yohanan ben Zakkai, Two palm trees are in the valley of Ben Hinnom, and smoke goes up between them, and this is what we have learned, "the thorn palms of the Iron Mount (a hill near Jerusalem) are valid (for the palm branches on Sukkot), and this is the entrance to Gehinom."

[2] On esoteric speculation as a private (possibly secret) activity, cf. Hagigah 2.1 and parallels. Cf. also Kadushin, *Rabbinic Mind*, 260-1, G. Scholem, *Major Trends in Jewish Mysticism* (New York, 1954), 44-50; Moore, *Judaism*, I, 411. Cf. also Gershom G. Scholem, *Jewish Gnosticism, Merkabah Mysticism, and Talmudic Tradition* (New York, 1960). Note especially that Scholem demonstrates the antiquity of the *Shiur Komah* speculation, pp. 36-42.

[3] Cf. Finkelstein, *Pharisees*, I, 182-3; *Akiba*, 195-214. Epstein, *Mavo-ot*, 48, 50; Kohut, *Aruk*, s. v. Merkavah, V, 251; K. Kohler, "Cabala," *JE*, III, 456-9; L. Ginzberg, "Cabala, History and System," *JE*, III, 459-479; J. D. Eisenstein, *Ozar Yisrael*, s. v. Maaseh Bereshit, VI, 272-3; for later examples of the Merkavah mysticism, cf. Scholem, *Major Trends*, 42-3; A. Jellinek, *Bet HaMidrash* (Jerusalem, 1938), II, 40-47, 114-117, III, 83-108, 161-163, V, 170-190; A. Wertheimer, *Bate Midrashot* (Jerusalem, 1952), II, 15-28. Cf. also Weiss, *Dor*, I, 204. The expression, "lecture in his presence' (Hirzah) is apparently a *terminus technicus* in esoteric learning at this time, cf. *Aruk*, III, 248, s. v.; also VII, 296, s. v. raz.

First, some kind of ecstatic state seems to have been involved, though no evidence suggests how it was achieved. Nonetheless, unless the entire account is poetic or fraudulent, the recorded vision of clouds, rainbows, and heavenly fire suggests that Yohanan and his disciples saw sights most men do not regularly see, and believed these sights were real.[1] Second, a mystical tradition was handed down from master to disciple; Jonathan ben Uzziel engaged in some kind of theosophy,[2] and the tradition continued among the sages until the time of Akiba. Third, the answer to the boast of the "Babylonian king" suggests that such a boast, to conquer heaven, once again required a reply. Yohanan allegedly foresaw the destruction of the Temple. If so, the prophecies of Isaiah at the time of Sennacherib were especially relevant to him, and he may have been concerned with the prospect that a pagan king would once again aspire to conquer heaven, and claim, upon the ruins of the Temple, that he had. If so, the boast "I will ascend to heaven above the stars of God, I will set my throne on high" had likely become a troubling question again. Fourth, the answer Yohanan gave was an effort to describe the infinity of the distance between man and God, measured by firmaments, living creatures, legs, bellies, necks, and heads. The journey of five hundred times five hundred years conveyed a sense of the majesty and grandeur of the universe beyond which the Creator's throne was stationed. Fifth, the mention of the several levels of heaven indicates that Yohanan and his disciples were familiar with an earlier tradition, in Enoch, II Enoch, the Ascension of Isaiah, and a broader range of mystical speculation, for this was also a comprehensible image in the Christian community of Corinth:

> I know a man in Christ, fourteen years ago... such a one was caught up even to the third heaven, and I know such a man, how that he was caught up into paradise (II Corinthians 12.2-3).

The Corinthian Church, which does not seem to have included many Jews, was expected by the apostle Paul to understand such an experience.[3]

---

[1] K. Kohler, "Merkabah," *JE*, VIII, 498-500.

[2] Cf. ch. 2. TB Sukkah 28a, Megillah 3a. Cf. also TB Shabbat 80a, Hagigah 13a, a certain youth studied about the *hashmal* in Ezekiel's vision, and was consumed by the fire which sprang forth; also note the conversation of Eleazar, Johanan ben Hapaaha, and ben Azzai, Shir HaShirim Rabbah 1.10, Lev. R. 16. For discussions on metaphysical questions between Eliezer and Joshua, cf. TB Yoma 54b, Bereshit Rabbah 12.11, 13,9, 1.15.

[3] Note the parallel to Yohanan's journey in a dream in the Testament of Levi (Charles, *Pseudepigrapha*, 304-315), esp. 2.5-6. "Then there fell upon me a sleep and I beheld a high mountain and I was upon it. And behold, the heavens were opened, and an angel of God said to me, Levi, enter." On the seven divisions of

ℒℴ823

Sixth, the image of the chariot[1] so opaque after more than twenty-six centuries, would have had a particular appropriateness for Yohanan and his disciples. Ezekiel's vision had provided a manner of explaining precisely how God had left his sanctuary before the Chaldean conquest. One recalls Josephus' story about the day, before sunset, when chariots were seen in the air, and armed battalions hurtling through the clouds, and the holiday when the priests heard a voice, "We are departing hence."[2] Ezekiel himself had employed this image to meet the parallel situation in the sixth century: God, who was believed to be present in the Temple, abandoned the sanctuary before the enemy profaned and burned it. So too, the chariot may have provided a useful means of speculation in the first century. It had, at least, special relevance to the impending reenactment of an ancient disaster, which Yohanan was supposed to have foreseen in Scriptural prophecy, and which some, according to Josephus, were expecting.[3] Finally, Yohanan blessed his students with a peculiar word, "Happy

---

paradise and the seven classes of dwellers in Paradise, cf. L. Ginzberg, *Legends*, I, 11, 21, IV, 118, V, 30, 31, 32-33, and B. Cohen, *Index*, 426. I, 21, "Beyond Paradise begins Eden, containing three hundred and ten worlds, and seven compartments for seven different classes of the pious. In the first are the martyred victims of the government, like Rabbi Akiba and his colleagues; in the second, those who were drowned; in the third, Rabbi Yohanan ben Zakkai and his disciples; in the fourth, those who were carried off in the cloud of glory; in the fifth, the penitents who occupy a place which even a perfectly pious man cannot obtain; in the sixth are the youths who have not tasted sin in their lives; in the seventh, those poor who studied Bible and Mishnah, and led a life of self-respecting decency. And God sits in the midst of them and expounds the Torah to them." Ginzberg cites Sifre Deut. 10, 47; Midrash Tannaim 6; Midrash Tehillim 11.10, 16.128. Cf. also Yalkut I, 20:

> "In the midst of it (Paradise) there are seven houses. In the first are those who were martyred by the Government, like Rabbi Akiba and his colleagues. In the second, those drowned at sea. In the third, Rabban Yohanan ben Zakkai and his disciples. What was his power? That he would say, If all the heavens were parchment, and all the men scribes, and all the trees quills, they would not be able to write what I have learned from my teachers, and I did not take away from them more than a dog licks from the sea. In the fourth are those upon whom the cloud came down and rested. In the fifth, the truly penitent… in the sixth, the childless who never tasted the taste of sin in their lives; in the seventh, the poor who have Scripture and Mishnah and Derekh Erez in them."

Cf. also J. Klausner, *Jesus to Paul*, 326.

[1] On the Throne-Chariot vision, cf. H. G. May, "The Departure of the Glory of Yahweh," JBL, LVI, 309-21; H. G. May, "Ezekiel, Introduction," Interpreters Bible, VI, 46-47; also, cf. my essay, "Essay on the Works of the Chariot" (in Hebrew), *Student Annual of the Jewish Theological Seminary Teachers Institute*, 1961, p. 31-42, and bibliography cited there.

[2] *War*, VI, 5. 3 (300). Cf. also Tacitus, *History*, 5, 13. Compare Ezekiel 1, 10.

[3] *War*, VI, 5, 3 (300-309).

are you... who expound well and perform well." It is difficult to understand these words as a one-dimensional reference to ethical preaching and ethical action. Praise for moral consistency was hardly relevant in this context. One recalls Yohanan's student, Haninah ben Dosa, who taught "He whose works exceed his wisdom, his wisdom shall endure." At face value, these words express praise for one who founds his learning on the practice of good deeds. But one also remembers that Haninah was a wonder-worker, and "wisdom" in his terms would have had a metaphysical, theosophical dimension. If so, what were these works? It appears possible that the blessing was for the achievement of a fully realized gnostic experience: those who preach the chariot should themselves be able to behold it.[1] It would seem, therefore, that Yohanan and his disciples drew upon a continuing tradition of theosophical speculation, using a fund of contemporary, common images as well as ancient Scriptural forms, and, in moments of mantic ecstasy, confronted the impending disaster in its metaphysical and theological dimensions.

Some have argued that hidden knowledge was suspect in Israel's "normative" religious life.[2] (Certainly later generations of sages did wipe out most traces of Pharisaic mysticism and theosophy.[3]) On the contrary, at this time, such visions appear to have been crucial to the very survival of the faith. With disaster impending, new questions were raised, and old perplexities renewed.[4] The force of extreme despair must have swept away the shallow certainties. Neither wisdom, nor wonder-working, nor sacrifice saved Jerusalem. When it was destroyed, some men lost the will to live, but Yohanan and his disciples endured the disaster. Some regarded the destruction as the last, worst day in Israel's history, expecting the last judgment to take place then. With Romans in the Holy of Holies and flames round about them, they awaited the conclusion of history:

---

[1] Professor Jacob Taubes suggests a possible polemical quality to the words "Teach well – act well," that they may be a comment on the activities of antinomians who do not act well, or gnostics, who, blaspheming the creator-revealor God of Israel, do not teach well. Cf. especially R. M. Grant, *Gnosticism and Early Christianity*, New York, 1959. Note also that Akiba was taught by Eliezer how to create and destroy a field of cucumbers by means of an incantation.

[2] Cf. L. Baeck, *The Pharisees and Other Essays* (New York, 1947), 99-101; L. Ginzberg, "Some Observations on the Attitude of the Synagogue towards the Apocalyptic-Eschatological Writings," *JBL*, XLI, 115-137; F. C. Burkitt, *Jewish and Christian Apocalypses* (London, 1914).

[3] Cf. Epstein, *Mavo-ot*, 50; Scholem, *Major Trends*, 41-43.

[4] M. Buber, *The Prophetic Faith*, 183. Extreme despair can have "but one of two results: the sapping of the last will of life or the renewal of the soul."

They then proceeded to the one remaining portico of the outer court, on which the poor women and children of the populace and a mixed multitude had taken refuge... the soldiers, carried away by rage, set fire to the portico... and out of all that multitude, not a soul escaped. They owed their destruction to a false prophet who had on that day proclaimed to the people of the city that God commanded them to go up to the Temple court, there to receive the tokens of their deliverance...[1]

For Yohanan ben Zakkai, the disaster evidently proved to be occasion for renewal of the soul.[2] Having escaped from the city, he and his disciples established a new center for the study, interpretation, and application of the Torah, at Yavneh. Thus they affirmed their faith that the Torah remained the will of their unvanquished God, and that it remained their duty to obey him. In retrospect, it seems that the immediate source of this faith was the Scriptural record of the earlier disaster and subsequent recovery. Yohanan apparently succeeded in using the ancient images of prophecy once again to embody religious experience, for he found in the visions of Ezekiel viable and appropriate forms for his own vision. If our understanding of what these visions meant to him is correct, one discerns a very practical consequence of Yohanan's dedication to the study of Torah: when Jerusalem lay in ruins, he and his disciples found the faith to continue their study.

---

[1] *War*, VI, 5, 2 (286). Cf. also VI, 7, 2 (364).

[2] It is not necessary to argue that the speculation on the Merkavah took place before the destruction for this point to be valid. However, I do believe it did, first, because sources specify that the speculation took place on the road out of Jerusalem (cf. Mekilta de Rabbi Simeon bar Yohai, 158 1. 13), and though this is not conclusive, it is suggestive. Second, *if* Eleazar left Yohanan at any point before his death, the warm relationship depicted here would indicate a time before the destruction (cf. chapter 8).

CHAPTER SIX

LIGHT OF THE WORLD

In 66 C.E., Jewish rebellion overthrew Roman rule in some parts of the land, particularly in the vicinity of Jerusalem and in the Galilee. The war began as a mere protest against temporary imperial misgovernment. Once unleashed, however, the emergent discontent within the Jewish population transformed a colonial mutiny into a broad, disordered, and partly utopian movement to reconstruct the political and social order. The rebels were hopelessly divided from the beginning. Some of the Sadducees and part of the upper classes in Jerusalem joined in the rebellion. The Pharisaic sect split, and Simeon ben Gamaliel led a wing of the revolutionary tribunal. Yohanan ben Zakkai apparently proposed a pacific policy, although the evidence of his opinions at this time is circumstantial and scant. In any case, it is certain that he escaped from the city before it fell in the summer of 70 C.E., possibly in the spring of 68, surrendered to the Romans, and was permitted by them to go to Yavneh (Jamnia), a town in the plain, where a number of pro-Roman Jewish loyalists had taken refuge.

While the rebellion began as a massive riot against maladministration, led by some of the Temple authorities and reformers within the native aristocracy, the consequent revolution was advanced mainly by two classes, a part of the peasantry, and the urban proletariat, aided by certain fervent messianic nationalists within all classes of society. In the light of the paramount importance of agriculture, one must regard the decline of the rural yeomanry, characteristic of large parts of the Empire at this period,[1] and the concentration of land in the hands of urban proprietors as fundamental causes of the discontent that led to war. Discontent in Jerusalem was accentuated by the widespread unemployment caused by the completion of the Herodian Temple, which threw 18,000 men out of work.[2] Of the peasant class, those in depressed areas supported the national cause most enthusiastically. These were in areas where agriculture was marginal, in the back country of the Galilee for example; but in the most prosperous agricultural areas, particularly in the Sharon, the Plain, the lower Galilee,

---

[1] M. Rostovtseff, *Social and Economic History of the Roman Empire* (Oxford, 1926), 248-9, 296. Cf. also S. G. F. Brandon, *The Fall Of Jerusalem and the Christian Church* (London, 1951), 155-6. On the decline of the rural yeomanry, cf. J. Klausner, *Beyme Bavit Sheni*, 68; *Jesus of Nazareth*, 189.

[2] Josephus, *War*, I, 401; V, 184-247. On unemployment, *Antiquities*, XX.

and Transjordania, the revolution took hold with difficulty. The larger commercial centers either did not oppose the Romans, like Sepphoris with its mixed population, or surrendered without a fight, like Tiberias. In many of the mixed cities, the Jewish population remained at peace. Thus Yohanan's act of surrender must have appeared neither unique nor treasonable to very large numbers of Jews.[1] If, however, the revolution was fought by classes which were economically and socially dispossessed, it was led by messianists, ecstatics, patriots, and zealots, who formed the revolutionary complex in Jerusalem. Thus the revolutionary cause benefited from several disparate groups, united by discontent with the status quo for economic, or religious, or political reasons,[2] but divided on everything else.

Yohanan's counsel of political caution may first have been offered more than two decades earlier.[3] During the reign of Caligula (37-41 C.E.), Jews had destroyed the brick altar erected by pagans at Jamnia. The pagan population had erected such an altar

> of the most contemptible materials, having made clay into bricks for the sole purpose of plotting against their fellow citizens...

When the Jews saw the altar, they destroyed it, and were ordered to replace it:

> So the sojourners immediately went to Capito, who was in reality the contriver of the whole affair; and he... writes to Caius dilating on the matter and exaggerating it enormously; and he, when he had read the letter, ordered a colossal statue gilt all over, much more costly and much more mangificient than the rich altar which had been erected in Jamnia, by way of insult to be set up in the temple of the metropolis...[4]

Petronius, the Syrian legate, was alarmed at the prospect of erecting a colossal statue in the Temple, and procrastinated, ordering the Sidonian craftsmen to work with special painstaking care; Agrippa

---

[1] *Pace* the Israeli revisionist historians, particularly G. Allon and J. Klausner. On Allon's view, see below. Klausner's view of Yohanan's action is presented in his *Historia shel HaBayit Ha Sheni* (Jerusalem, 1954), V, 211, 291.

[2] On the causes of the rebellion, cf. Klausner, *Beyme Bayit Sheni*, 55 f.; E. Schuerer, *A History of the Jewish People in the Time of Jesus Christ* (Edinburgh, 1890), I, ii, 207-218; J. Derenbourg, *Essai*, 247-261; F. M. Abel, *Histoire de la Palestine* (Paris, 1952), 2 vols.), I, 477-490. Cf. also S. Zeitlin, *La Revolution Juive de 65-70, La Revolution Francaise, et la Revolution Russe, Etude Comparative* (Paris, 1930). C. Roth also is at present preparing a study of the revolution.

[3] I am indebted to Professor Morton Smith for this date.

[4] Philo, *Gaius*, 200-201. Cf. Wolfson, Philo, II, 366-7. C. D. Yonge, *Works of Philo Judaeus* (London, 1855), IV, 144-156 *pass*.

eventually succeeded in having the order rescinded. On this event, Yohanan may have made the comment,

> Do not destroy their altars, so that you do not have to rebuild them with your own hands. Do not destroy those of brick, that they may not say to you, Come and build them of stone.[1]

If so, Yohanan could hardly have favored the irregular actions against native, pagan populations, the pillaging of villages and slaughter of their pagan populations,[2] which marked the onset of the revolution.

A second counsel of caution may likewise have proven particularly relevant in the spring of 66, although one cannot so date it with certainty.[3] Yohanan argued for the observance of biblical regulations on exemption of certain classes from military service. Scripture had commanded (Deut. 20.5-8):

> Then the officers shall speak to the people, saying, What man is there that has built a new house, and has not dedicated it? Let him go back to his house, lest he die in the battle and another man dedicate it. And the officers shall speak further to the people and say, What man is there that is fearful and fainthearted? Let him go back to his house, lest the heart of his follows melt as his heart.

On this verse, Yohanan commented, apparently in the manner of *homer*:

> This law was given in order that the cities of Israel should not be graveyards, and this was what Rabban Yohanan ben Zakkai said, Come and see how much the Omnipresent pitied the honor of his creatures. On account of the faint-hearted and fearful, when the commander goes through the ranks, he will say, perhaps one has built a house, perhaps another has betrothed a wife, and whoever (so claimed), let him bring witnesses to that effect. The exception is the fainthearted and fearful. His witness is at hand. He hears the sound of the clashing shields and is frightened, the sound of the neighing horses and trembles, the noise

---

[1] ARNb, ch. 31, Schechter 33b. Cf. also Midrash Tannaim, ed. D. Hoffman, p. 58; "Thou shalt surely blot them out... From here, Rabban Yohanan ben Zakkia said, Do not make haste to destroy the altars of the gentiles, so that you do not have to rebuild them with your own hands; do not destroy brick altars, so that will say to you, build them of stone, of stone and they say, of wood..." For another comment on this verse, posisbly by Yohanan, cf. Semahot 8.17, and chapter five, n. 29. Cf. also Yalkut, I, 878, "Rabban Gamaliel says, And would it enter your mind that Israel would destroy their altars, God forbid? But that they should not do deeds like their deeds, and their evil deeds cause the destruction of the sanctuary of their fathers.

[2] Cf. Josephus, *War*, III, 18, 1 (457-8).

[3] This is the date assigned by C. Roth, "The Pharisees in the War of 66," unpublished mss.

of the horns blasting and is confused, sees the edge of the sword and water runs down between his knees.[1]

Thus Yohanan seems to have urged that the revolutionists keep in mind the importance of long-term Jewish settlement in the land, and, more important, the abiding dignity of man.

Seeing the world as the men of Jerusalem saw it at the beginning of the rebellion, one wonders, nonetheless, how Yohanan ben Zakkai could have remained aloof from the popular enthusiasm. Rome was suffering its own internal disorders.[2] The Eastern Empire was turbulent, and the revolutionaries apparently hoped that the Jews of the Diaspora, particularly on the other side of the Euphrates, would join them.[3] After

---

[1] Sifre Deut. 192; cf. also TB Sotah 44b, TP Sotah 5.9, Midrash Tannaim, ed. Hoffman, p. 120. Compare the Scroll of the war of the Sons of Light, in which the same admonition is given, plate X, lines 1-10 (Tr. M. Burrows, *The Dead Sea Scrolls*, New York, 1955, 397):

> ... and he taught us of old for our generations, saying 'When you draw near to the battle, the priest shall stand and speak to the people saying, Hear O Israel, you draw near this day to battle against your enemies: do not fear, and let your heart not faint; do not tremble or be in dread of them, for your God goes with you to fight for you against your enemies to save you.' And our officers shall speak to all those ready for battle, willing volunteers, to make them strong in the power of God, and to turn back all the fainthearted, to make them strong together with all mighty men of valor..."

Note also the midrash on this verse in Luke 14.14 f. Cf. also Tos. Sotah 7.14. Note that the Yalkut I 923 specifically assigns the words, "that the cities of Israel should not be graveyards" to Yohanan, and continues as in Sifre Deut. 192. Cf. also Epstein, Mevo-ot, 402-3, who concludes that the essential parts of chs. 8-9 of Mishnah Sotah were written by Yohanan ben Zakkai. If so, then the extended discussion of Sotah 8.1-7 on military exemptions would reveal a certain leniency to permit draft exemptions; cf. especially 8.2, 3, 4.

[2] Cf. Josephus, *War*, I, i, 2 (4-5). Rome had burned in July, 64 C.E., and to pay for rebuilding it, Nero imposed heavy taxes, with consequent discontent leading to several conspiracies against him. Cf. A. Momigliano, "Nero," *Cambridge Ancient History* (hereafter – CAH), ed. S. A. Cook, F. E. Adcock, M. P. Charlesworth, Vol. X, Cambridge, 1952, Vol. XI, Cambridge 1936. Cf. also B. H. Stevenson, "Year of the Four Emperors," *CAH*, X, 808 f., and B. H. Stevenson and A. Momigliano, "Rebellion within the Empire," *CAH*, X, 840 f. Cf. also Tacitus, *Annals*, XV, 38.

[3] Cf. A. Schalit, "Roman Policy in the East," *Tarbiz*, VII, 159-180. Throughout this period, Rome and Parthia remained at peace, with Parthia even acknowledging the suzerainty of Nero's government. However, earlier Rome had been preparing an advance into the east, and the failure of Nero's plans mainly on account of the Jewish revolt had world-wide consequences. When the rebellion began in the spring of 66, the Romans decided that they could not fight on a northern front against Armenia and on a southern front in Judah, and diverted troops to the south. The diaspora community in Parthia was not allowed to participate in the rebellion, and there is no evidence that it wanted to; nor was any support whatever received from the diaspora communities in the Hellenistic parts of the Roman Empire. The only exception to the rule of the Diaspora's indifference at this time

the death of Nero in 68, the rebellion of Gauls, Celts, and other peoples augured to some the immanent collapse of Roman hegemony. Jerusalem had, moreover, strategic advantages; it was well-fortified, had an excellent water supply, and access to it was difficult. The first successes of the rebels, in addition, certainly raised hoped of final victory.[1] These hopes, together with economic, social, and political discontent, and the messianic expectations of some circles of Jews,[2] combined to render many men indifferent to counsels of caution. Those who shared Yohanan's opinion were mainly the upper clergy of the Temple, the part of the upper classes responsive to Herodian influence, and a segment of the Pharisees. These argued that misgovernment was both temporary and, at that time, not the private tribulation of Judah, and that the maintenance of public order depended on submission to Rome. Thus Hanina, the Prefect of the Priests, had said:

> Pray for the peace of the ruling power, since but for fear of it, men would swallow each other up alive.[3]

The subsequent hostility between Jewish parties proved the wisdom of this warning. Indeed, later generations reflected that Jerusalem was

was Adiabene. But after 70, Diaspora opinion may have changed, on account of the destruction of the Temple. See also my essay, "The Parthian Background of Jewish History in the First Two Centuries C.E." (in Hebrew), *Midwestern Annual of Jewish Studies* (Chicago, 1962-3).

[1] It is conjectured that after the defeat of Cestius, the Sanhedrin was reconstituted and returned to the Hewn-Stone Chamber, cf. S. Hoenig, *The Great Sanhedrin*. Certain measures were likewise apparently issued at this time, to cut off Jewish intercourse with the gentile population, cf. Mishnah Shabbat 1.7 f., S. Zeitlin, "Les Dixhuit Mesures," *REJ*, LXVIII, 22-36, esp. p. 24; Klausner, Historia, V, 156-7; I. HaLevi, *Dorot HaRishonim*, I, v, 64a-65b. Derenbourg calls this a "general boycott against the gentile world," and dates it in the late summer-early autumn of 66, cf. *Essai*, 274. Cf. also S. Zeitlin, *Megillat Taanit*, 105; and H. Tchernowitz, *Toldot Halakhah*, IV, 313-314.

[2] On the messianism of the revolutionaries, cf. S. G. F. Brandon, *The Fall of Jerusalem and the Christian Church;* C. Roth, *Historical Background of the Dead Sea Scrolls* (Oxford, 1958), 9. Also C. Roth, "The Zealots in the War of 66-73," *Journal of Semitic Studies*, IV, 332 f.

[3] Avot 3.2. Hanina transmitted many traditions concerning the Temple and its rites. He witnessed the destruction of Jerusalem and survived it, cf. TB Taanit 13a, Bazah 2.2. Note also his teaching, like Yohanan's, on the sanctity of peace, Sifre Numbers 144, "Great is peace, for it is equivalent to the works of creation." Cf. A. Hyman, *Toldot HaTannaim ve-HaAmoraim* [History of the Tannaim and Amoraim] (London, 1910), II, 511; Z. Frankel, *Mishnah*, 61-2; Bruell, *Mavo*, 52. Frankel dates this saying at the outset of the rebellion. Cf. also Mishnah Pesahim 1.6, Shekalim 4.4, 6.1; Eduyot 2.1, 2, 3; Zevahim 9.3, 12.4; Menahot 10.1; Negaim 1.4, Para 3.1; TB Pesahim 14a, 15a, b; Yoma 8a, 21b, 39a; Ketuvot 106b; Sotah 42a; Avodah Zara 4a; Zevahim 84a, 85b, 103b, 104a; Menahot 63b, 64a; T. P. Terumot 8.4, Peshaim 1.6, Shekalim 4.2, Bezah 2.2.

destroyed in 70 on account of causeless hatred.[1] The insurgents
silenced their opponents with their successful siege of the Roman
garrison resident in Jerusalem. They also ended the sacrifices offered
in behalf of the emperor.[2] Thus they confronted the country with a
fait accompli, and by the winter of 66-67 C.E. the war had begun.
The social revolution was not long in following, for the revolutionists

> fired the palaces and public archieves, to destroy the money-lenders
> bonds and to prevent the recovery of debts... and to cause an uprising
> of the poor against the rich.[3]

They established a coalition revolutionary government,[4] many
loyalists fled the city, and the moderates were silenced.[5]

Yohanan ben Zakkai apparently remained in the city for more than
a year, probably until the spring of 68 C.E. Nothing is known about
his actions or opinions in this period. Indeed, one of the conspicuously
silent periods of his life is that of the early war years. If conjecture is
possible on his earlier political opinion, Talmudic literature does not
preserve a reliable record of his viewpoint on the period between the
spring of 66 C.E. and his flight two years later. Yohanan had probably
spoken out twenty-five years earlier to say that destroying altars was
unwise when Rome could compel rebuilding them. It is possible that
some of his statements against forced conscription and in praise of
peace ("Whole stones – stones which make peace...")[6] may date from
this period, but they have survived in forms so abstract and indirect
that it would be unfair to him suppose this was all he had to say at
such a crucial period. Josephus does not mention him. What, if
anything, he said and did, his successors did not preserve. What they
did preserve were several extremely confused accounts of his escape,

---

[1] TB Yoma 9b.

[2] *War*, II, 17, 3 (411-15). Cf. C. Roth, "The Debate on the Loyal Sacrifices,"
Harvard Theological Review, LIII, 93; also F. M. Abel, *Histoire*, I, 483-4.

[3] *War*, II, 17, 6 (427).

[4] On the composition of the first coalition regime, cf. Schuerer, *History*, I, ii,
214, "The men who now had the power in their hands belonged exclusively to
the higher ranks. The chief priests, the most distinguished of the Pharisees were
those who directed the organization of land defenses..." I find it difficult to harmonize this fact with the burning of the archives. Perhaps it was an act of popular,
rather than Governmental, origin.

[5] On the flight of the loyalists, cf. Abel, *Histoire*, I, 489. He suggests that it
was at this time that the Christian-Jews fled the city. On the composition of the
revolutionary movement, cf. Roth, "Zealots in the War of 66-73," 340, who discerns these groups: moderates who eventually were willing to come to terms, nationalists who were prepared to fight to the end, zealots, and the Qumran group.

[6] Mekilta Bahodesh 11. Cf. ch. five.

which are likely to have been based on historical events, but which are nonetheless neither wholly congruous with the events of that period, nor internally consistent. All accounts agree, however, that he escaped from the city when escape was still possible, and when, at the same time, the city was under siege, met Vespasian and prophesied his immanent rise to imperial power, and was permitted by him to go to Yavneh, there to take refuge from the war.

Vespasian had been sent to quell the rebellion and to forestall revolt in the neighboring lands.[1] He had grown grey in the imperial service, fighting in Germany, Britain, and elsewhere; his long career had seen numerous good omens, and if he believed in them, he had sufficient cause to regard his current assignment as highly auspicious. The belief was current that "out of Judea would come rulers of the world.[2] Signs and wonders had long ago allegedly pointed to his future distinction. Suetonius reported, for example, that an ancient oak tree on the Flavian estate near Rome

> put out a shoot for each of the three occasions when his mother was brought to bed; and these clearly had a bearing on the child's future. The first slim shoot withered quickly, and the eldest child, a girl, died with the year. The second was long and healthy, promising good luck; but the third seemed more like a tree than a branch.[3]

Later in life men saw, in both commonplace and uncommon events in Vespasian's long life, evidence that he had been destined to become Caesar. A stray dog picked up a human hand at the crossroads and brought it to Vespasian, "a hand being an emblem of power." A plough ox shook off its yoke and burst into his dining room, falling at his feet and lowering its neck, which was interpreted as a sign of the world's immanent submission. In Greece, he dreamed that he and his family would prosper the moment Nero lost a tooth; the next day, Nero had a tooth extracted. In Judea, when he finally arrived, men fell over one another in their haste to predict his coming enthronement. He consulted the god of Carmel, and was promised that he would never be disappointed in what he planned or desired, no matter how lofty his ambitions.[4] When he captured Josephus, the Jewish general predicted that he would be released from his chains by the very man who had now put him there when that man would be emperor.[5] Further reports of

---

[1] *War*, III, 1, 2 (3).

[2] Suetonius, *The Twelve Caesars* (translated by R. Graves; London, 1957), Vespasian 4 (276-7). Cf. also Tacitus, *History*, 5.13.

[3] Suetonius, Vespasian, 5 (277).

[4] *Ibid.*

[5] *War*, III, 8.9 (399-408). Cf. also other omens mentioned by Tacitus, *History*,

omens came from Rome. Nero had been told in a dream to take the sacred chariot of Jupiter the Greatest and Best from the capitol to the circus, calling at Vespasian's house as he went. While Galba was on the way to the elections which gave him his second consulship, a statue of Julius Caesar turned of its own accord to face east, and at Betriacum, when the battle was about to begin, two eagles fought in full view of both armies, but a third appeared from the rising sun and drove off the victor.[1] While at Alexandria on his way to battle in the land of Israel, Vespasian had seen many wonders which pointed to him as object of the gods' partiality. Thus one of the common people of the city, a blind man, threw himself at Vespasian's knees and implored him with groans to heal him:

> This he did by the advice of the god Serapis... Another with a diseased hand... prayed that the limb might feel the imprint of a Caesar's foot... and so Vespasian, supposing that all things were possible to his good fortune, and that nothing was any longer past belief, with a joyful countenance, amid the intense expectation of the multitude of bystanders, accomplished what was required. The hand was instantly restored to its use, and the light of day again shone upon the blind.[2]

When finally Vespasian drew near Jerusalem, and a Jewish sage named Yohanan ben Zakkai greeted him (according to Jewish tradition) with the words *Vive Imperator* one thing is perfectly certain: Vespasian was neither surprised nor especially displeased. Yohanan was

---

I, 10, II, 1, V, 13. Cf. also Dio Cassius 46b. Cf. also Schuerer, *History*, I, ii, 223, n. 41. Professor Gershon Cohen points out that Pharisaic prophecy often depended on Scriptural exegesis, as in Yohanan's prophecy of the destruction, noted earlier (ch. 3) and of Vespasian's coming rise. Josephus, by contrast, reports that his prediction was based on dreams as well as prophecy (III, 8, 3, 1. 340):

> "But as Nicanor was urgently pressing his proposals and Josephus overheard the threats of the hostile crowd, suddenly there came back into his mind those nightly dreams, in which God had foretold to him the impending fate of the Jews and the destinies of the Roman sovereigns He was an interpreter of dreams, and skilling in divining the meaning of ambiguous utterances of the deity; a priest himself and of priestly descent, he was not ignorant of the prophecies in the sacred books. At that hour, he was inspired to read their meaning, and recalling the dreadful images of his recent dreams, he offered up a silent prayer to God..."

Cf. also III, 8, 9 (400):

> "You imagine, Vespasian, that in the person of Josephus you have taken a mere captive? But I come to you as a messenger of greater destinies... To Nero do you send me? Why then? Think you that those who before your accession succeed him will continue? You will be Caesar, Vespasian, you will be emperor, you and your son here... For myself I ask to be punished by stricter custody if I have dared to trifle with the words of God."

[1] Suetonius, Vespasian, 4.
[2] Tacitus, *History*, 4.81. Cf. also 5.13.

not the first such "holy man" to bring him good news, nor the last.

Vespasian reached Jerusalem after having pacified the Galilee, the Sharon, and finally, the Judean hills. He had moved in no apparent haste; the situation in Rome was increasingly fluid, and the battlefields of the land of Israel must have seemed safer than the Roman forum for an ambitious general, especially one who had so often received auguries of coming distinction. Vespasian had thus begun to campaign in the spring of 67, a year after the rebellion, and nine months or so after the subsequent revolution, and had conquered the lowlands as the Jewish levies faded before his advancing forces. By the autumn of 67, only Gush Halav (Gischala) and Mount Tabor, in Galilee, and Gamala in Gaulanitis, remained in rebellion in the north, and these cities fell during the coming season. For the spring campaign of 68, therefore, there could be only one objective: Jerusalem, and final pacification. Vespasian waited out the winter of 67-8, but the Jews did not. They pursued a vigorous civil war, and when the head of the defeated armies of the north, Yohanan of Gush Halav (In the Greek accounts, John of Gischala) reached Jerusalem in November of that winter, young and enthusiastic warriors followed him into the teeming city.[1] Reenforcing the extreme elements already in the city, they overthrew the coalition regime of Simeon ben Gamaliel[2] and Gorion ben Yoseph, with the help of the Idumeans from the south. Thus in the winter preceding Yohanan's escape, the "party of order" lost its hold completely, and a reign of terror began in Jerusalem. The former leaders of the revolution were accused of treason and secret communication with Rome,[3] the new coalition slaughtered Hananiah ben Hananiah the former high priest, and other nobles and moderates. Yohanan ben Zakkai must at this time have determined to escape from the city. Toward the end of the winter, the Roman general staff advised Vespasian to order an immediate general assault, but Vespasian temporized cautiously, preferring to let the Jews fight the Roman's' battle against one another. At this time, with moderate rebels (and others[4]) deserting the city, Vespasian must

---

[1] *War*, IV, 3, 2-4 (128-142).

[2] On the participation of Simeon ben Gamaliel in the revolutionary coalition, cf. *Life*, 38, 39, 44, 90.

[3] *War*, IV, 4, 1 (224-232), IV, 6, 1 (353-361). On the allegations of Simeon's death at this time, cf. J. L. Maimon, "On the Death of Simeon ben Gamaliel," *Sinai*, XXII, 229 f.; J. Klausner, *Historia*, V, 162.

[4] It seems to me that this was the most likely time for the Jewish-Christians to escape from the city. (Cf. Eusebius, *Ecclesiastical History*, 3.5.2-3). Under the moderate regime, they had no reason to fear the government, for the policy of the Pharisees toward them had always been tolerant and even friendly. But with

have had excellent intelligence of what was happening there. After the winter rains, in March, 68, Vespasian reviewed his armies, and sent them off to clear the rest of the country of rebellion, himself invading Judah and taking Antipatris, Lud, and Yavneh, and finally reaching as far as Emmaus, a mere hour's journey from the city. Only the capital remained. Vespasian went around it from Emmaus to Jericho,[1] investing the city at all sides with camps and garrisons. He only needed to throw up siegeworks. The campaign of spring, 68, ended with the news, received late in June, that Nero had died. Vespasian postponed his assault on Jerusalem, and began the long wait for good news from Rome. The closest he came to the city was, therefore, Emmaus at the west and Jericho at the east. Since the traditions agree that Yohanan escaped from a besieged city, escape then being possible, and met Vespasian, predicting his immanent rise to the imperial throne, one must conclude that this happened in the spring of 68 C.E., between April and June. Before that time, Vespasian was never near Jerusalem; and Yavneh, to which Yohanan went, was not in his hands until then; after that time, and before the siege of Titus in 70 C.E., escape became increasingly difficult, and access to the Roman commander required a trip to Caesarea. This must have been Yohanan's last chance to surrender by escaping through the rebel lines and into the Roman camp. By every evidence, he took it.[2]

---

the change of government, they could hardly hope to have the favor of the Zealot radicals. Hence the conditions of flight which Eusebius suggests, namely an actual escape, under difficult conditions, possibly even of siege, which are so similar to those surrounding Yohanan's escape, would probably best be met at this time. It would certainly have been difficult to escape after the summer of 68 C.E., especially for an entire community. At this time, the moderate rebels did begin to desert, cf. *War*, IV, 7, 3 (410-413):

> "Of these proceedings, Vespasian was informed by deserters. For although the insurgents guarded all the exits and slew anyone who for whatever reason approached them, there were notwithstanding some who evaded them, and, fleeing to the Romans, urged the general to protect the city and rescue the remnant of its inhabitants, assuring him that it was owing to their loyalty to the Romans that so many had been slain and the survivors were in peril. Vespasian, who already pitied their misfortunes, broke up his camp with the apparent purpose of taking Jerusalem by siege, but in reality to deliver it from siege..."

[1] *War*, IV, 9.1 (486).

[2] Some have held that Yohanan escaped to Titus, not Vespasian. Cf. S. Dubnow, *Divre Yemei Am Olam* [History of the Eternal People] (Tel Aviv, 1936), II, 282-3. I believe this is because the burning of the stores of food, reported in one recension of the event, took place later than the spring of 68 (cf. below). But then the details on Yohanan's prediction are meaningless, while they are meant, in fact, to be the point of the stories. It might well be argued, that the prediction of Vespasian's

The sources which record this event reveal two traditions on Yohanan's action.[1] According to the first, he left the city after the Zealots refused to surrender to Vespasian, because he was opposed to the war and hoped to save the Temple. Vespasian had spies in the city, and knew that Yohanan favored his cause. When he came to the Romans, therefore, they recognized him, brought him directly to Vespasian, who received him kindly and asked what he could do in Yohanan's behalf. Yohanan thereupon made his famous request for Yavneh, and *then* prophesied Vespasian's rise to power. According to a second body of tradition, Yohanan surrendered not because he opposed the war, but because he opposed the war policies of the Zealots. He apparently favored remaining in the besieged city for a defensive war, rather than making sorties against the Roman lines. The Romans, according to this account, knew nothing about him, had no special regard for him, and at his interview with Vespasian, he had to justify his actions. Having nothing to his credit, he made a prediction, and when it came true, he was granted a small favor.

---

coming rise to power is a literary device, an effort by the Pharisees to prove that they too, like the pagans and Josephus, had known of his coming reign, because their Scriptures so informed them. But I do not see what is to be gained by so postulating; an economy of skepticism is sufficient, when, in fact, so very little is known for certain. Cf. also J. Klausner, *Historia*, V, 135, 191-2, 211-213, 220; N. Krochmal, *More Nevuche HaZeman*, 89; Derenbourg, *Essai*, 281 f., 302 f. Cf. also H. Graetz, *Geschichte*, III, 12 (Leipzig ed., 1888) and II, 323-4 (Philadelphia ed., 1893, tr. H. Szold). Graetz holds that he went to Titus, "who received him in a friendly manner and gave him permission to make some request of him." Why Titus? Graetz in fact confuses (or, at least, fuses) the two major traditions, that of the Midrash and Talmud and that of ARNa (cf. below, n. 1). Cf. also Javitz, *Toldot*, VI, 5 f.; HaLevi, *Dorot*, I, v, 1-2, 18a, f; D. A. Bertholet, *Das Ende des juedischen Staatswesens* (Tuebingin, 1910), 153-4; Bacher, *Agadot*, I, i, 18 f. On Yavneh, cf. TP Demai 2.4, Ber. R. 76, HaLevi, *Dorot*, I, v, 22b-23a. It was not destroyed in the war, cf. also Derenbourg 302. Finkelstein, *Akiba*, 67, and 324, n. 92, dates the escape at the spring or summer of 68 also. On the strange aftermath of Yohanan's escape and meeting with Vespasian in European Jewish history, G. Kisch, "A Talmudic Legend as the source for the Josephus Passage in the Sachsenspiegel," *Historia Judaica* (1939), 105 f. One wonders whether it was so very clear in the spring of 68 C.E. that the Jews were likely to lose (cf. Klausner, Historia, V, 220-221). It seems to me that it was, for the Jewish armies had not stood before a professional Roman legion on any battlefield since the victories of 66; neither in the field nor in siege was there evidence that the Jews would stand. Cf. also Kaminka, *Mehkarim*, 99-100, who rejects the historicity of the entire account.

[1] The sources are as follows: ARNa ch. 4, Schechter 22-24; Goldin 35 f.; ARNb ch. 6, Schechter 19f.; Lamentations Rabbah to vs. 1.31. TB Gittin, 56a-b. Midrash Mishle ch. 15 (this last is copied from ARNb). The story of Ben Battiah is also in Kohelet Rabba 7. The story of burning the wheat (below) stands by itself. The following analysis of the sources is that of G. Allon, *Mehkarim*, I, 238-251.

The classic recension of the first account is as follows:[1]

Now when Vespasian came to destroy Jerusalem, he said to the inhabitants, Fools, Why do you seek to destroy this city, and why do you seek to burn the Temple? For what do I ask of you but that you send me one bow or one arrow [as signs of submission] and I shall go off from you? They said to him, Even as we went forth against the first two who were here before thee and slew them, so shall we go forth against thee and slay thee. When Rabban Yohanan ben Zakkai heard this, he sent for the men of Jerusalem and said to them, My children, why do you destroy this city, and why do you seek to burn the Temple?[2] For what is it that he asks of you? Verily he asks naught of you save one bow or one arrow, and he will go off from you. They said to him, Even as we went forth against the two before him and slew them, so shall we go forth against him and slay him. Vespasian had men stationed inside the wals of Jerusalem. Every word which they overheard they would write down, attach an arrow, and shoot it over the wall, saying that Rabban Yohanan ben Zakkai was one of the emperor's friends. Now after Rabban Yohanan ben Zakkai had spoken to them one day, two, and three days, and they would still not listen to him, he sent for his disciples, Rabbi Eliezer and Rabbi Joshua. My sons, he said to them, Arise and take me out of here. Make a coffin for me that I may lie in it. Rabbi Eliezer took hold of the head and of it, and Rabbi Joshua took hold of the foot, and they began carrying him as the sun set, until they reached the gates of Jerusalem. Who is this? the gatekeepers demanded. It is a dead man, they replied, do you now know that the dead may not be held overnight in Jerusalem? If it is a dead men, the gatekeepers said to them, take him out. So they took him out, and continued carrying him until they reached Vespasian. They opened the coffin, and Rabban Yohanan stood up before him. Art thou Rabban Yohanan ben Zakkai? Vespasian

---

[1] ARNa ch. 4. The basis of Yohanan's prediction may be that *Lebanon* provides a play on words, from lavan (clean, white) – Lebanon, that which washes white, clean of iniquity. See p. 39 n. 5. Cf. Is. 1.18. Cf. also Bacher, *Agadot*, -I, i, 18. Cf. also ARNb, ch. 6, Schechter 10a-b. Comparing the two accounts, one finds the following major differences in ARNb from the account that follows in the text (ARNa): first, when they reached the gate, the guards wanted to stab him (to be certain that he was dead), and the students answered, If so, you will give your state a bad name. They will say, even Rabban Yohanan they stabbed as in the Midrash-Talmud account. Second, Yohanan greeted Vespasian, Redumani Imperatorion. He said to him, Are you ben Zakkai? He said, yes [as in the ARNa account]. Third, he predicts the fall of the city by Scripture, and is then incarcerated until the word comes from Rome that the prediction was correct. At this point, Vespasian called Yohanan, and said, "Ask a favor for yourself. Yohanan replied, I ask of thee Yavneh, and I shall study Torah there and offer prayer, and do all the other commandments. He said to him, behold it is given to thee as a gift. This follows the Talmudic-Midrashic account in that Vespasian waited until prediction was proven true before granting his wish, while in ARNa, Yohanan was given his three favors before the prediction was made. Thus ARNb apparently confuses the two traditions.

[2] Cf. Allon, *Mehkarim*, I, 211.

inquired. Tell me what I may give thee? I ask nothing of thee, Rabban
Yohanan replied, save Yavneh, where I might go and teach my disciples,
and there establish a prayerhouse, and perform all the commandments.
Go, Vespasian said to him, By thy leave, may I say something to thee?
Speak, Vespasian said to him. Said Rabban Yohanan to him, Lo thou art
about to be appointed king. How dost thou know this? Vespasian asked.
Rabban Yohanan replied. This has been handed down to us, that the
Temple will not be surrendered to a commoner but to a king, as is
said, "And he shall cut down the thickets of the forest with iron, and
Lebanon shall fall by a mighty one" (Is. 10.34). It was said, No more
than a day or two or three days passed before messengers reached him
from his city announcing that the emperor was dead, and that he had
been elected to succeed as king.

The picture of Yohanan was evidently drawn from the outlines of
Jeremiah's portrait. As the Babylonians had known about Jeremiah
through their agents in the city, so Yohanan was known to Vespasian.
He was therefore received cordially, and was given the right to re-
establish the religious life, whereupon he predicted Vespasian's coming
election. Josephus reports that he himself reminded the besieged city
of Jeremiah's warnings,[1] and one may conclude that the Jeremiah's
example was not forgotten when later generations considered Yohanan's action at the time of the second destruction. (One notes that
Vespasian's election, however, did not take place for a year after the
Judean campaign.)

The second and third recensions of the event presented a very
different view of the event. The second was as follows:[2]

"Her adversaries are become the head" – this refers to Vespasian.
"Her enemies are at ease" (Lam 1.5) – this refers to Titus. For three and
a half years, Vespasian surrounded Jerusalem, having four generals with
him, the general of Arabia, of Africa, of Alexandria, and of Palestine...
in Jerusalem there were four councillors, Ben Zizit, Ben Gurion, Ben
Nakdimon, and Ben Kalba Sabua.[3] Each of them was capable of supply-

---

[1] *War*, V, 9. 4 (391-394).

[2] Lamentations Rabbati, 1.5.31. Tr. by J. Rabinowitz, Soncino ed., *Midrash
Rabbah* (London, 1956), ed. H. Freedman and M. Simon, Vol. VII, 100-105.

[3] Yohanan signed the marriage contract of Nakdimon's daughter. Cf. ch. 7.
When Eliezer gave his first exposition, Ben Zizit, Nakdimon, and Ben Kalba
Sabua were supposedly present at Yohanan's academy, cf. ch. 4. Yohanan thus
had connections with the leading men of the city, according to the rabbinic
traditions. Note also that Ben Battiah, Yohanan's alleged nephew, was a leading
Zealot. This account is thus internally consistent in emphasizing the relationship
between Yohanan and the moderate revolutionary party, and in emphasizing his
opposition not to the war (any more than the upper class leaders Ben Zizit, Nakdimon, and Ben Kalba Sabua) but to the Zealots' conduct of it. On the burning
of the grain cf. below. Note that in this account, Yohanan was respected by the
Zealots, which would have been less likely if he were completely opposed to war.

ing food for the city for ten years. There was also Ben Battiah, nephew of Rabban Yohanan ben Zakkai, who was appointed in charge of the stores. He burned all the stores. When Rabban Yohanan ben Zakkai heard of this, he exclaimed "woe." It was reported to Ben Battiah, Your uncle exclaimed woe, He sent and had him brought before him, and asked, Why did you exclaim woe. He replied, I did not exclaim "woe" but wah [a note of approval]. And why did you make that exclamation? He answered, Because you burned all the stores, and I thought that so long as the stores were intact, the people would not expose themselves to the dangers of battle. (Through the difference between "woe" and "wah," Rabban Yohanan ben Zakkai escaped death, and the verse was applied to him (Ecc. 7.12), "The excellence of knowledge is that wisdom preserveth the life of him that hath it.") Three days later Rabban Yohanan ben Zakkai went out to talk in the market place, and saw how people seethed straw and drank the water, and he said, Can the men who seethe straw and drink the water withstand the armies of Vespasian? He added, I have come to the conclusion that I must get out of here. He sent a message to Ben Battiah, Get me out of here. He replied, We have made an agreement among ourselves that nobody shall leave the city except the dead. He said, Carry me out in the guise of a corpse. Rabbi Eliezer carried him by the head, and Rabbi Joshua by the feet, and Ben Battiah walked in front. When they reached the city gates, the guards wanted to stab him. Ben Battiah said to them, Do you wish people to say that when our teacher died, his body was stabbed? On his speaking to them in this manner, they allowed him to pass. After going through the gates, they carried him to a cemetery and left him there and returned to the city. Rabban Yohanan ben Zakkai went out and went among the soldiers of Vespasian. He said to them, Where is the king? They went and told Vespasian, A Jew is asking for you. He said to them, Let him come. On his arrival, Yohanan exclaimed, Vive domine imperator. Vespasian remarked, You give me a royal greeting, but I am not a king; and should the king hear of it he will put me to death. He said to him, Well if you are not the king, you will be eventually, because the Temple will only be destroyed by a king's hand, as it is said, "And Lebanon shall fall by a mighty one (Is. 10.34). They took and placed him in the inner-most of seven chambers, and asked him what hour of the day it was, and he told them. (How did Rabban Yohanan ben Zakkai know? From his study. That is, he was accustomed to recite studies from memory, and knew how long it took.) Three days later, Vespasian went to take a bath at Gophna [fifteen miles northwest of Jerusalem]. After he had bathed and put on one of his shoes, a messenger arrived, and it was announced to him that Nero had died, and the Romans had proclaimed him king. He wished to put on the other shoe, but it would not go on his foot. He sent for Rabban Yohanan ben Zakkai and asked, Will you not explain to me why all these days I wore two shoes which fitted me, but now one fits and the other does not. He answered, You have been informed of good news, because it is written (Prov. 15.30), A good report maketh the bones fat. He asked, What must I do to get them on? He replied, If there is anybody whom you hate, or who has done you wrong, let him pass in front of you and your flesh will shrink, because it is written (Prov. 17.22), A broken spirit drieth the bones. Then they began to speak to him in parables. If a snake rested in a cask, what is to be done with it? He answered, Bring a charmer and charm the snake and leave the cask intact. Panger, the Arab general, said, Kill the snake and break the cask. Then they asked, If a snake nested in a tower, what is to be done with it? He replied, Bring a charmer and charm the snake, and leave the tower intact. Panger said, Kill the snake and burn the tower. The snake meant Israel, the cask, Jerusalem, the tower, the Temple. Said Rabban Yohanan to Panger, All neighbors who do harm do it to their neighbors. Instead of putting in a plea for the defence, you argue for the prosecution against us. He replied, I seek your welfare. So long as the Temple exists, the heathen kingdoms will attack you, but if it is destroyed, they will not attack you. Rabban Yohanan said to him, "The heart knows whether it is for *akkel* or *akalkalot* (woven or crooked). Vespasian said to Rabban Yohanan ben Zakkai, Make a request of me and I will grant it. He answered, I beg that you abandon this city of Jerusalem and depart. He said to him, Did the Romans proclaim me king that I should abandon this city? Make another request of me and I will grant it. He answered, I beg that you leave the western gate which leads to Lud (Lydda) open, and everyone who departs up to the fourth hour will be spared. After Vespasian had conquered the city, he asked him, Have you any friend or relative there? Send and bring him out, before the troops enter. He sent Rabbi Eliezer and Rabbi Joshua to bring out Rabbi Zadok. They went and found him at the city gate. When he arrived, Rabban Yohanan stood up before him. Vespasian asked, Do you stand up before this emaciated old man? He replied, By your life, if there had been in Jerusalem one more like him, though you have double your army you would not have been able to conquer it. He asked, what is his power? He replied, He eats one fig, and on the strength of it, teaches at one hundred sessions of the academy. Why is he so lean? On account of his numerous abstinences and fasts. Vespasian sent and brought physicians who fed him on small portions of food and doses of liquid until his physical powers returned to him. His son Eliezer said to him, Father give them their reward in this world, so that they should have no merit with respect to you in the world to come. He gave them calculation by fingers and scales for weighing. When Vespasian had subdued the city, he assigned the destruction of the four ramparts to the four generals, and the west gate to Pangar. Now it had been decreed by heaven that this should never be destroyed, because the Shekhinah abode in the west. The others demolished their sections, but he did not demolish his. Vespasian sent and asked, Why did you not destroy your section? He replied, by your life, I acted so for the honor of the kingdom, for if I had demolished it, nobody would know what it was that you had destroyed, but when people look at the western wall, they will exclaim, see the might of Vespasian, from what he destroyed! He said to him, Enough! You have spoken well but since you have disobeyed my command, you shall ascend to the roof and throw yourself down. If you live, you will live, and if you die, you die. He ascended, threw himself down, and died, and thus the curse of Rabban Yohanan ben Zakkai alighted on him.

A third formulation, from the same viewpoint, is as follows:[1]

Abba Sikra, leader of the revolutionists in Jerusalem, was the son of Rabban Yohanan ben Zakkai's sister. He sent word to him, Come in secret to me, and he came. He said to him, How much longer will you persist in killing the people with hunger? He replied, What am I to do? If I should say anything to them, they would kill me. Rabban Yohanan ben Zakkai said, Think of some plan for me that I may get out of the city. Perhaps there may be some slight salvation. He answered, Pretend that you are ill, and let everyone come and inquire after you. Then place a decayed thing alongside yourself, and spread the rumor that you have died, and allow only your disciples to handle you, and no one else, so that none may feel that you are light, for men know that a live person is lighter than a dead one. And he did so. Rabbi Eliezer entered at one side, and Rabbi Joshua at the other. When they reached the gate, the guards wanted to stab the body. He said to them, People will say they stabbed their teacher. They wanted to push him, and he said, People will say that they pushed their teacher. Finally they opened the gate to him. When he reached there, he exclaimed, Peace be to you, O king, peace be to you, O king. He said to him, you are twice liable to death, for you have called me a king when I am not a king, and second, if I were a king, why did you not come before this? He said to him, As for your saying I am not a king, indeed you are a king, for if you were not king, you would not have Jerusalem given into your hand, as it is written (Is. 10.34), "The Lebanon shall fall by a prince," and prince (or, mighty one) means king, as it is written, "And their prince shall be of themselves" (Jer. 30.21), and Lebanon means the Temple as it is written (Deut. 3.25), the Goodly mountain, the Lebanon. And as for your saying, if I am king, why have you not come to me sooner, the revolutionaries who are among us did not let me. He answered him, If one has a cask of honey, and a reptile is curled about it, would one not break the cask in order to get rid of the reptile? He fell silent. (Rabbi Joseph, and some say, Rabbi Akiba, applied to him the passage, He turned the wise backward, and marketh their knowledge futile (Is. 44.25). He should have answered him, One takes a pair of tongs, removes the serpent and kills it, and saves the cask.) In the meantime a messenger arrived from Rome saying, Caesar has died and the leaders have chosen you emperor! He had one shoe off at the time, and he wanted to put it on, and could not, and then he wanted to remove the other and could not. He said, What could the trouble be? Rabban Yohanan said to him, Do not be alarmed, you have heard good news, as it is written (Prov. 15.30), A good report swelleth the bones. What

---

[1] TB Gittin 56b, tr. by Maurice Simon, Soncino ed., *Babylonian Talmud, Seder Nashim*, I. Epstein (London, 1936), VII, 255-9.

shall be done? Let someone you dislike appear before you, as it is
written, "But a depressed spirit drieth up the bone" (Prov. 17.22). He
did so, and was cured. He said, If you are so wise, why did you not come
before this? He replied, But have I not told you already? He answered,
But have I not also told you? He continued, I will soon leave, and
someone else will be sent in my place. Now ask me what I may grant
you. He said, Give me Yavneh and its sages, and the chain of Rabban
Gamaliel, and a physician to heal Rabbi Zadok. (Rabbi Joseph said, and
some say, Rabbi Akiba said, "He turneth the wise backward" (Is. 44.25).
For he should have asked him to leave them alone that time, but he
thought that perhaps so much he would not grant, and then there would
have been no relief whatever.)

The second account is clearly a reformulation of the third, for it has
already "corrected" the request of Yohanan to conform to the later
criticism, and expanded the story of Yohanan's healing Vespasian's
temporary dropsy.

Thus all three accounts agree first, that Yohanan escaped from the
city and received Vespasian's permission to go to Yavneh, and second,
that he predicted Vespasian's victory on the basis of Isaiah 10.34.[1]
They differ,[2] as we have noted, on whether Vespasian knew that
Yohanan was a loyalist. According to the Talmudic-Midrashic tradition, Yohanan had either no war policy, or, possibly, favored
fighting a long, defensive war. He was unknown to the Romans,

---

[1] Sifre Num. 134, Deut. 6, 28. Note also that a midrash on the verse is found
in the Qumran literature, cf. J. M. Allegro, "Further Messianic References in
Qumran Literature," *JBL*, LXXV, 174 f. Cf. also G. Vermes, "The Symbolical
Interpretation of *Lebanon* in the Targums: The Origin and Development of an
Exegetical Tradition," *Journal of Theological Studies*, IX, 1 f.; Vermes' article in
Melanges bibliques rediges en l'honneur de Andre Robert, Paris, 1957, 269 f.; and H.F.D.
Sparks, "The Symbolical Interpretation of Lebanon in the Fathers," *Journal of
Theological Studies*, X, 264 f. Cf. Pesher Habbakuk, 12.3-4. In the Targumin, Vermes
points out, Lebanon is interpreted as king, the rich, the nations, Jerusalem, and
the Temple. Specifically, Is. 10.34, "God will slay the warriors of his army, strong
as iron, and they shall fall that make war against the land of Israel"; Zech. 11.1,
"Open your gates, O *nations*, that fire may destroy your strongholds." However,
at the time of the destruction, Lebanon was reinterpreted in these two Scriptures
to mean the Temple, rather than the nations, and the "mighty one" as the destroyer
of the Temple. Vermes comments that the destruction of the Sanctuary by the
Roman army was absorbed into the tradition that Lebanon means Temple, rather
than the nations, as earlier. Vermes ascribes the identification of Lebanon and the
Temple by reference to Deut. 3.25, Is. 60.13, and Ps. 92.13-14. Cf. also chapter 3,
It seems possible that Yohanan was, therefore, in an ancient exegetical tradition,
and modified that tradition in the light of events. If so, one must question the
historicity of the earlier prediction, cited in ch. 3, and suggest that the exegesis came
after the event, and represents the reinterpretation of the verse in the light of it.

[2] Cf. Allon, *Mehkarim*, I, 248 f.

granted an interview grudgingly, and obtained favor only after his supernatural powers of prediction were substantiated by events.[1] In the first account, he requested permission to go to Yavneh, to establish an academy, a house of prayer, and to do all the commandments. This considerable request may have represented a statement of the Pharisaic loyalist policy, that if Rome would grant inner autonomy, the Pharisaic loyalists would willingly counsel political submission to Rome. In the second and third accounts, he won the right to make any request at all through authenticating prescience and then asked only "Yavneh and its sages," the chain of Rabban Gamaliel (possibly meaning to save the life of Gamaliel II, son of Simeon ben Gamaliel), and a physician to heal Zadok[2]; or, merely, the right for refugees to escape through the Western gate. These two accounts are more congruent to the period close to the destruction of the city. The burning of the stores took place in the winter of 69-70, but at that time, flight was extremely difficult; it was unlikely either that the gatekeepers were then permitting free egress for any reason whatever, or that corpses were removed from the city, or that Titus would accept refugees. By Passover of 70, he had ordered refugees to be slaughtered. At that time, therefore, it seems quite unlikely that even if Yohanan ben Zakkai had escaped from the city, he would have avoided torture or would have been permitted to go to Yavneh. The conditions of the first account, met at the spring of 68 C.E., are therefore more likely to have been met in the historical events than those of the second and third accounts, congruent to the spring of 70 C.E. when no such Roman action is indicated by Josephus.[3]

---

[1] Note that Josephus recorded the existence of such "holy men" who have prescience because of their knowledge of Scriptures, cf. *War*, 8, 12 (159). These men, he says, were in the Essene circles. Thackeray notes three such instances of Essene predictions, *War*, i, 78; II, 113, and *Antiquities*, XV, 373 f. This was an art which was taught to the disciples, cf. *Antiquities*, XIII, 311. Cf. Thackeray, II, 384.

[2] Other traditions have it that Zadok was brought to Rome.

[3] Cf. *War*, V, 1, 4 (21-26); Tacitus, *History*, 5.12. Josephus says that in the winter of 69-70, John's party burned the buildings stocked with provisions, and Simon did the same, "as though they were purposely serving the Romans by destroying what the city had provided against a siege... The city was converted into a desolate no man's land..." Flight was impossible then, cf. *War*, V, 1. 5 (29-30);

"Loyal citizens, for their part, were in dire despondency and alarm, having no opportunity for planning any change of policy, no hope of coming to terms or of flight, if they had the will; for watch was kept everywhere, and the brigand chiefs, divided on all else, put to death as their common enemies any in favor of peace with the Romans or suspected of an intention to desert, and were unanimous only in slaughtering those deserving of deliverance."

Yavneh, which had been attacked and burned by Judah Maccabee, had come under Jewish rule at the time of Simon, and incorporated into Jewish territory by Alexander Jannaeus. It was a mixed city, with a preponderance, by the first century, of Jewish settlers; thus during the war, Vespasian twice had to establish garrisons in the city.[1] Jewish tradition long regarded Yohanan's settlement there as the crucial nexus in the orderly transmission of the authority of the Sanhedrin in Jerusalem to rabbinical courts of later ages. While the rabbinic account is rather fanciful, one must ask whether its essential point is reasonable, namely, did the Romans willingly and knowingly permit Yohanan ben Zakkai to establish an academy there? The late Israeli historian, Gedaliahu Allon, has argued that they did not. He holds that the Romans moved loyalist Jews at Yavneh, Gophna, Lud, and elsewhere as a war-measure, establishing in these places detention camps, and not centers of voluntary, peaceful settlement.[2] He argues that if the Romans had created such settlements as an act of kindness, Josephus would not have failed to point this out. Rather, Allon thinks, Vespasian forcibly uprooted civilian populations, and settled them in such pacified regions as Yavneh and Lud,[3] to concentrate Jewish populations and to facilitate supervising them. He explains this policy, first, because the Romans suspected that the refugees would rejoin the rebellion when they could, and second, because in fact the Romans were fighting a

---

Furthermore, even corpses were no longer removed from the city, *War*, V, 11.1 (446-451) and Titus refused to receive refugees:

> "... The general... sent a detachment of horses with orders to lie in wait for any who issued from the town into the ravines in quest of food...
> The majority were citizens of the poorer class, who were deterred from deserting by fear for their families, for they could neither hope to elude the rebels if they attempted to escape with their wives and children, nor endure to leave them to be butchered by the brigands. Famine, however, emboldened them to undertake these excursions, and it but remained for them if they escaped unobserved from the town to be taken prisoners by the enemy. When caught... they were scourged and subjected to torture of every description... Titus... recognized the risk of dismissing prisoners of war, and that the custody of such numbers would amount to the imprisonment of their custodians..."

[1] Schuerer, *History*, II, i, 78-9. Cf. ch. 8.

[2] Cf. Allon, *Mehkarim*, I, 219-238. Cf. Josephus, *War*, 4.8.1 (444). Yavneh (Jamnia) is mentioned by Josephus in I, 50, 156, 166; II, 98, 167, 335 f.; III, 56; IV, 130, 444, 663. Cf. IV, 444; "Having reduced the neighborhood of the province of Thamna, he moved to Lydda and Jamnia; both these districts being already subdued, he quartered upon them an adequate number of residents from those who had surrendered, and passed to Ammaus..."

[3] Allon, 223.

war against the Jewish people, and not merely (as Josephus claimed)
against rebels and revolutionaries.[1] He attempts to demonstrate that
this was an ethnic war by citing many of the atrocity stories that
Josephus related. Thus he shows that the Romans did not distinguish
between combatants and non-combatants, or even between loyalists
and moderates. Therefore, he concludes, the Roman war against the
Jews was directed not against revolutionaries, but against any element
of Jewish autonomy. The Romans intended to annul the authority
of autonomous institutions such as the Sanhedrin, and to destroy the
spiritual and material strength of the Jewish people, so that the Jews
in the land of Israel would never again be able to revolt against Roman
rule.[2] Allon holds that the Romans exiled the captured refugees to
concentration camps, mainly by the sea and amid mixed populations;
and that Yohanan and his disciples were sent to Yavneh not because
they requested it, but because this was part of a continuing policy of
suppression. All Yohanan asked, and all that he was granted (if anything) was that he be given a special right in the Yavneh camp to
practice the Jewish faith. Yohanan could not have received any
favorable treatment of lasting significance, or any power or authority,
but only a small personal kindness. When, after the destruction, the
nation began to recover its strength, and at Yavneh, an autonomous
and limited Jewish government evolved, the sages looked back on
Yohanan's mission, and assigned to it a significance that it acquired
only as a consequence of later events. Thus it is concluded the academy
first consisted of a group of scholars discussing their tradition quite
unofficially, with neither Jewish nor Roman recognition.[3]

One must agree with Allon that the settlements at Yavneh, Lud,
and elsewhere were, as Josephus makes abundantly clear, created as a
war measure. Allon's contention, however, that the refugees were
forcibly incarcerated there is nowhere supported by the facts he cites.
He argues that if the Roman intention were to benefit the refugees,
Josephus would have said so. But this begs the question. Josephus'
silence proves nothing, but (presumably) that he thought the Roman
intent was sufficiently clear to his readers throughout the Empire.
If the Romans had made a practice of forcibly and malevolently im-
prisoning loyal refugees in detention camps in other revolted parts of

---

[1] Allon, 234.
[2] Allon, 237-8.
[3] G. Cohen, "The Talmudic Age," *Great Ages and Ideas of the Jewish People*, ed.
L. Schwarz (New York, 1956), 160-1.

the Empire, then Josephus ought to have pointed out their contrary, benevolent intention in Judah; not having done so, Josephus might provide support for Allon's interpretation. But Allon does not prove that the Romans acted in such a manner elsewhere, and there is no evidence that they did. His silence proves nothing, therefore, except that to him the intention of the Roman policy of resettlement was self-evident, namely, to provide the loyalists a secure shelter from the vagaries of war.

Allon's main contention, however, is that the war was in fact directed by Rome against the Jewish nation and people in the land of Israel, and that it was waged with unusual cruelty. Allon ignores comparable Jewish atrocities; he omits the question of war guilt; he does not consider how the Romans regarded the slaughter of their garrison in Jerusalem. He regards the revolutionaries as faultless, and holds that they were treated as unjustly as possible by the vengeful imperial power. They fought a national war, but were treated with the severity due to treasonable seditionists, not to legitimate combatants. If, one must note, the Romans did not abide by the higher ethics of war, neither did the Jews. They did not distinguish any more carefully than Rome between civil and military populations, nor were their troops more responsive to the requirements of a higher morality. Furthermore, it is gratuitous to cite numerous actions of cruelty on the field of battle. Armies in war do not commonly take measures to distinguish between innocent bystanders and guilty combatants. Even in modern times, armies of enlightened nations have carried out military action against civilian cities. Atrocities against prisoners of war and soldiers who want to surrender are not uncommon. Allon cannot, therefore, cite Roman atrocities in military areas to prove that Rome intended to wage war against the Jewish people in the land of Israel. These atrocities only prove that the Roman armies were no more scrupulous in their conduct of war than the Jewish zealots, or, indeed, most armies in most periods of history.

The Romans certainly knew that they had an ethnic revolt on their hands. They were anxious not to meet an underground revolution throughout the diaspora. Therefore they did not transform the war into a religious persecution. Their policy was to divide and conquer. They always tried to find allies among the enemy, and to discern who could be won over and neutralized. If as Allon contends, they considered the war an ethnic struggle, this did not in any case prevent them from trying to win over all Jews they could reach. It is clear that they succeeded. First of all, large sections of the Jewish population remained at peace throughout the war. The rebellion in no sense enlisted the support of the entire Jewish population in the land of Israel, and progressively lost what support it had at the outset. Second, the consequences of the war did not include the destruction of the economy or social foundations of Jewish settlement in the land. The Jewish populations in the mixed cities were molested, but mostly survived the war. The Roman policy after the war was certainly not generally to enslave or to deport non-combatant, loyal civilian populations except from the revolted regions. Most important, there *is* evidence of the reconstitution of limited self-government, if not under Yohanan, then under Gamaliel II at Yavneh (as Allon admits). If the Romans intended to destroy Jewish settlement in the land, they had sufficient information about what was going on at Yavneh to know that the activity of the sages there endangered such a policy. They had sufficient force to destroy that work. They did not do so.

What, then, was the Roman policy toward the Jews? It was, first of all, to pacify the country, and this policy was effected by military action. It was, more important, to conciliate Jewish opinion in the Diaspora during the war, and in the land itself after it. That the Romans succeeded in substantially retaining the loyalty of the Jewish populations in the Diaspora is proven by the absence throughout the entire course of the war of significant military or political support for the revolutionaries on the part of diaspora communities. Indeed, the one instance of exilic support, that given by the Jewish converts in Abiadene, proves that such support was possible, and, yet, never rendered in a meaningful way by most of the exilic settlements. Josephus wrote his *Jewish War* as a part of the Roman propaganda effort, designed to conciliate the diaspora, and, specifically, the Mesopotamian settlements, and

> to demonstrate that the rebels had brought their ruin upon themselves by their own wickedness, that the Romans were not hostile to Judaism, but had acted in Palestine regretfully, as agents of divine vengeance, and that therefore submission to Roman rule was justified by religion as well as common sense.[1]

If this was the purpose of the Roman propaganda, what then was their policy in the land itself? One concludes that it was to reconstitute limited self-government among the Jewish population of the land, through loyal and non-seditious agents. Such a policy would have two

---

[1] M. Smith, "Palestinian Judaism in the First Century," in M. Davis, ed., *Israel. Its Role in Civilization*, New York, 1956, 74-5.

favorable consequences. First, it would further conciliate the diaspora communities, and demonstrate in action the theory of war-guilt advanced by the Roman propaganda effort. The destruction of the Temple and enslavement of thousands of Jewish soldiers and civilians must certainly have weakened the bonds of loyalty which held the diaspora communities to the Imperial government. By genuinely constructive and conciliatory actions after the war, the Romans could manifest their true Jewish policy: not persecution but tolerance and legal scrupulousness. Second, the survival of the Jewish settlements in the land of Israel necessitated some form of government. One means, which Rome had pursued for almost a century, had been through the constitution of native, pro-Roman authorities to continue the type of religious-legal jurisdiction which was so important to the Jews themselves. Jewish law was obviously going to remain operative among the Jewries of the land and the Empire. The Romans made no attempt to stamp out the Jewish legal autonomy at this time. If, therefore, they expected to continue it, their best policy would have been, and, probably was, to continue its operation through instrumentalities loyal to the government. Indeed, the situation of the Jews in the land of Israel made such loyalty imperative; they were close to the Parthian frontier, where additional numbers of their people lived. It was essential to Rome to regain the sincere loyalty of the Jews, and through loyalists such as Yohanan ben Zakkai, they attempted to do so.[1]

Whether, however, the Romans did so in the manner described by the Talmudic traditions is an open and conjectural question. As we have seen, the several accounts are neither internally consistent nor congruent with the facts of the imperial succession.[2] They were, moreover, written by later generations, who received an account of the events in question after the reconstitution of Jewish self-government had become well established. Thus one may indeed regard the account of a smooth transition from Jerusalem to Yavneh with some suspicion. Nonetheless, if in detail the several accounts present difficulties, one legitimately concludes that their common point is congruent to the course of events: Yohanan did escape from Jerusalem before its destruction; he did go willingly and with Roman approval to Yavneh; and he did begin in an elementary way to reconstitute legitimate Jewish authority there.

A final question remains: why did the Romans choose the Pharisaic party, which had been one among a number of contending sects before

---

[1] Finkelstein, *Akiba*, 66-8.
[2] None seems to take account of the year of the three emperors (68-69) for instance.

the destruction, to become the instrument of reconstituting Jewish autonomy afterward? Their influence before the war was supposedly widespread, but if, as Josephus maintains,[1] they favored peace with Rome, their authority was insufficient to effect at least that one crucial policy, and, as we have seen, they were unable to force the priests and Sadducees to conduct the Temple affairs according to their doctrines. Furthermore, at the time of Herod, their number was, according to Josephus, not more than six thousand. Faced with the question, which Jews of those who will work with the government at all can command sufficient popular support to maintain the stability of the Jewish communities in the land of Israel, the Roman government very likely was guided by two main considerations. First, Josephus wrote his *Antiquities* to provide an answer:

> The Pharisees, he says again and again, have by far the greatest influence with the people. Any government which secures their support is accepted. Any government which alienates them has trouble... The Sadducees, it is true, have more following among the aristocracy... but they have no popular following at all, and even in the old days when they were in power, they were forced by public opinion to follow the Pharisees' orders.[2]

The other parties, as Josephus represents them, were ineligible for consideration: The Essenes were "a philosophical curiosity" and the Zealots were, as everyone knew, anti-Roman:

> So any Roman government which wants peace in Palestine had better support and secure the support of the Pharisees.[3]

Thus Josephus himself was probably instrumental in obtaining the recognition of Pharisaic hegemony. Second, the Pharisees for their part actively advanced their own candidacy as Roman supporters, and (possibly after Yohanan's death) negotiated for it.[4] If so, one discerns significant evidence that Yohanan ben Zakkai's policies took hold among the refugee sages at Yavneh, and that he, above any other in his generation, was responsible for the ultimate prevalence of Pharisaic Judaism, which was made possible by Roman encouragement and, in unequal measure, by the Pharisaic policy and program.[5] If Rome did recognize the sages of Yavneh as a legally constituted and legitimate authority in the Jewish community in the land of Israel, one may well regard the accounts of Yohanan's escape from Jerusalem as a legendary, but ultimately accurate, representation of that recognition.

---

[1] Smith, "Palestinian Judaism," 78.
[2] *Ibid.*, 76. [3] *Ibid.* [4] *Ibid.*, 77. [5] Cf. Chapters seven and eight.

Yohanan probably spent the last year and a half of the war isolated from the tragedy at Jerusalem; one does not know how much war news actually reached him at Yavneh, but he must have had some idea that his escape was providential. As the Roman armies pressed closer to the city walls, he might well have seen the fulfilment of his alleged expectation, that only a "slight salvation" was possible. For all the rest of 68 C.E., Vespasian awaited news from Rome; he waited until June of 69, during which time, the Roman armies were mostly idle. The Zealots were not. The Jewish forces overran the southern parts of the land, surprised and took Hebron, a major stronghold, and recovered territories in the land of Judah which Vespasian had conquered the preceding year. Vespasian had to return in June of 69 to recapture Gophna, Acrabata, and Hebron. By early summer, Rome held the whole land, except for Jerusalem, and the fortresses of Herodion, Masada, and Machaerus, south of the city. On July 1, 69, the Eastern legions proclaimed Vespasian to be Caesar, he marched to Antioch, thence to Alexandria, and in January of 70, to Rome.

Titus carried on the war, advancing on the city with four legions, and numerous auxiliary units of confederated kings (as the midrashic sources knew). In the spring of 70 he began the siege, pressing the lines forward and surrounding the city with a continuous stone wall to cut off escape. The walls were breached in the summer of 70, and the city fell by stages. By September, 70, Jerusalem was once again subjected to Roman authority. Many were killed, many more sold into slavery until Jewish captives glutted the slave markets and arenas of the Empire. The Temple was burned, and only the Western wall remained. When word reached Yavneh that Jerusalem had fallen, Yohanan ben Zakkai and his students sat down and wept:

> Meanwhile Rabban Yohanan ben Zakkai sat and waited trembling, the way Eli had sat and waited, as it is said "Lo Eli sat upon his seat by the wayside watching, for his heart trembled for the ark of God" (I Sam. 4.13). When Rabban Yohanan ben Zakkai heard that Jerusalem was destroyed, and the Temple was up in flames, he tore his clothing and his disciples tore their clothing, and they wept, crying aloud and mourning.[1]

---

[1] ARNa, ch. 4, Schechter 12b, Goldin 37. Cf. also ARNb, ch. 7, Schechter 21, "He stood and tore his clothing and removed his tefillin, and sat down and wept, and his students with him. And they say that even Abraham, Isaac, and Jacob were with them, as it is said (Zech. 11.2)..." etc. Rabbinic sources on the siege and famine of Jerusalem are summarized in the study by A. Lettofsky, *Milhemet HaYehudim ba-Roma-im Lefi Yosephus ve-HaMekorot HaTalmudi-im* The War of the Jews against the Romans according to Josephus and the Talmudic Sources, unpublished bachelor's honors thesis, Brandeis University Library, 1959.

CHAPTER SEVEN

HAPPY ARE YOU, O ISRAEL!

At Yavneh, Yohanan ben Zakkai began the task of reconstruction. His attention may have been drawn, first of all, to the deep despair that characterized Jewish morale. With Jerusalem in Roman hands and the Temple in ruins, some Jews saw themselves as the rejected children of God, who had been born to disaster.[1] Others accepted the prophetic teaching that suffering was punishment for sin, and reflected more thoughtfully on the nature of human transgression. They reconsidered ancient analyses of man's shortcoming in the light of the fresh catastrophe. Still others, both on the Roman and the Jewish sides, as well as within the nascent Christian community, offered an explanation of the cataclysm in terms of their own understanding of human history. Most thus focused upon the recent unfortunate events, taking as their problem how to confront the national disaster. The result was a preoccupation with the future and hope for quick recompense. Yohanan ben Zakkai differed from the rest of his generation in that he concerned himself with the present needs of the surviving remnant of Israel. While he shared the common sense of tragedy and endured the despair of his generation, he did not fix his vision on what had happened and what would come to compensate for the catastrophe. He attempted rather to devise a program for the survival and reconstruction of the Jewish people and faith. Thus retrospectively a paradox emerges: out of preoccupation with the sufferings of the past came obsession with the secret of future redemption, while from stubborn consideration of present and immediate difficulties came a practical plan by which Israel might in truth save what could be saved from the disaster. Others offered the comfort that as surely as punishment has followed sin, so surely would He who chastised the people comfort them, and therefore Israel ought to wait for inexorable redemption. Yohanan on the other hand proposed a program and a policy for the interim during which the people had to wait.[2]

---

[1] On the widespread bitterness after the war, cf. Dio Cassius, *Epitome*, 69:11-15, in *Extra-Biblical Sources for Jewish History*, ed. S.A.B. Mercer (London, 1913); cf. also Edersheim, *Life and Times*, I, 167-9; Lamentations Rabbati 7.2; Song of Songs Rabbah 11.7; B. Helfgott, *The Doctrine of Election in Tannaitic Literature* (New York, 1954), 42-49. Cf. also below, n. 2.

[2] For a survey of rabbinic reactions to the destruction, cf. A. Lettofsky, *Milhemet*

The people had to be told why they suffered. The Romans and Jewish loyalists, Jewish-Christians, Jewish apocalyptics, and Yohanan ben Zakkai advanced answers to this question, agreeing that the sin of Israel had brought disaster, but disagreeing on precisely what that sin was. The obvious answer, given by the victorious party, was that Israel had sinned by relying on force of arms and by rebelling against Roman rule. Josephus emphasized that the sins of the nation had guaranteed the Roman victory:

> ... invariably arms have been refused to our nation, and warfare has been the sure signal of defeat. For it is, I suppose, the duty of the occupants of holy ground to leave everything to the arbitrament of God, and to scorn the aid of human hands, can they but conciliate the Arbiter above...[1]

(Josephus, in the *War*, was particularly concerned to drive home this point, because the Romans had hired him to write the book partly in order to dissuade the Jews of Mesopotamia from trying to secure Parthian intervention in Palestine.) The Romans likewise regarded the catastrophe as direct recompense for rebellion against Rome, a sin compounded by the sheer inconvenience of the war, coming when the imperial succession was in doubt, other lands in revolt, and the armies fighting a civil war. So, Josephus reported, Titus addressed the city:

> You who without bestowing a thought on our strength or your own weakness have through inconsiderate fury and madness lost your people, your city, and your Temple...[2]

> You were incited against the Romans by Roman humanity... We allowed you to occupy this land, and set over you kings of your own blood; then we maintained the laws of your forefathers, and permitted you... to live as you willed.[3]

Nonetheless, Israel had rebelled. Whose fault was it, then, that the Temple was destroyed? Israel sinned by the act of war, and was punished by conquest. In later decades, even some Jews came to see matters in this way, but only after the utter devastation of vast territories in the Bar Kokhba rebellion sixty-five years later.[4]

HaYehudim baRomaim lefi Yosephus veHamekorot Ha Talmudiim The War of the Jews against the Romans according to Josephus and the Talmudic Sources.

[1] *War*, V, 9. 4 (399-400).

[2] *War*, VI, 6.2 (328). Cf. also Tacitus, *History*, V, 10. On the Roman view cf. E. Kaufman, *Toldot HaEmunah HaYisraelit* History of the Israelite Faith (Jerusalem, 1956), VIII, 24-5.

[3] *War*, 6.6.2 (333-4).

[4] Cf. S. W. Baron, *Social and Religious History of the Jews*, II (Ancient Times, Part 2), 126-8. Cf. also S. Krauss, *Paras va-Romi baTalmud u-vaMidrash*, Persia and

The Christian community in Jerusalem had held the Temple sacred for thirty years, participating in its rites and frequenting its courts. After the destruction, they held that the final punishment had at last come on the people who had rejected the savior, and thus the Church regarded the catastrophe as a vindication of Christian faith. The historian Eusebius preserved the Christian viewpoint:

> ...Those who believed on Christ migrated from Jerusalem, that when holy men had altogether deserted the royal capital of the Jews... the judgment of God might at last overtake them for all their crimes against Christ and his apostles, and all that generation of the wicked be utterly blotted out from among men... Such was the reward of the iniquity of the Jews and of their impiety against the Christ of God...[1]

The Christians thus thought that Jerusalem had suffered the punishment of its inhabitants, who had sinned against Christ.

The Jewish apocalyptics[2] likewise blamed Israel's sins for the dis-

---

Rome in the Talmud and Midrash (Jerusalem, 1947), 5. Cf. especially TB Avoda Zara 18a, "When Rabbi Yosi ben Kisma fell ill, Rabbi Hanina ben Teradion went to visit him. He said to him, Hanina my brother, do you not know that this nation has been endowed with sovereignty by Heaven, for it has destroyed his house, and burned his sanctuary, and slaughtered his pious ones, and still endures..." This was at the time of the Hadrianic persecutions.

[1] Eusebius, *Ecclesiastical History*, III.5.1-5. Cf. also J. Weiss, *Earliest Christianity, A History of the Period A.D. 30-150* (New York, 1959), II, 715; A. Schlatter, *The Church in the New Testament Period* (London, 1955), 307. But S.G.F. Brandon, *Fall of Jerusalem and the Christian Church* (London, 1951), 181-2, projects a Jewish-Christian view of the destruction as seen by those who remained loyal to the Jewish people. Since Brandon's hypothesis has not been widely accepted by New Testament scholars, I do not include it in discussing the main responses to the destruction. Cf. also H. Leitzmann, *The Beginnings of the Christian Church* (tr. B. L. Woolf, New York, 1959), 177-82; L. Baeck, *Judaism and Christianity* (Philadelphia, 1958), 78-9; R. T. Herford, "Separation of Christianity from Judaism," in *Jewish Studies in Memory of Israel Abrahams* (New York, 1927), 209 f.

[2] Cf. Burkitt, *Jewish and Christian Apocalypse*, 12, who finds in the following midrash a summary of the view of Yohanan's view of apocalypse: "In that day the Lord made a covenant with Abram (Gen. 15. 18). R. Judah said, Rabban Yohanan ben Zakkai and Rabbi Akiba disagree. One maintains, this world he revealed to him, but not the next; the other maintains that he revealed to him both this world and the next (Ber. R. 44.22)." According to Burkitt, this saying implies the renunciation of the apocalyptic idea, the "notion that the kingdom of God was an external state of things which was just upon the point of being manifested, and... that the person of insight could know something about it before hand... It was this idea that inspired the whole series of Jewish Apocalypses that was the central thought of the earliest preaching of Christianity, that intoxicated the Jewish people in their wild struggle with Rome." Yohanan ben Zakkai, Burkitt feels, had no such false hopes; he was content "to let the future age wait for God's good time..." Burkitt's view would be better founded if one knew for certain which of the two rabbis held what opinion.

aster, meditated on the nature of sin, comforted the people with the promise of impending redemption, of which they declared, "thrice blest the man who lives until that time."[1] Two documents, the apocalypse of Ezra, and the vision of Baruch, are representative of the apocalyptic state of mind. The author (or editor) of the Ezra apocalypse (II Ezra 3-14),[2] who lived at the end of the first century C.E., looked forward to a day of judgment, when the Messiah would destroy Roman power, and the rule of God would govern society. He wondered, at the same time, how Israel's continued sufferings might be reconciled with divine justice. To Israel God's will had been revealed, but God had not removed the evil inclination which prevented the people from carrying it out:

> For we and our fathers have passed our lives in ways that bring death... but what is man that thou art angry with him, or what is a corruptible race that thou art so bitter against it... (Ezra 8.26)

Ezra was told that God's ways are inscrutable (4.10-11), but when he repeated the question, "Why has Israel been given over to the gentiles as a reproach," he was given an answer characteristic of this literature: a new age is dawning which will shed light on such perplexities. Thus he was told,

> ...if you are alive, you will see, and if you live long, you will often marvel, because the age is hastening swiftly to its end. For it will not be able to bring the things that have been promised to the righteous in their appointed times, because this age is full of sadness and infirmities... (4.26-20)

An angel told him the signs of the coming redemption:

> ...the sun shall suddenly shine forth at night and the moon during the day, blood shall drip from wood, and the stone shall utter its voice, the peoples shall be troubled, and the stars shall fall... (5.4-5)

---

[1] Sybilline Oracles, IV, 15-26. The fourth book was written shortly after 76 C.E., cf. R. H. Charles, *Apocrypha and Pseudepigrapha of the Old Testament* (Oxford, 1913, 2 vols.), II, 373. Cf. also IV, lines 162-191.

[2] Cf. Charles, Apocrypha, II, 542 f. Charles summarizes the problem set out by IV Ezra as follows: "Why is the chosen people given up as a prey to the heathen? If it is because of its sins, the sins of the heathen far outweigh those of Israel. Why then should the heathen be allowed to lord it over and oppress the latter? To these questions, no satisfactory answer can be found in the law alone. The law is impotent to redeem and save the sinner... The utmost that the seer can hope from the law is that while many are born to perish, but few shall be saved. The answers to the problem... are the following: a. God's ways are inscrutable... b. human intelligence is finite and limited... c. The course and duration of the present world have been predetermined. Evil must run its course... but the predetermined moment... will soon arrive. In spite of all the appearances to the contrary, God loves Israel now and always..."

and he was admonished to wait patiently:

> The righteous therefore can endure difficult circumstances, while hoping for easier ones, but those who have done wickedly have suffered the difficult circumstances, and will not see easier ones (6.55-6)

One finds, therefore, first that Ezra regarded the catastrophe as the fruit of sin, more specifically, the result of man's natural incapacity to do the will of God; second, that he prayed for forgiveness; and third, that he found hope in the coming transformation of the age and the promise of a new day when man's heart will be as able, as his mind even then was willing, to do the will of God. The pseudepigraph in the name of Jeremiah's secretary, Baruch, likewise brought promise of coming redemption, but with little advice for the intervening period.[1] The document exhibited three major themes, first, that God acted righteously in bringing about the punishment of Israel:

> Righteousness belongs to the Lord our God, but confusion of face to us and our fathers... The Lord has brought them upon us, for the Lord is righteous in all his works... (Baruch 2.6)

Second, the catastrophe came on account of Israel's sin:

> Why is it, O Israel... that you are in the land of your enemies?... You have forsaken the fountain of wisdom, if you had walked in the way of the Lord, you would be dwelling in peace forever. (3.10)

---

[1] Charles, *Apocrypha*, II, 553 f. Although the apocryphal book of Baruch has been divided into three documents, I have not dealt with these divisions, since my main point is that the other approaches to the destruction all rested on an eschatological expectation that I do not find in Yohanan's thought. The dating of the documents, according to Charles, is between 74 and 79 C.E. Charles (I, 574) would assign the pseudepigraph to the circle of Yohanan ben Zakkai at Yavneh, on the grounds that Yohanan also counselled peace, mourned the destruction, and was a devoted student of Torah. I do not find this conclusive, for these qualities were not unique to him. Furthermore, part B (3.10. f.) might well have been written abroad. It is true that the final lines of B are appropriate to Yohanan (3.35-4.4): "This is our God... He found the whole way to knowledge and gave her to Jacob his servant... Turn O Jacob and take her Wisdom – Torah, walk toward her shining light... Do not give your glory to another, or your advantages to an alien people." Cf. TB Ketuvot 66b, a later rescension of the story in Mekilta, Bahodesh 1. The Syriac and Greek Apocalypses of Baruch likewise emphasized the imminence of coming redemption. Compare the Greek recension (II Baruch 10.6 f) with TB Ketuvot 113a, TP Taanit 4.8, and ARNa, ch. 4. III Baruch (the Greek recension) contains an account of the seven heavens, which Yohanan's academy apparently discussed also, but there is no connection with what is known of Yohanan's conclusions. Cf. also F. Rosenthal, *Vier Apokalyptische Bücher* (Leipzig, 1885), on the authorship of the main post-70 apocalypses. His theory has not won wide acceptance, cf. R. Pfeiffer, *History of New Testament Times* (New York, 1949), 274. I see no reason, therefore, to include the book of Tobit in this discussion as Rosenthal's theory would require.

Third, as surely as God had punished the people, so certainly would he bring the people home to their land and restore their fortunes. Thus Jerusalem speaks:

> But I, how can I help you? For he who brought these calamities upon you will deliver you from the hand of your enemies... Take courage, my children, cry to God, and he will deliver you from the power and hand of the enemy... For I sent you out with sorrow and weeping, but God will give you back to me with joy and gladness forever... (4.17-18, 21, 23)

Finally, Baruch advised the people to wait patiently for redemption:.

> My children, endure with patience the wrath that has come upon you from God. Your enemy has overtaken you, but you will soon see their destruction, and will tread upon their necks... Take courage, my children, and cry to God, for you will be remembered by him who brought this upon you. For just as you purposed to go astray from God, return with tenfold zeal to seek him, for he who brought these calamities upon you will bring you everlasting joy with your salvation. Take courage, O Jerusalem, for he who named you will comfort you (4.25, 27-30).

This theme came very close to Yohanan's comments on the destruction, for it emphasized, as did he, the comfort to be found in the very authorship of the calamity. Yohanan emphasized the duty of the people to repent and return to God, however, as the condition of redemption. Baruch regarded the redemption as a very present hope, which would be fulfilled in a little while, while Yohanan gave no indication until his very last breath, and only then, that he expected the redemption in the near future.[1] So far as the consolation of Baruch depended on immediate redemption, it was not consonant with the known opinions of Yohanan ben Zakkai, who never said "Endure with patience..." because redemption is very close at hand.

On the contrary, Yohanan was skeptical of the messianic movements among the people, and taught:[2]

> If you have a sapling in your hand, and it is said to you, Behold, there is the Messiah – go on with your planting, and afterward go out and receive him. And if the youths say to you, Let us go up and build the Temple, do not listen to them. But if the elders say to you, Come, let us destroy the Temple, listen to them, for the building of youth is destruction, and the destruction of old age is building – proof of the matter is Rehoboam, son of Solomon.

---

[1] Cf. chapter nine.
[2] ARNb, ch. 31, Schechter 34a.

We shall see that Yohanan offered not hope of speedy redemption, but rather a conditional promise, that just as punishment surely followed sin, so certainly will redemption follow *repentance*.

Yohanan was not immune to the widespread sense of despair, for he changed his interpretation of the verse (Prov. 14.34), "Righteousness exalteth a nation, but the kindness of the peoples is sin."[1] Earlier he had taught, that just as a sin-offering makes atonement for Israel, so does lovingkindness make atonement for the heathen, but after the destruction, he apparently accepted an xenophobic interpretation:

> Rabban Yohanan ben Zakkai said to his disciples, My sons, what is the meaning of the verse, Righteousness exalteth a nation, and the kindness of the peoples is sin (Prov. 14.34)? Rabbi Eliezer answered and said, Righteousness exalteth a nation – this refers to Israel, of whom it is said, "Who is like thy people Israel, one nation in the earth" (II Sam. 7.23), and the kindness of the peoples is sin – the good deeds are a sin to the nations of the world, for they do it only to make themselves great, as it says, That they may offer sacrifices of sweet savor unto the God of Heaven, and pray for the life of the king of his sons (Ezra 6.10).
>
> Rabbi Joshua answered and said, Righteousness exalteth a nation – this refers to Israel, of whom it is written, Who is like thy people Israel, one nation in the earth? And the kindness of peoples is sin – all the kindness and charity that the heathen do is counted sin to them, because they only do it to prolong their dominion, as it says, Wherefore O King let my counsel be acceptable to thee, and break off thy sins by righteousness and thy iniquities by showing mercy to the poor, that there may be a lengthening of thy tranquility. (Daniel 4,27f.)
>
> Rabbi Eleazar ben Arakh answered and said, Righteousness exalteth a nation, and [so does] kindness – this is Israel, but to the nations of the world [belongs] sin.
>
> Rabban Yohanan ben Zakkai said, I prefer the words of Rabbi Eleazar ben Arakh to my and your words, for he assigns righteousness and kindness to Israel, and sin to the nations of the world.

This seems to show that he also had given an answer. What had it been? As it has been taught, Rabban Yohanan ben Zakkai had said to them, Just as the sin-offering makes atonement for Israel, so charity makes atonement for the heathen.[2]

---

[1] The Revised Standard Version translated, "Righteousness exalts a nation, but sin is a reproach to any people." I have followed the rabbinic translation, in order to clarify the midrash that follows.

[2] TB. Baba Batra 10b, Pesikta de Rav Kahana, ch. Shekalim, ed. S. Buber 12b, and Yalkut II, 952 (on the verse). I have reconstructed the account following the comment (in part) of Bacher, *Agadot*, I, i 26, n. 4. The original texts are as follows: TB Baba Batra 10b:

> "Rabban Yohanan ben Zakkai said to his disciples, My sons, what is the meaning of the verse, Righteousness exalteth a nation, but the kindness of

Continued notes from page 135.

the peoples is sin? Rabbi Eliezer answered and said, Righteousness exalteth
a nation – this refers to Israel, of whom it is said, Who is like thy people
Israel one nation in the earth? (II Sam. 7.23) But the kindness of the peoples
is sin – all the charity and kindness done by the heathens are counted to
them as sin, because they only do it to magnify themselves, as it says, That
they may offer sacrifices of sweet savor unto the God of heaven and pray
for the life of the king and of his sons (Ezra 7.10). (But is not an act of this
kind charity in the full sense of the word, seeing that it has been taught, If
a man says, I give this sela for charity in order that my sons may live, and that I
may be found worthy of the future world, he may all the same be a righteous
man in the full sense of the word? There is no contradiction, in the one case
we speak of an Israelite, in the other, of a heathen). Rabbi Joshua answered
and said, Righteousness exalteth a nation – this refers to Israel, of whom
it is written, Who is like thy people Israel, one nation in the earth? The
kindness of the peoples is sin – all the charity and kindness that the heathen
do is counted sin to them, because they only do it in order that their dominion may be prolonged, as it says (Dan. 4.27), Wherefore O King let my
counsel be acceptable to thee, and break off thy sins by righteousness, and
thy iniquities by showing mercy to the poor, if there may be a lengthening
of they tranquility. Rabbi Gamaliel answered and said, Righteousness exalteth a nation – this refers to Israel (etc.) And the kindness of the peoples is
sin – all the charity and kindness that the heathen do is counted as sin to them,
because they only do it to display haughtiness, and whoever displays haughtiness is cast into gehinnom, as it says, The proud and haughty man, scorner
is his name, he worketh in the wrath of pride (Prov. 21.24), and wrath
connotes gehinnom, as it is said (Zeph. 1.15), A day of wrath is that day.
Said Rabban Gamaliel, We have still to hear the opinion of the Modite.
Rabbi Eliezer the Modite says, Righteousness exalteth a nation – this refers
to Israel, of whom it is written, Who is like thy people Israel (etc.). The
kindness of the peoples is sin – all the charity and kindness of the heathen
is counted to them as sin, since they do it only to reproach us, as it says,
The Lord that brought it and did according as he spoke, because ye have
sinned against the Lord and have not obeyed his voice, therefore this thing
is come upon you (Jer. 40.3). Rabbi Nehuniah ben HaKaneh answered and
said, Righteousness exalteth a nation, and there is kindness for Israel and
a sin-offering for the peoples. Said Rabban Yohanan ben Zakkai to his
disciples, the answer of Rabbi Nehuniah ben HaKaneh is superior to my
answer and to yours, because he assigns charity *and* kindness to Israel, and
sin to the heathen. This seems to show that he also gave an answer. What was
it? As it has been taught, Rabban Yohanan ben Zakkai said to them, Just
as the sin-offering makes atonement for Israel, so charity makes atonement
for the heathen."

The recension in Pesikta de Rav Kahana is as follows:

"Righteousness exalteth a nation and the kindness of the peoples is sin.
Rabbi Eliezar and Rabbi Joshua and the Rabbis. Rabbi Eliezar says, Righteousness exalteth a nation – this is Israel. And the kindness of the nations
is sin – good deeds are a sin to the nations of the world, for they take pride
in them. And Rabbi Joshua said, Righteousness exalteth (etc.). And the
kindness of the nations is sin – it is a pleasure to the nations of the world,
that is, when Israel sins, they do subjugate them. Rabban Gamaliel
said, Righteousness exalteth (etc.) and the kindness of the nations of the
world is a sin for them, for so Daniel said to Nebuchadnezzar (Dan. 4.27),

Continued note from page 136.

Break off thy sins by thy righteousness ... (etc.). Rabbi Eleazar ben Arakh said, Righteousness exalteth (etc.). But sin is of the nations of the world. Said Rabban Yohanan, I prefer the words of Rabbi Eleazar ben Arakh over your words, for he gives righteousness and kindness to Israel; and sin to the nations of the world... [There intervenes a passage in the name of Abin bar Judah.] Rabbi Nehuniah ben HaKaneh said, Righteousness exalteth a nation – this is Israel. And the kindness of the nations is sin – the kindness which nations of the world do is a sin to Israel..."

The recension in Yalkut Shimoni is as follows:

"It was taught, Rabban Yohanan ben Zakkai said to his students... (etc., as in TB Baba Batra). Answered Rabbi Eliezer and said, The righteousness and kindness which the nations of pagans do is a sin to them, because they only do so to puff themselves up, as it is said (Ezra 7.10) etc. Rabbi Joshua answered and said, Righteousness exalteth (etc.) Righteousness and kindness which the pagans do is a sin to them, for they only do so to extend the life of their kingdoms, as it is said (Dan. 4.27), etc. Rabban Gamaliel answered and said, Righteousness (etc.). And the kindness of the peoples is a sin – the kindness and righteousness that the pagans do is a sin to them, as they only do so in order to be proud, and whoever is proud falls into gehinnom, as it is said (Prov. 21.24) etc. Rabban Simeon ben Gamaliel said, We still need the Modite, as we learn, Rabbi Eleazar the Modite said, Righteousness exalteth (etc.). And the kindness of the peoples is a sin – the kindness and righteousness which the pagans do is a sin to them, as they only do so in order to blaspheme us (citing Jer. 40.3). Rabbi Nehumiah ben HaKaneh said, Righteousness exalteth... (etc.). Rabban Yohanan ben Zakkai said, I see his words above your words, for he gives righteousness and kindness to Israel and to the nations, sin... And what did he say, Just as righteousness..."

Following Bacher's comment and the precedents of the Avot sources cited in ch. 4, the form of which is repeated for several stories, I suggest that the proper order should be the three famous students of Yohanan: Eliezer, Joshua, and Eleazar. Before the words of Eleazar, the opinion of Gamaliel II is included, and afterward, that of Abin; that of Nehuniah ben HaKaneh's opinion in the TB is that of Eleazar praised by Yohanan, in the Pesikta. Thus:

TB		Pesikta
Nehuniah ben HaKaneh	–	Eleazar ben Arakh
Joshua ben Hananiah	–	Gamaliel
Eliezar ben Hyrkanus	–	Gamaliel (very close)
Eliezer the Modite	–	Abin ben Judah.

Bacher continues that the appearance of Gamaliel and Eliezar the Modite among the students of Yohanan is surprising, especially in the TB Beraita, and there is apparently a confusion of two stories (or, perhaps, two separate conversations). In one, Yohanan speaks with his students, and in this conversation, Nehuniah ben HaKaneh took part, and Yohanan ben Zakkai praises the opinion of Nehuniah; in the second, Gamaliel presided, and after hearing the opinion of Eliezer and Joshua, he asked the opinion of Eliezer the Modite, as happened elsewhere (cf. Berahot 40a, Hullin 92b).

However, although Joshua, Nehuniah, Eliezer, and Eleazar were contemporaries (on the former three, cf. Eduyot 6.3), I find it difficult to understand why Yohanan should be represented as praising the words of Nehuniah over Eleazar's, There is no precedent for such a deed, and if there are specific patterns in which

If Yohanan hated the pagans who had destroyed the Temple, he had a detailed, practical program to offer for the repair of the soul and reconstruction of the social and political life of Jewry in the land of Israel.[1]

Yohanan's program was, first, to provide a source of genuine comfort, by showing the people how they might extricate themselves

---

the words of Yohanan ben Zakkai were cast for transmission to future generations, it is difficult to understand why the form of the transmission was broken here. Second, I find it extraordinary that Gamaliel II is included in such a discussion, for this would represent the only source in which he so appears. The Yalkut's reading is useless, for it implies that a conversation was held between Simeon ben Gamaliel I, Gamaliel II his son, and Yohanan ben Zakkai *after* the destruction, which is contrary to all that is known and suspected on Simeon's fate. The Yalkut apparently fuses the TB beraita and the Pesikta tradition, but I do not know how Simeon ben Gamaliel was included.

It seems to me that one will best understand the source in the following pattern, as I have presented it in the text:

I. The question of Yohanan ben Zakkai (as in the TB).
II. The answer of Eliezer ben Hyrkanos ”   ”   ”
III. The answer of Joshua ben Hananiah ”   ”   ”
IV. The answer of Eleazar ben Arakh (as in the Pesikta).
V. Yohanan's praise for Eleazar.
VI. The tradition, added later, of Yohanan's earlier midrash on the verse.

I see no way to include Eliezer the Modite, who appears in a similar relationship to Gamaliel II elsewhere, nor Nehuniah ben HaKaneh, nor, certainly, Simeon ben Gamaliel I. As Bacher suggests, the second discussion on the verse may have been transmitted in confusion with the first; I cannot, however, agree with him that Gamaliel II was included in the first discussion, or that Yohanan praised Nehuniah ben HaKaneh in preference to Eleazar ben Arakh. If this reconstruction is accepted then the words of Eleazar as preserved in the Pesikta actually do *differ* substantially from both those of Eliezer and those of Joshua, and I do not have deal with an impossibly close relationship between the serveral opinions, which would otherwise lead one to wonder why Yohanan should have so selected Eleazar's opinion for praise. Thus I reconstruct the source from the following elements:

Paragraph I, II, III	–	TB Baba Batra
Paragraph IV	–	Pesikta
Paragraph V	–	TB Baba Batra.

I do not make use of any other material in TB Baba Batra, or in the Pesikta, or, of course, in the Yalkut. If my reconstruction is correct, then the likelihood that the Eleazar ben Arakh left Yohanan after the exodus from Jerusalem seems most remote (assuming that this source, in whatever recension, truly represents a change in Yohanan's midrash of the verse, as I believe it does). It seems to me, therefore, that Eleazar came to Yavneh, remained with Yohanan until Yohanan's death, and then went to Emmaus, as has always been the common assumption; and not that he went to Emmaus in protest against Yohanan's pacifist policy, as Allon suggests. Cf. ch. 8 for further discussion of Allon's thesis.

[1] Cf. L. Ginzberg, "The Attitude of the Synagogue," 134, who says, "The apocalyptics cut loose from life, the rabbis were the guardians and leaders of a nation."

from the consequences of their sins; second, to give new emphasis to the means of service to the creator which had survived the devastated sanctuary, and, finally, to offer a comprehensive program for the religious life which was capable of meeting any vicissitude in Israel's history. By concentrating on the immediate problems of the day, Yohanan showed how to transcend history itself, not through eschatological vision, but through concrete actions in the workaday world.

His message of comfort was preserved in the following story:
> "Because thou didst not serve the Lord thy God with joyfulness and gladness of heart, by reason of the abundance of all things, therefore thou shalt serve thine enemies whom the Lord will send against thee in hunger and thirst, in nakedness and in want of all things..." (Deut. 28.47). Once Rabban Yohanan ben Zakkai was going up to Emmaus in Judea, and he saw a girl who was picking barley-corn out of the excrement of a horse. Said Rabban Yohanan ben Zakkai to his disciples, What is this girl? They said to him, She is a Jewish girl. And to whom does the horse belong? To an Arabian horseman, the disciples answered him. Then said Rabban Yohanan ben Zakkai to his disciples, All my life I have been reading this verse, and I have not until now realized its full meaning, "If you will not know, O fairest among women, follow in the tracks of the flock, and pasture your kids beside the shepherds' tents." (Song of Songs 1.8). You were unwilling to be subject to God, behold now you are subjected to the most inferior of nations, the Arabs. You were unwilling to pay the head-tax to God, a beka a head (Ex. 38.26). Now you are paying a head-tax of fifteen shekels under a government of your enemies. You were unwilling to repair the roads and streets leading up to the Temple, now you have to keep in repair the posts and stations on the road to the imperial cities. And thus it says, "Because thou dist not serve..." Because thou didst not serve the Lord thy God with love, therefore thou shalt serve thine enemy with hatred. Because thou didst not serve the Lord thy God when thou hadst plenty, therefore thou shalt servce thine enemy in hunger and thirst. Because thou didst not serve the Lord thy God when thou wast well clothed, therefore thou shalt serve thine enemy in nakedness. Because thou didst not serve the Lord thy God by reason of the abundance of all things, therefore shalt thou serve thine enemy in want of all things...[1]

---

[1] Mekilta de R. Ishmael, Bahodesh, 1; Friedman ed. 61; Lauterbach ed. and trans. II, 193-4. Cf. also TB Ketuvot 66b, TP Ketuvot 5.11, Tosefta Ketuvot ch. 5, Pesikta Rabbati ch. Nahamu; Sifre Deut. 305; Mekilta Yitro; Midrash HaGadol Deut., section Ki Tavo, ad. loc.; Lam. R. 1.16, ARNa ch. 17, Schechter 33a; Yalkut Shimoni II, 982. Cf. also Gaster, Folklore, 135, and note on p. 213. Cf. also TB Gittin 57a,

> "Said Rabban Yohanan ben Zakkai about her (apparently in context, Martha daughter of Roethus, who died of hunger.) The woman, the most tender among thee, and the most delicate, who hath never adventured to set the sole of her feet upon the ground" (Deut. 28.56).

Continued note from page 139.

In the other sources, particularly ARNa ch. 17, the woman is identified with the daughter of Nakdimon ben Gorion, as follows (tr. Goldin 88f):

> "One time as Rabban Yohanan ben Zakkai was walking in the market-place, he saw a girl picking up barley grains from under the feet of Arab cattle. My child, he asked her, who art thou? She did not answer. Again he asked her, My child, who art thou? But she would not answer. Finally she said to him, Wait a moment. She covered herself with her hair, and sat down before him; Master, she said, I am the daughter of Nakdimon ben Gorion. My child, he asked, the wealth of thy father's house – where is it? Master, she replied, is this not how the proverb goes in Jerusalem, Your wealth you will keep if you don't keep it, and some say, if you give alms. And your father-in-law's, where is that wealth? Master, she said, the one went down and dragged the other down with it. Thereupon Rabban Yohanan ben Zakkai said to his disciples, all my life I have read this verse, "If thou know not..." and not understood what it meant and now I come along and learn what the meaning is, that Israel has been surrendered to the meanest of peoples, and not merely to a mean people, but to their cattle dung. Moreover she said to him, Master, do thou remember when thou didst sign my marriage deed? Indeed I do, he answered. By the temple service, he exclaimed to his disciples, I signed this girl's marriage deed, and it read, "A million gold denarii in Tyrian coin." In the prosperous days of the household of this girl's father they did not go from their home to the Temple service unless woolen carpets were laid for them to walk on."

Cf. L. Finkelstein, *Mavo*, 113, who comments on the parallels that the *agada* is based on two events, one concerning Yohanan ben Zakkai, and the other concerning Eleazar the son of Zadok. The most ancient source of the event concerning Yohanan is that of the Mekilta, which I have cited. That concerning Eleazar son of Zadok happened in Acre, and the most ancient source for it is in the TP Ketuvot 5.11, where it is told concerning the daughter of Simon ben Gurion that the sages arranged for her a daily allowance for cosmetics of five hundred dinarii, and she was only awaiting Levirite marriage, and even so, she cursed them and said to them, "May you give thus to your own daughters." Upon this, Eleazar son of Zadok said, "May I see comfort if I did not see her tied by her hair to the tail of a horse in Acre, and I said concerning her this verse, The woman, the most tender among the..." In the TB, the story was influenced by that concerning Yohanan ben Zakkai. According to the parallel there, the event happened to Martha daughter of Boethus, and of this incident, Eleazar commented, "...if I did not see her gathering barley-corn from between the legs of the horses in Acre, and I said concerning her this verse, "The most tender among thee," and "If thou dost not know..." Certainly the Tanna of ARNa, as cited above, changed the basic style of the incident. In the Tosefta Ketuvot 5, the incident is brought in the second recension, and there the name of the woman is already changed to the daughter of Nakdimon. In the TB Ketuvot 67a, the incident is presented in the language of the Tosefta. The Tanna of ARNa united the two incidents, and identified the girl whom Yohanan ben Zakkai saw (who is not mentioned in the primary source that the Mekilta presents) with the daughter of Nakdimon, and he further ornamented the story; in this form, the story is brought in Sifre Deut. 305, TB Ketuvot 66b. Compare also the remarks of Bacher, *Agadot*, I, i, 22, n. 2, who thinks, also, that the Mekilta was the primary source and that in the Sifre and the TB and ARN ch. 17 representations, it is joined to the meeting of Eleazar son of Zadok with another woman, who was very rich, the daughter of Nakdimon, concerning whom the verse in Song of Songs 1.8 was applied.

In a second recension, Yohanan was reported thereupon to have exclaimed:

> Happy are you, O children of Israel! When you obey the will of God, then no nation or race can rule over you! But when you do not obey the will of God, you are handed over into the hands of every low-born people, and not only into the power of the people, but even into the power of the cattle of that low-born people.[1]

This incident epitomized Yohanan's viewpoint on the disaster. One does not find the idea that comfort is to be found because in a little while, suffering will cease. Yohanan called on the people to achieve a better fortune through their own effort. Like Josephus, he taught that Israel can be happy if they submit to God and to the Romans, and follow the laws laid down by both. Both conceive of the fulfilment of Jewish law as interpreted by the Pharisees as the good life in this world and assurance of a portion in the next. (In later years Akiba became impatient with the results of Yohanan's limited program, and allowed his followers to dare to rebel once again. This act represented a failure of the courage to wait. Because the people had grown impatient with their own capacities, they looked to God for immediate deliverance. The consequence was a new revolution, led by Bar Koseba, whom Akiba said was the Messiah. Akiba was rebuked,

> Grass will grow on your cheeks, Akiba ben Joseph, and the messiah will not have appeared.[2]

In the meantime, however, the nation was plunged once again into revolution, and met a greater disaster than before.)

Yohanan had taught, in commenting on the words Kohelet "Let your garments be always white, and let not oil be lacking on your head" (Koh. 9.8), that Jews should clothe themselves in Torah, commandments, and acts of kindness. Each of these categories represented a fundamental concern of the pious man: through the study of Torah, man learned what the will of God for him was; through doing the commandments, he carried out that will; and through acts of lovingkindness, he honored God who gave the Torah. These

---

[1] TB Ketuvot 66b. Since the TB beraita clearly distinguishes between the two incidents, I think it is legitimate to assume that the added quotation may have been said by Yohanan, although it does not appear in any of the parallels. The question was raised in a later generation, what had been the particular sin of the girl in question. It was postulated that her father's acts of charity had not been done disinterestedly.

[2] Cf. TP Taanit 4.7, Lam. R. 2.2. Cf. also Finkelstein, *Akiba*, 219-20, 269.

elements were probably a transformation of the teachings of Simeon the Righteous two centuries earlier:

> On three things the Age stands, on the Torah, on the Temple service, and on acts of piety.[1]

By Torah, Simeon had meant, the books of the Torah; by the Temple service, the sacrificial cult in Jerusalem; by acts of piety, he meant acts of loyalty and obedience to God.[2] Yohanan survived the end of the Temple; he came at the end of a long struggle for the authenticity and legitimacy of the Torah, both written and oral, which had been interpreted by the Pharisees; and acts of obedience to God seemed to him to comprehend a broader obligation than piety. He therefore infused these categories with a new content.[3] It was told;

> Once as Rabban Yohanan ben Zakkai was coming out of Jerusalem, Rabbi Joshua followed after him, and beheld the Temple in ruins. Woe unto us, Rabbi Joshua cried, that this place, the place where the iniquities of Israel were atoned for, is laid waste. My son, Rabban Yohanan said to him, be not grieved. We have another atonement as effective as this, and what is it? It is acts of lovingkindness, as it is said, "For I desire mercy and not sacrifice" (Hos. 6.6).[4]

Yohanan's treatment of the verse, "For I desire mercy and not sacrifice" was consistent with the contemporary hermeneutic. In biblical times, *hesed* had meant (in part) the mutual liability of those who

---

[1] Avot 1.2.

[2] J. Goldin, "The Three Pillars of Simeon the Righteous," *PAAJR*, XXVII, 43-56. Cf. in particular 50-51: "What he gives us... therefore is three purely religious pillars. The *olam* (age) rests on the books of the Torah, the Temple cult, and the acts of *pietas*."

[3] *Ibid.*, pp. 50-51:

> "Now... we are able truly to appreciate the grandeur of Rabban Johanan ben Zakkai's achievement. We read in Abot de Rabbi Natan that when Rabban Johanan was finally received by Vespasian, and the conqueror allowed the Sage to make a request. Rabban Johanan said, I ask of you only Jabneh, where I might go, and teach my students, and arrange prayer, and do all the mitzvot. Here are the three pillars of Simeon the Righteous brought to reenforcement ... Johanan made of Ha-Torah, the pillar of studying and teaching Torah... Out of Temple worship... he now redefined in terms of prayer... Out of gemilut hasadim, acts of pietas,... he would underscore those acts which man carries out in an exemplary relation with his fellow man. And gemilut hasadim thus become the acts of lovingkindness as typical of those who are known as merciful men sons of merciful men."

Goldin feels that the teachings of Eliezer, Joshua, and Yosi, in Avot 2.10 f. (cf. chap. 4) are based on Yohanan's reinterpretation. While I certainly agree, I think the program of Torah, commandments, and good deeds may have been articulated before the destruction, and that one need not date these discussions in Yavneh; in fact, one cannot date them with any certainty at all.

[4] ARNa ch. 4, Schechter 11a, Goldin 34. Cf. ARNb ch. 7, Schechter 11b.

are friends and relatives, master and servant,[1] or any relationship of joint responsibility. In relationship to God, *hesed* meant acts in conformity with the covenant between man and God. Thus Hosea meant that God demanded loyal adherence to his covenant, rather than sacrifice.[2] By Yohanan's time, however, the word had acquired a different connotation. It meant mercy, or an act of compassion and lovingkindness.[3] Thus Jesus of Nazareth had understood the verse:

> Those who are well have no need of a physician, but those who are sick. Go and learn what this means, I desire *mercy* (eleon) and not sacrifice. For I came not to call the righteous, but sinners (Matt. 9.13).[4]

---

[1] Cf. L. Koehler and W. Baumgartner, *Lexicon in Veteris Testamenti Libros* (Leiden, 1953), s. v. p. 318. Cf. also J. Gur, *Milon Ivri* (Tel Aviv, 1957), 217, who emphasizes the quality of *grace: Hesed* is something done not out of obligation but out of love. Also A. Even-Shoshan, *Milon Hadash* (Tel Aviv, 1949), II, s.v.; Aruk, III, 453; J. Levy, *Neuhebraischer Wörterbuch* (Leipzig, 1876), I, 86; B. Krupnick and A. M. Silberman, *Milon Shimushi LaTalmud* (London, 1927), s.v.; C. F. Keil, *Biblischer Commentar über die Zwölf Kleinen Propheten* (Leipzig, 1866), 72, "Hesed ist die in Gerechtigkeit sich betätigende Nächstenliebe, welche in der Erkentnis Gottes wurzelt, daher hier, wie 4.1, mit Daat Elohim verbunden." W. R. Harper, *Amos and Hosea* (New York, 1910, in *International Critical Commentary on the Holy Scriptures of the Old and New Testaments*, vol. XXIII), 286-7. Cf. also F. Brown, S. R. Driver, and C. A. Briggs, *A Hebrew and English Lexicon of the Old Testament* (Oxford, 1955), 338-9. Cf. especially, N. Glueck, *Das Wort Hesed in Alttestamentlichen Sprachgebrauche als menschliche Verhaltungsweise in profaner und religiöser Bedeutung* (Jena, 1927), cited by Köhler-Baumgartner also.

[2] Harper, Amos and Hosea, 286-7. Cf. also J. Pedersen, *Israel, Its Life and Culture* (Copenhagen, 1953, 4 vols.), IV, 535-544. Pedersen translates *hesed* to mean, constancy in love (loyal love). Cf. p. 540-1, "Hesedh is the feeling of fellowship between the Israelites themselves and between them and their God... Right conduct meant a knowledge of God, because it was a subordination to Yahwehs will... nothing can affect the covenant in a similar way; this puts the cult in the second place..."

[3] On *hesed*, cf. N. N. Glatzer, *Geschichte der Talmudische Zeit* (Berlin, 1937), 21, who points out (as I shall below) that hesed meant bringing harmony between men and nations. Cf. also Javitz, *Toldot*, VI, 6 f., who suggests that ARNa ch. 4 continues in the words of Yohanan as follows, "For thus we find concerning Daniel... that he was engaged in acts of lovingkindness all his days..." Cf. Goldin 34-5, however, who holds that this was a separate comment based on Yohanan's teaching, but not a part of it. Halevi, *Dorot*, I, v, 106-7, emphasizes that this was a consolation and surrogate for the cult, and neither criticism of it nor an effort to denigrate its former, and future importance; I agree entirely with Halevi's judgment. Cf. also Finkelstein, *Mavo*, 133, for an examination of the several readings of ARNa. Cf. also, Goldin, "Three Pillars," 54-5.

[4] Cf. also Matthew 12.7, I Timothy 1.15. Cf. W. C. Allen, *The Gospel according to S. Matthew* (New York, 1907, I.C.C. XXVI), 91-2. The NT quotation follows closely the Septuagintal translation, which is *Dioto eleos thelo e phusian;* eleos means pity, mercy, or compassion (cf. Lidell & Scott, *Lexicon*, s. v.); but hesed is translated variously in the LXX, sometimes by dikaos or agape, cf. F. E. Hatch and H. A. Redpath, *Concordance to the Septuagint* (Graz, 1954), I, 451.

Later rabbinic sources likewise preserved this connotation in commenting on the verse.[1] The verse was understood by Clement of Alexandria in an exegesis strikingly similar to Yohanan's:

> This place which seemed chosen for a time, often harassed as it had been by hostile invasions and plunderings, was at last to be wholly destroyed. And in order to impress this upon them even before the coming of the true prophet, who was to reject at once the sacrifices and the place, it was often plundered by enemies and burnt with fire, and the people carried into captivity among foreign nations, and then brought back when they betook themselves to the mercy of God; that by these things they might be taught that a people who offer sacrifices are driven away and delivered up into the hands of the enemy, but they who do mercy and righteousness are without sacrifices freed from captivity and restored to their native land...[2]

Yohanan likewise thought that through *hesed* the Jews might make atonement, and that the sacrifices now demanded of them were love and mercy. His choice of the Scripture in Hosea thus emphasized the ethical element of his earlier trilogy (study of Torah, doing the commandments, and acts of lovingkindness), and like Clement, he emphasized the primacy of *hesed* itself in the redemptive process: just as the Jews needed a redemptive act of compassion from God, so they must act compassionately in order to make themselves worthy of it.

This primary emphasis on personal moral quality, rather than specific external action, either ritual or legal, is in accordance with the increasing emphasis on the inner aspect of religion which was characteristic of this period. One recalls the strikingly similar emphasis of Paul in his letter to the Corinthians (I Corinthians 13), that no external manifestations of religion will take the place of *agape*, which one might

---

[1] Cf. Midrash on Psalms, 9.3, 89.1; Pirke de Rabbi Eliezer 12.16; Eliahu Rabbah ch. 6; Yalkut II, 321, 522, 840. For the use of *hesed* in rabbinic sources, cf. Levy, cited above; *Aruk*, cited above; H. J. Kassovsky, *Ozar Lashon HaMishnah* (Jerusalem, 1957), II, 717, s.v. and Mishnah Shavuot 4.13; *Ozar Lashon HaTosefta* (Jerusalem 1942), III, s. v., cf. Tosefta Peah 4.21, Sanhedrin 13.3. Neither Philo nor Josephus comment on Hosea 6.6.

[2] *The Recognitions of Clement*, ch. 37, in A. Roberts and J. Donaldson, eds., *Tatian Theophilus and the Clementine Recognitions* (Edinburgh, 1867, *The Antenicene Christian-Library*, III, p. 163). It seems to me that this is precisely the meaning that Yohanan attached to the verse. Cf. also Tertullian, *Against Marcion*, Roberts and Donaldson, *Antenicene Library*, VII, 86; Pope Anterus, *Antenicene Library* (XI, p. 243); *Treatises of Cyprian, Testimonies: Of the Benefit of Good Works and Mercy*, XIII, p. 138; Tertullian, *On Repentance*, ch. 8 (XI, i, 272); *On Modesty* (XI, iii, 60); Clement of Alexandria, *Who is the Rich Man that Shall Be Saved*, ch. 39 (XXII, 212); also Augustine, City of God, Book X, ch. 5 *(Library of Nicene and Post-Nicene Fathers*, Grand Rapids, 1956, II, 183), "All the divine ordinances therefore which

translate with the Hebrew *hesed* as Yohanan, Jesus, and other contemporaries understood the word. The act of compassionate fellowship which was the foundation of true religion, in Yohanan's opinion, became the central focus of his consoling message for the new and troubled age.

Thus Yohanan shared the common sense of grief, and taught, like others, that the sins of the nation had brought the disaster; but, he added, its virtues might bring redemption. He differed from others in rejecting the eschatological focus of consolation, advancing, rather, the idea of *hesed*, a means by which Jews might change their own hearts. He provided an interim ethic, by which the people might live while they awaited the coming redemption. If the earlier age had stood on the books of the Torah, the Temple rites, and acts of piety, the new age would endure on the foundation of studying the Torah, doing the commandments, and, especially, performing acts of compassion, embodying that very quality which the brutality of war must have accentuated, paradoxically, in his thinking, man's capacity to act compassionately to his fellow-man.

The consequence of Yonanan's lesson may have been embodied in a later encounter between Joshua and a group of apocalyptists. One recalls that II Baruch had lamented:

> Blessed is he who was not born, or he who having been born has died,
> But as for us who live, woe unto us. because we see the
> afflictions of Zion, and what has befallen Jerusalem...
> Ye husbandmen, sow not again,
> And earth, wherefore givest thou thy harvest fruits,
> Keep within thee the sweets of thy sustenance.
> And thou, vine, why further dost thou give thy wine
> For an offering will not again be made therefrom in Zion,
> Nor will first-fruits again be offered.
> And do ye, O heavens, withhold your dew,
> And open not the treasuries of rain;
> And do you, sun, withhold the light of thy rays,
> And you moon, extinguish the multitude of thy light,
> For why should light rise again
> Where the light of Zion is darkened.

---

we read concerning the sacrifices in the service of the tabernacle or the Temple refer to the love of God and of neighbor..." Cf. also City of God, Book XX, ch. 24. Also St. Chrysostom, *Homilies on Timothy*, VI (Nicene Fathers, XIII, 498), "God made heaven and earth and the sea – great works are these... but by none of these has he so powerfully attracted human nature to himself as by mercy and the love of mankind."

Would that thou hadst ears, O earth,
And that thou hadst a heart, O dust,
That ye might go and announce in Sheol,
And say to the dead,
Blessed are ye more than we who live.

(II Baruch, 10.6-7, 9-12, 11.6-7.)

Yohanan's student Joshua apparently met such people, for it was reported:

When the Temple was destroyed, ascetics multiplied in Israel, who would not eat flesh nor drink wine. Rabbi Joshua dealt with them. He said to them, My children, On what account do you not eat flesh and drink wine? They said to him, Shall we eat meat, from which they used to offer a sacrifice on the altar – and now it is no more? And shall we drink wine, which was poured out on the altar, and now is no more? He said to them, If so, we ought not to eat bread, for there are no meal offerings any more. Perhaps we ought not to drink water, for the water-offerings are not brought any more. They were silent. He said to them, My children, come and I shall teach you: not to mourn at all is impossible for the evil decree has already come upon us. But to mourn too much is also impossible, for one may not promulgate a decree on the community unless most of the community can endure it... But thus have the sages taught, A man plasters his house with plaster, but leaves a little piece untouched. A man prepares all the needs of the meal, but leaves out some morsel. A woman prepares all her cosmetics, but leaves off some small item...[1]

---

[1] TB Baba Batra 60b. For further comment on this incident, cf. Gershon D. Cohen, "Zion in Rabbinic Literature," in Abraham Halkin, editor, *Zion in Jewish Literature* (N. Y. 1961), p. 52-54, and p. 63, notes 63-66, as well as the sources cited by Professor Cohen, in particular, Adolph Buechler, *Die Priester und der Cultus in Letzten Jahrzehnt des Jerusalemischen Tempels* (Vienna 1895) p. 22, and the article "Abele Ziyyon", *Encyclopedia Hebraica*, I, p. 167.

CHAPTER EIGHT

TALL PILLAR

If Israel might enjoy better fortune by faithfulness to God's will, then Yohanan ben Zakkai's task at Yavneh was to show how to do his will with neither sanctuary, nor holy city, nor (at the outset) national tribunal. The most pressing problems were liturgical, for the observance of holy days and festivals were commemorated in the sacrificial cult. Yohanan therefore decreed a series of specific modifications of law necessitated by the disaster. Somewhat later, he and his successors came to define the authority of the academy which issued these ordinances. Apparently they claimed the academy held the authority formerly exerted by the Sanhedrin in Jerusalem,[1] for Yavneh was regarded as a high court capable of issuing such authoritative enactments. Yohanan's method was that of Hillel, Gamaliel I, and Simeon ben Gamaliel before him: to issue decrees on specific legal problems. His ordinances met some opposition, particularly from the priests, but in the main, they came to be accepted.[2] The opposing parties had been weakened by the war. The Pharisees, in the persons of Yohanan and his disciples and succeeding colleagues at Yavneh, were eventually able to attain national recognition. The other parties were doubtless represented among the people, but from the destruction onward, the issues of Israel's religious life were debated in terms of the Pharisaic formulation of Judaism.

The Jewish-Christians, for example, had escaped to Pella, in Transjordan, and the war had marked the beginning of their separation from Jewry.[3] The Herodians retired to their distant lands, to rule mainly gentile populations.[4] The Essene communes were devastated. Bereft of their separate communities, the surviving Essenes, if any, must have pursued their austere discipline with difficulty, and trans-

---

[1] J. Goldin, "The Period of the Talmud," in L. Finkelstein, ed., *The Jews, Their History, Culture, and Religion* (New York, 1949), I, 147. Compare, however, G. Cohen, "The Talmudic Age," 160-1. Cf. also H. Graetz, History, II, 333; Javitz, *Toldot*, VI, 1 f.

[2] Cf. G. Allon, "The Presidency of Rabban Yohanan ben Zakkai at Yavneh," *Mehkarim*, I, 254-273, which I shall discuss below. Cf. also G. Cohen, "Age," 161.

[3] On the separation of the Jewish Christians, cf. ch. 6.

[4] On the subsequent history of the Herodians, cf. Schuerer, *History*, I, ii, 191-206; A. H. M. Jones, *Herods of Judaea* (Oxford, 1938), 258-61; S. Perowne, *The Later Herods* (Nashville, 1959), 187-192.

mitted it, if at all, with diminishing success.[1] The Sadducees suffered
both from the present inadequacy of their doctrine and from their
social position. They could cope only awkwardly with the problems
posed by the destruction. One may speculate that the Sadducees could
not provide adequate answers to help the people meet the disaster.
They could not promise retribution or recompense in the world to
come. Israel no longer worshipped at the Temple, but the Sadducees,
for whom the sacrificial system had been so central, had no bastion
prepared for a retreat. They had no temporary surrogate to receive
the piety once lavished on the altar. Their view of law likewise must
have rendered it almost impossible to legislate for the new era. They
had denied the authority of oral tradition, and held that interpretation
was to be settled by *ad hoc* decisions of the court of the High Priest. The
end of the High Priestly authority therefore meant the end of their
supreme court, and of any authority able to legislate or to reinterpret
the law. Thus, for the Sadducees, the authority to adapt the law to
rapidly changing needs had disappeared. Furthermore, the Sadducees,
many of whom were upper-class priests and wealthy land-owners in
the Judean region, lost considerable wealth in the war and concomitant
social upheavals. Hence while remnants of the Sadducees did survive
the war, the policies and attitudes fostered by their party, even when
relevant and congruent to the new dilemmas, received less attention
than when, earlier, they had been advanced by the leading men of
Jerusalem.[2]

The Pharisees, on the contrary, had several particular advantages.
First of all, they advanced, as we have seen, a comprehensive program
for the religious life temporarily to replace the sacrificial system.
Second, their doctrines of providence, life after death, retribution, and
recompense for suffering offered meaningful consolation to men who
lived daily with the ancient perplexity of monotheism: why do good men
meet evil days? Third, their hermeneutical principles permitted them to
give to ancient laws the broader construction which, under changing
circumstances, was essential for the practical administration of the
public polity. Fourth, they enjoyed the confidence of the Romans, as
we have seen, on account of the loyalism of some of their sages; and
they had the articulate support of Josephus to advocate their cause in

---

[1] On the Essenes, cf. Milik, *Ten Years of Discovery*, 94-7.
[2] On the Sadducees after the war, cf. B. Z. Bokser, *Pharisaic Judaism in Transition*
(New York, 1935), 1-6. We know almost nothing about the other groups after
the war, however, and this judgment is based on conjecture.

Rome. Fifth, they also had the confidence of large parts of the nation, and the ambivalence of their war-policy, with Simeon taking a leading part in the revolutionary coalition and Yohanan among the pacifists, left them with the possibility to claim extraordinary prescience, whatever the war's outcome. Sixth, the Pharisees now vigorously pressed their earlier claims to represent the one legitimate authority in, and interpretation of, Judaism. In the absence of organized opposition from other groups, the hour was particularly opportune to press such a claim, and as it turned out, the Romans accepted it. Thus in time the Pharisees transformed their status. Earlier they had been a sectarian religious group among several competing parties, and now began the process by which they eventually came to constitute "normative Judaism."[1] Thus as the decades passed, the larger part of the Jewish people came to embody what Pharisaism had conceived as a "holy congregation," that is, a community whose essential definition and foundation was the Mosaic faith as taught by the Pharisaic sages. Finally, the Pharisees had the benefit of Yohanan ben Zakkai's leadership, and the advantage of the central institution at Yavneh which began to take shape during his last years. If Yohanan began the successful effort to bring the whole people to recognize the Pharisaic academy as legitimate successor and heir to the Sanhedrin's authority, the reason was that in his judgment, he and his colleagues and disciples had the obligation and right to reconstitute the social and religious order.[2] Asserting this right, they carried on the prophetic teaching that Israel was to be more than an ethnic and cultural entity, but was to form rather a "kingdom of priests and a holy people," whose constitution was revelation and whose citizenship imposed ethical and religious obligations.[3]

---

[1] Perhaps Moore's term is less felicitous historically than "regnant" or "official" Judaism, as the varieties of Judaism even in later centuries render it difficult indeed to determine what, if anything, was widely "normative".

[2] L. Finkelstein, *Perushim ve-Anshe Kenesset HaGedolah* [Pharisees and Men of the Great Assembly] (New York, 1950), 38.

[3] Bokser, *Pharisaic Judaism*, 3-6; G. Cohen, "Talmudic Age," 161, "...the priesthood and sacrifices had become... a vestigial relic, necessary only because the Torah prescribed them. With the Temple in abeyance, the Jewish population of the Holy Land itself became a quasi-Diaspora community. Who therefore could logically assume the new leadership if not the apprentices and protagonists of lay religion, of synagogal community, the rabbis." Cf. also M. Weber, *Ancient Judaism* (Glencoe, 1952; tr. H. Gerth and D. Martindale), 385-404. Weber says that the community now became the bearer of the religion, "this was no longer the function of a hereditary charisma of priests and Levites..." (pp. 387-8). Cf. also E. Kaufman, *Golah VeNekhar* [Exile and Alienation] (Tel Aviv, 1930), I, 208-256, especially 208-226; and 433-455.

The possibility of concentrating attention on liturgical and religious issues was the consequence of the relatively fortunate situation of most of the land and of large parts of the people of Israel.[1] Although Jerusalem was mostly in ruins, many major cities survived the war intact. According to Josephus, up to 1,500,000 men, women, and children perished or were enslaved on account of the rebellion, and although there is reason to consider this figure exaggerated, certainly large numbers were killed, or enslaved.[2] Several limited areas of the land, however, had born the brunt of the losses, as follows: in Jordan, Gamala; in the Galilee, the northern strip of the Kinneret (Sea of Galilee), and the areas around Jotapata including the town, and around Sepphoris but not including the city; Beth Shean and isolated areas in the Emek; in the Sharon, the region around Garvata; in the Plain, the region between Antipatris and the sea, including Yaffo (Jaffa) and southward to Lud (Lydda); in the Judean hills, the territories around Jericho, Jerusalem, and Bet Netufah, north of Hevron, but not including Hevron.[3] Even in these territories, however, many of the inhabitants fled before the fighting, and survived the war. The economy of the land suffered considerably, and famine, and probably also a depression, followed the reconquest. Many families certainly lost their fortunes. The areas ravaged by the war, mainly agricultural lands, had

---

[1] This is indicated by the contrast between the *takkanot* (ordinances) of Yohanan ben Zakkai at Yavneh, and those of the synod at Usha, held after the collapse of the Bar Kokhba revolt. The war of 132-5 led to the destruction of the economic and social order. Cf. S. Krauss, "Synod of Usha," *JE*, XI, 645-6. The synod took place at about 140 C.E., after the Hadrianic persecutions; as at Yavneh, some ritual and calendrical questions were discussed, but mainly the ordinances dealt with matters of family law, for example, parents must care for their children so long as they are minors; if a parent deeded his property to his sons during his lifetime, the sons must support their parents from the estate; the father must be patient in teaching his sons until they are twelve years of age, then he may send them out into the world, etc. None of the ordinances of Yavneh reflect such conditions. On the Usha enactments, cf. also TB Ketuvot 49b-50a, Frankel, *Mishnah*, 179. On the date of the Usha enactments, see especially Mantel, *Studies in the History of the Sanhedrin* p. 166-168, and notes 137-146.

[2] Cf. Josephus, War, VI.9.3 (420). Also G. Allon, *Toldot*, I, 34-5. A great many prisoners were ransomed and freed. Cf. also Graetz, *History*, II, 311; G. Cohen, "Talmudic Age," 161, "The overwhelming majority of the country was still Jewish." Cf. also J. Juster, *Les Juifs dans L'Empire Romain* (Paris, 1914, 2 vols.), I, 209 f.

[3] Cf. S. Yeivin, *Milhemet Bar Kokhba* [The War of Bar Kokhba] (Jerusalem, 1952), 1-49, especially map, p. 24. Cf. also M. Avi-Yonah, *Georgraphia Historit shel Erez Yisrael* [Historical Geography of the land of Israel] (Jerusalem, 1951), 67-73; and A. Buechler, *The Economic Conditions of Judea after the Destruction of the Second Temple* (London, 1912), *pass*.

to be restored to productivity but while trees and vineyards had suffered, the fields had been refreshed by lying fallow. Still, large territories
had not suffered at all, and the economy of the land sustained a greater
war sixty-five years later, certainly an indication that it had substantially survived the earlier war with minimal damage. The Romans,
moreover, applied and collected heavy taxes, a second indication that
the economy retained substantial strength, and although there were
great changes in the pattern of land tenure, as Jewish properties were
expropriated or confiscated for taxes,[1] the former Jewish-held territories remained in Jewish hands for the most part, except in the immediate vicinity of Jerusalem.

The country was now administered by a series of legates, including
Sextus Vettulenus, commander of the Tenth Legion at Jerusalem, in
70-71; Lucilius Bassus, 71-72, who reduced the final pockets of re-
sistance; L. Flacius Silva, 72-80; M. Salvidenus, 80-86; and Cn. Pom-
peius Longinus, 86. Except for the few details on military operations,
however, nothing is known about these governors of Judea.[2] One
fact is absolutely certain concerning their administration, however:
they did not institute systematic religious persecutions.[3] In war time,
the Roman policy of tolerance may have been suspended; but afterward, only isolated incidents, such as the effort at Antioch to force
Jews to desecrate the Sabbath, disturbed the free exercise of Judaism.
The Romans did impose a *Fiscus Judaicus*, a head tax to be paid to Rome

---

[1] On the taxes imposed after the reconquest, cf. especially G. Allon, *Toldot*, I,
36-42. Cf. also S. Krauss, *Paras ve Romi*, 260-8; Yeivin, *Milhemet Bar Kokhba*, 32-36.

[2] Paulus de Rohoen, *De Palaestina et Arabia Provinciis Romanis* (Berlin, 1885),
33 f. Cf. also Schuerer, *History*, I, ii, 258-9. Sextus Vettulenus Cerialis commanded
the Fifth Legion at the siege and remained as commander of the Garrison troops
(the Tenth Legion). Lucilius Bassus took Herodium and Machaerus in the south,
L. Flavius Silvus conquered Masada. I shall consider the alleged conversation of
Yohanan with a Roman officer below. Also cf. AviYonah, *Geographia*, 67-73.

[3] Cf. Abel, Histoire, II, 50-2; the Government apparently pursued anyone who
claimed Davidic descent, and Gamaliel II met some difficulty on this account.
But contrast the policy enunciated by Titus at Antioch (Josephus, *War*, VII, 5.2
(109 f): "Their own country... has been destroyed, and no other place would
receive them." He therefore confirmed the Jewish rights as they had been. Compare Allon, *Toldot*, I, 43-6. Cf. however the more widely accepted opinion of J.
Juster, *Les Juifs*, I, 224, which I have followed. Most of the examples of persecution
that Allon cites happened during or immediately after the war. Cf. also G. Cohen,
"Talmudic Age," 163, "The Jewish community owed its survival largely to the
Roman policy of toleration... Rome must candidly be acknowledged to have dealt
with the Jews harshly but not viciously... At no point did it proscribe the Jewish
religion..." Cf. also Baron, *History*, II, 105. In any event, the extant sources contain
no parallel to the atrocity stories told about the years after the Bar kokhba war,
under Hadrian.

rather than, as earlier, to the Temple in Jerusalem, but this tax represented symbolic submission to Rome, not the cessation of Israel's licit existence; and the tax was abrogated before the turn of the century. Flavian religious policy did not, to be sure, encourage Jewish proselytism, but it also did not extend to concerted persecution of Judaism. Jews retained their civil rights, and nothing altered the individual's right to enjoy whatever type of citizenship he had formerly held.[1]

The social structure was considerably altered, however, for some men profited from the war to rise in social standing. Thus a class of Jews arose,[2] who through acquisition of large properties were able to assume authority in villages and towns throughout the land.[3] Thus one reads about "lying judges" and men who increased their capital at the expense of the depressed classes. The masses certainly bore the cost of the dislocation of the social economy, and the standard of living declined. Thus Hananiah, prefect of the priests, testified to the general suffering after the war:

> Rabbi Hananiah prefect of the priests says, "And they shall be upon thee for a sign and a wonder and upon thy seed forever. Because thou didst not serve the Lord thy God with joyfulness and with gladness of heart, by reason of the abundance of all things, therefore thou shalt serve thine enemy whom the Lord shall send against thee in hunger and in thirst and in nakedness and in want of all things" (Deut. 28.46). In hunger – for example, when one craves food and cannot find even coarse bread, the heathen nations demand from him white bread and choice meat. And in thirst – for example, at a time when one longs for drink and cannot find even a drop of vinegar or a drop of bitters, the heathen nations demand from him the finest wine in the world. And in nakedness – for example, at a time when one is in need of clothing and cannot find even a wool shirt or a flaxen one, the heathen nations demand from him silks and the best cloth in the world. And in want of all things – that is, in want of light, of knife, of table. Another interpretation: in want of vinegar and salt...[4]

When at Yavneh, therefore, Yohanan ben Zakkai considered the situation in the land, he saw suffering and want, but he could well have discerned that the nation had survived the calamity substantially intact. It could rely upon a damaged, but viable economy. It enjoyed strict,

---

[1] S. Baron, *Social and Religious History*, II, 103, 108.

[2] Allon, *Toldot*, I, 47-9, cf. Mishnah Sotah 9.15; TB Gittin 37a; Tosefta Sotah 14.3-5, cited by Allon. Cf. also S. Baron *Social and Religious History*, II, 104-5.

[3] These men may have represented de facto authorities competing with the Yavneh academy.

[4] ARNa ch. 20, Schechter 71; Goldin 94-5. Compare the midrash on this verse given by Yohanan, ch. 7.

sometimes harsh, but bearable and law abiding government. Its social structure had sustained both loss in population and rearrangements of social status, but, again, survived fundamentally unchanged by the revolutionary upheaval.

Yavneh itself was pleasantly situated; consisting of two parts, a port and an inland borough, the town was a commercial center, in the richest part of the plain.[1] Nearby were Lud, Gimzo, Bene Brak, and Emmaus. The town held a large number of merchants and craftsmen, augmented by the loyalist refugees who settled there after their escape, and who remained, one may assume, having no better place to go after the war. The populace had been spared most of the trials of wartime. It had been a center of loyalism during the latter part of war, and one may assume that the populace did not bear ill-feelings toward the refugee rabbis and disciples. The warm climate of the coast permitted the sages to conduct most of their discussion in the open air, and they could make the small living they needed either through the crafts or in trade, perhaps more easily than in Jerusalem. Yohanan apparently met with his students in a vineyard in the town.[2]

At Yavneh, Yohanan, his disciples and colleagues had the first opportunity to effect their religious program. They had hoped to transform the community of Israel in deed and in fact into the bearer and representation of the faith of Israel as they understood it; this social policy was the logical and natural consequence of their theology, as we have noted, that Israel ought to be a holy people. In Jerusalem, however, they were one among a great number of sects, and they themselves exhibited internal divisions.[3] Now at Yavneh, they exerted what remained of Jewish autonomous authority with very little interference from other Jewish groups, nor did the Romans on the whole, interfere with the operation of their court.[4] Their agents (apostoloi) were able to carry out their missions like the collectors of the Temple

---

[1] Cf. S. Krauss, *Sefer HaYishuv*, 74; W. M. Christie, "The Jammia Period in Jewish History," *Journal of Theological Studies*, XXVI, 347; A. Neubauer, *La Geographie du Talmud* (Paris, 1868), 73 f.; S. Seligsohn, "Jabneh," *JE*, VIII, 18; H. Graetz, *Monatschrift*, II, 108-110; Schurer, *History*, II, 1, 78; M. Stein, "Yavneh and Her Scholars," *Zion*, n. s. III, 118 f.; Avi-Yonah, *Geographia*, 34, 36, 39, 43, 46, 49, 54, 58, 60, 65, 69-9; Finkelstein, *Akiba*, 68.

[2] On the "vineyard at Yavneh" (*Kerem BeYavneh*), cf. Finkelstein, *Akiba*, 68; explained figuratively in Eduyot 2.4, TP Berahot 4.1; Neubauer, *Geographie*. 74-5; S. Krauss, "Die Versammlungsstätten Der Talmudgelehrten," *Festschrift zu Israel Lewy*, ed. M. Brann and J. Elbogen (Breslau, 1911), 21.

[3] M. Smith, "Palestinian Judaism in the First Century," 71-74.

[4] Juster, *Les Juifs*, I, 391 f.

taxes before the destruction.[1] The transition of authority, from the
tribunal in Jerusalem to that at Yavneh, as embodied in the ordinances
which Yohanan issued, took place first though the assumption of the
liturgical authority formerly vested *de facto* in the Temple priests to
determine the proper calendar, second through the later exercise of judicial and legal authority formerly held by the Sanhedrin in Jerusalem,
and third through the performance of certain rites formerly reserved for
the Temple.[2] Yohanan did not, of course, unveil at Yavneh a fully developed institution to replace the earlier court. He did not, so far as we
can determine, legislate on a very wide range of subjects, nor was his
authority accepted everywhere without question. (One may assume,
for example, that the local strong men simply ignored the sages' opinions.) Yohanan enacted certain limited measures, which at first may
have applied only at Yavneh; this was the opinion of Eliezer ben
Hyrkanus on the jurisdiction of one of the ordinances. In the time
of Gamaliel II, the authority of the academy broadened, and in succeeding decades, received widespread acceptance and apparently formal *de jure* recognition from the Roman officials.[3] The broadening
concerns of the later rabbis would seem to illustrate a widening range
of problems brought for their adjudication and growing popular
acceptance of their hegemony. Yohanan ben Zakkai himself left very
few legal traditions, while his students, Eliezer and Joshua, are among
the most important legislators in Jewish history. What accounts for
the difference? Part of the answer may be found in the difference in
authority exerted by his students and their generation. Before the
destruction, when the Pharisees competed for power, the growth of
their particular legal traditions may have been limited to the problems

---

[1] A. Buechler, "Apostoli," *JE*, II, 20-21.

[2] See below.

[3] On the history of the court at Yavneh after the death of Yohanan ben Zakkai,
cf. G. Allon, *Toldot*, I, 114-201. I shall deal only with the period from 70 to the
death of Yohanan. Cf. also for this period and Gamaliel's, Graetz, *History*, II,
325; A. Gulak, *Yesodot HaMishpat HaIvri* [Foundations of Hebrew Jurisprudence],
IV, 23-29; A. Buechler, *Das Synedrion in Jerusalem und das Grosse Beth Din in der
Quaderkammer des Jerusalemischen Temples* (Vienna, 1902), 39, n. 33; 42-6; Weiss,
Dor, II, 33-8; J. Goldin, "Period of the Talmud," 147, "... a series of takkanot
were at once proclaimed to underscore that Jabneh, in everything but sacrificial
offerings, was to enjoy the prerogatives of Jerusalem..."; N. N. Glatzer, *Geschichte*
(Berlin, 1937), 20-22; H. P. Chajes, "Les Juiges Juifs en Palestine de l'an 70 B.C.E.
a l'an 70 C.E.," *REJ*, XXXIX, 39f.; Frankel, *Mishnah*, 66-8; Bruell, *Mavo*, 57-9;
S. Hoenig, *Great Sanhedrin*, 10, 56, 63, 122, 192-3. On the career of Gamaliel II
during Yohanan's hegemony at Yavneh, cf. Hugo Mantel, *Studies in the History
of the Sanhedrin*, p. 34, n. 198. He holds that Yohanan was "nasi in all but name,"
which accords with the sources we shall treat.

that came up before their own tribunal. As we have seen, the Pharisees had their own legal traditions, but the city's municipal courts dealt with the main matters of civil law which Jewish autonomy was competent to govern. (Titus had noted that the Jews were permitted their own law, even after the procuratorial regime was established.) Hence while the Pharisees had and adhered to their own civil law, and advanced their own viewpoint on the common law, the country as a whole was not administered by them or in accordance with their opinions. After the destruction, as the sages successfully, though gradually, expanded the area of their authority, they may have met new and previously unconsidered issues of law. If, for example, they had general principles of law before the destruction, now they must have had to apply them to a multiplicity of specific cases which they were allowed to judge for the first time. The result seems to have been a gradual, but perceptible expansion of the areas of their juridical concern, and consequently an increase in the disputes on individual cases. Yohanan's successors dealt with a wider variety of cases than he did,[1] for at Yavneh he was concerned mainly with religious and ritual questions, while his students Eliezer and Joshua, and his successor Gamaliel II, had to adjudicate many other kinds of legal matters. If this is so, one can explain the multiplicity of disputes between Eliezer and Joshua, both of whom studied with the same master. Yohanan might well have given them general principles on many questions (or, possibly, no opinions at all on some), and they had to apply them. Hence one may partially understand both the alleged conservatism of Eliezer,[2] and the broad legal constructions of Joshua, both disciples of the master. Thus, one may conjecture, the extension of Pharisaic authority led to an expansion of Pharisaic law, formerly applied to a limited sect, and now to an entire nation.

The specific ordinances[3] issued by Yohanan provide insight into the

---

[1] Allon, *Toldot, loc. cit.*

[2] Cf. Bokser, *Pharisaic Judaism in Transition, pass.*

[3] An extensive discussion, from the viewpoint of traditional rabbinic scholarship, of the various ordinances will be found in Bloch, *Institutionem*, II, 211-251. On the shofar, 211-16; the lulav, 216-20; the day of waving, 220-3; receiving testimony, 223-39; on the priestly blessing, 239-41; on the proselyte 241-2; and on the fourth fruits, 245-51. Kaminka proposes another enactment made by Yohanan at this time, cf. *Mehkarim BaTalmud* (Tel Aviv, 1951), 101-7. He cites the Mishnah Yadayim 4.3 (cf. Hagigah 3.2, Midrash Tehilim 25.13), which notes a tradition held by Eliezer from Yohanan ben Zakkai, that the Jews in Moab and Ammon give poor man's tithe in the seventh year. Kaminka thinks (p. 107) that Yohanan taught this matter because it was necessitated by Jewish settlement in the surrounding countries after the destruction. (One notes that Joshua likewise supported this

nature of the court he was founding, and into precisely in what manner
he sought to ground its authority, as well as into how he met the
specific problems of the day. It seems likely that the first issue came
with the advent of the New Year shortly after 70 C.E. (certainly
between 70 and 77), when the holy day happened on the Sabbath.
The outcome was the assertion that the academy at Yavneh possessed
the same prerogative as the Temple in Jerusalem. The source is as
follows:

> If a festival day of the New Year fell on a Sabbath, they might blow
> the shofar in the Holy City, but not in the provinces. After the Temple
> was destroyed, Rabban Yohanan ben Zakkai ordained that they might
> sound the shofar wherever there was a court. Rabbi Eleazer said,
> Rabban Yohanan ben Zakkai ordained it only for Yavneh. They
> replied, It is all one whether it was Yavneh or any other place in which
> there was a court.

A second source adds:

> Once it happened that Rosh Hashanah fell on the Sabbath, and all
> the villagers gathered in Yavneh to hear the shofar. Rabban Yohanan
> ben Zakkai said to the Men of Bathyra, Let us sound the shofar. They
> said to him, Let us discuss (whether it is proper to do so or not). He said
> to them, Let us sound the shofar, and afterward, Let us discuss. After
> they blew the shofar, they said to him, Let us discuss. He said to them,
> Already the horn has been heard in Yavneh, and one does not reply
> after the fact.[1]

While the shofar was blown in synagogue and Temple alike, if the
New Year came on the Sabbath it might only be sounded in the
Temple; now, Yohanan arrogated to the rabbinical courts the prerogative of the Temple. In so doing, he advanced a claim to broad authority for the sages' academies. The men of Bathyra may possibly have
been descendants of the Babylonian Jews whom Herod had settled
in the northeast marches almost a century earlier, from whom the
chiefs of the Sanhedrin had been chosen before Hillel's time, and
during the time of Agrippa I and II likewise. During the war, one
may assume, they were among the loyalists, and settled at Yavneh,
like Yohanan, to escape the war. The doubtless regarded themselves

---

tradition.) This law, Kaminka adds, belongs to the list of those enacted at Yavneh.
Yohanan, however, claimed that this was a tradition he had learned from his
teacher, and there is no reason to assume otherwise, since when he did have an
ancient tradition, he did not hesitate to promulgate his own opinion. There is no
motive, therefore, for him to have claimed authority from the past if he did not
have such a tradition, and hence I do not include this law in discussing the *takkanot*
of Yavneh.

[1] Mishnah Rosh Hashanah 4.1. TB Rosh Hashanah 29b.

as authorities in such matters as this, and were not prepared to accept Yohanan's decision, or the authority by which he made it, but demanded for themselves at least equivalent recognition.[1] Hence the significance of this action in establishing the new institution is twofold. First, it represented a claim to recognition as legitimate surrogate for the sanctuary, and second, it represented a policy to exclude from authority former Temple officials who had come to claim it.[2]

In a second series of enactments, Yohanan met questions on the observance of Tabernacles, on the permission to eat new produce when the *omer* was no longer brought to Jerusalem, on receiving testimony concerning the new moon, on the manner of the priestly blessing, on the offering that a proselyte had formerly to bring to the Temple, and on the disposal of the fourth-year fruits. All these matters

---

[1] This is the viewpoint of G. Allon, *Mehkarim*, I, 263-7. Graetz originally suggested it, and Allon defends his interpretation from the criticism of Halevi and Klausner. Cf. p. 263. Cf. also Finkelstein, *Perushim ve Anshe Kenesset HaGedolah*, 6, 8, 14, 15. Finkelstein holds that the Bathyrites were a Temple Commission on the Observance of the Sabbath. Cf. also S. Hoenig, *Great Sanhedrin*, 38, 107, 141, 199, who interprets the name as "an opposition group in matters of law." Cf. also Finkelstein, *Pharisees*, II, 643-681; n. 6; and Buechler, *Economic Conditions*, 13.

[2] For other interpretations of this and the following ordinances, cf. Kaminka, *Mehkarim*, 107-9 who sees as the governing principle the idea that Jewish religious life did not depend on the altar, Temple, or Holy City; and that Yohanan was trying to free Judaism from connection to one place, and enhance its universal qualities. While Yohanan disputed with the priests, he did not reject the Temple, but prayed for its restoration, and sought only to provide an interim form for certain ritual observances. To say more than this is to be guilty of anachronism. He was seeking equivalent forms for the religious life, not replacements for the sacrifices. I have followed the interpretation of Finkelstein, *Akiba*, 69-70; also Frankel, *Mishnah*, 64; Graetz, *History*, II, 326; Dubnow, *Divrei Yemei Am Olam*, III, 12-13; Javitz, *Toldot*, VI, 8-9. Graetz points out that Yohanan "actually released Judaism from the observance of the rite of burnt-offerings, and rendered it independent..." It was the destruction of the Temple that "released Judaism from the rite of burnt-offerings," and no action of Yohanan ben Zakkai. Cf. also Derenbourg, *Essay*, 302-310; Weiss, Dor, II, 34-39, both of whom agree that the *takkanot* were designed to make Yavneh the heir of the high court in Jerusalem. On this question, cf. also Sifre Deut. 153, TP Sanhedrin 11.4, but there is no way to date these sources. Halevi, *Dorot*, I, v. 60a-64b holds, in the Talmudic tradition, that Yohanan was merely restoring the law to its state before the Temple; he says that enactments were an act of public pedagogy, to teach people what the law had always been. Thus two tendencies become evident, the first of Weiss, Graetz, Javitz, and other historians, who hold that the ordinances represented innovations in law, either (as Kaminka says) to replace the sanctuary, or (Weiss, Graetz, Finkelstein) to endow the new court with the rights and authority of the destroyed sanctuary and the second, of Halevi, who holds that Yohanan ben Zakkai was not an innovator. Allon on the whole follows the viewpoint of Halevi, emphasizing that many of the *takkanot* were not legal innovations at all. Cf. *Toldot*, II, 66-70.

required immediate attention on account of the destruction of the Temple, on which their observance formerly depended. By his ordinances, Yohanan preserved the memory of the cultic ritual without permitting its ancient forms to render obsolete the liturgical life of the people.[1] The record of these ordinances is as follows:

> Before time, the lulav was carried seven days in the Temple, but in the provinces, on one day only. After the Temple was destroyed, Rabban Yohanan ben Zakkai ordained that in the provinces it should be carried seven days in memory of the Temple.[2]
>
> Also he ordained that on the whole day of waving, it should be forbidden [to eat of the new produce]. [Scripture commands (Lev. 23.10), "When you... reap the harvest, you shall bring the sheaf of the first fruits of your harvest to the priest, and he shall wave the sheaf before the Lord... On the morrow after the Sabbath the priest shall wave it, and you shall eat neither bread, nor grain... until this same day, until you have brought the offering of your God."] After the *omer* was offered, the new grain was immediately permitted to be eaten, but for those that lived away from Jerusalem, it was permitted only after midday. After the Temple was destroyed, Rabban Yohanan ben Zakkai ordained that it should be forbidden throughout the day of waving. [In the Temple days, it had been permitted earlier in the day because the people in the provinces knew that the offering would be brought in its proper time.]

Of this action, the Talmud commented,

> What was the reason? Quickly may the Temple be rebuilt, and they may say, Last year did we not eat when it was light in the east? Now too let us eat early in the morning, and they will not know that last year, there was no *omer*, and therefore when it was light in the east, it was immediately permitted, but now that the *omer* is brought again in the Temple, the *omer* and not the advent of the day, permits eating of new food.[3]

Other liturgical enactments, touching the testimony for the new moon, were as follows:

> Before time, they used to admit evidence about the new moon throughout the day of the new year. After sunset on the night after the 29th of Elul, they treated the coming day as a festival day, in case witnesses arrived the next day to report that the new moon was visible the preceding evening. If they did not come that day, the following day

---

[1] G. Cohen, "Age of the Talmud," 168.

[2] Rosh Hashanah 4.3. Sukkah 3.12. Cf. TB Sukkah 41b, TP Sukkah 3.11, TP Rosh Hashanah 4.3. Sifra Emor 16.9. Cf. also TB Rosh Hashanah 30b, Sukkah 41a, Epstein, *Mavo-ot*, on the passage as it appears in Sukkah, 350 f., in Rosh Hashanah, 159, 163, 366, and 366, n. 25.

[3] Rosh Hashanah 4.3. Cf. TB Menahot 66a, Tosefta Menahot 10.26, Mishnah Menahot 10.5. Cf. also Eruvin 32a, Sukkah 41a, Sifra Emor 10.10. On Menahot 10.5, cf. Epstein, *Mavo-ot*, 287, 291.

(also) was made a festival day, and the day before was considered as the 30th of Elul. Once the witnesses tarried so long in coming that the Levites were disordered in their singing [of the Psalm at the daily whole offering. The usual afternoon daily whole offering was slaughtered at 2:30 p.m., but if it was the first of the month, additional offerings had to be brought (Num. 28.1) besides the daily whole offering. Therefore the offering was delayed as long as possible for the arrival of witnesses, to know whether or not additional offerings should be brought and whether the Levites should sing the psalm for an ordinary day or for a festival day. This time, however, the delay was so long that there was not time for the prescribed psalm.]

So it was ordained that evidence could be admitted only until the afternoon offerings. And if witnesses came from the time of the afternoon offering and onward, then that day was kept holy and also the following day. After the Temple was destroyed, Rabban Yohanan ben Zakkai ordained that they might admit evidence about the new moon throughout the day [since it would not affect the singing of the proper psalms.][1]

Rabbi Joshua ben Karha said, Rabban Yohanan ben Zakkai ordained this also, that wheresoever the chief of the court might be, witnesses should go only to the place of assembly [of the tribunal to testify about the new moon].[2]

Before time, they would profane the Sabbath to bring testimony on the new moon for all months. When the Temple was destroyed, Rabban Yohanan ben Zakkai said to them, And do we now have a sacrifice [to offer in addition to that of the Sabbath] that we should permit the Sabbath day to be profaned? They ordained that they should not profane the Sabbath to bring testimony except for Nisan [on account of the coming Passover festival] and Tishre [account of the New Year] only.[3]

This same decision was preserved in an anonymous mishnah, as follows:

Because of two new moons may the Sabbath be profaned, the new moon of Nisan and the new moon of Tishre, for on them, messengers used to go forth to Syria [to announce the calendar to the Diaspora], and by them the set feasts were determined. And while the Temple still stood, the Sabbath might also be profaned because of any of the new moons, to determine the right time of the offerings.[4]

Yohanan, on the other hand, preserved a Temple ritual in its precise form:

The priests are not permitted to go up [to bless the people with the priestly blessing] onto the platform with their shoes on [but rather, barefooted, as in the Temple].[5]

---

[1] Rosh Hashanah 4.4.

[2] Rosh Hashanah 4.4.

[3] TB Rosh Hashanah 21a. Compare the takkanah of Gamaliel I on this matter, cf. Mishnah Rosh Hashanah 2.5.

[4] Mishnah Rosh Hashanah 1.4.

[5] TB Rosh Hashanah 31a. Cf. TB Sotah 40a. The reason given there is "on account of the honor of the congregation."

He prohibited (for so long as the Temple should be destroyed) the consecration of money or objects for use of, or sacrifice in, the Temple.

A proselyte who converts in this time [with the Temple in ruins] must separate a quarter [coin] for his bird offering [that is, he must put aside the cost of the offering even though he cannot actually make the sacrifice]. Rabbi Simeon ben Eleazar said, "Already Rabban Yohanan ben Zakkai has taken a poll against it and cancelled it, on account of the possibility of misusing [the money which had been set aside for profane purposes]. Rabbi Simeon said, Rabban Yohanan ben Zakkai cancelled it (entirely), as it is taught, One does not declare holy, or to be evaluated (for the sanctuary) or declare *herem*, or raise up heave-offerings and tithes, and if a man declared holy, or evaluated, or *herem*, or gave heave-offering or tithes, the garments should be burned, the cattle should be set out to pasture (until they are blemished and no longer sacred).[1]

Fruit of the fourth-year vineyard was taken up to Jerusalem (from any place which was distant) one day's journey in any direction.[2] (It was taught): Rabbi Eliezer (ben Hyrkanus) had fruit of a fourth-year vineyard east of Lud in the direction of Kefar Tabi, and Rabbi Eliezer wanted to declare it ownerless property for the benefit of the poor [since the city would not benefit from the fruits]. His students said to him, Rabbi, your colleagues have already outvoted you, and permitted [the fruits of the fourth year to be eaten without their being brought to Jerusalem, and hence such action was superfluous],

A later teacher added,

And who were the "colleagues"? Rabban Yohanan ben Zakkai.[3]

On all the ordinances of Yohanan ben Zakkai at Yavneh, Rabbi Judah said,

These things Rabban Yohanan ben Zakkai brought to pass in the world when the Temple was destroyed, and when it will be rebuilt, these matters will return to their original condition.[4]

What do these ritual and liturgical ordinances reveal about the policy of Yohanan's academy at Yavneh? They apparently fall into three

---

[1] TP Shekalim 8.4. TP Hallah 1.1. But compare below, n. Cf. Allon, Mehkarim, I, 139-40; TB Rosh Hashanah 31b.

[2] Maaser Sheni 5.2.

[3] Mishnah Maaser Sheni 5.2. Compare TB Rosh Hashanah 31b, Bezah 51-b, and the discussion below.

[4] Tosefta Rosh Hashanah 4.3. For other possible ordinances, cf. p. 155 n. 3 above; cf. also TB Bezah 5b, that it is permitted to redeem 2nd tithe and bring the money to Jerusalem rather than the fruit itself even after the destruction of the Temple. Cf. also TB Ketuvot 14a for another ordinance issued by Yohanan; and ch. 3; and the report of Ben Bukhri cited there, cf. Mishnah Shekalim 1.4, but it seems to me that this was not a takkanah at Yavneh but an earlier opinion, which Ben Bukhri reported after Yohanan's death to the academy of Gamaliel II.

groups, the first on the celebration of the new moon and festivals and on receiving testimony concerning their proper dates, the second on the priestly privileges, and the third, on the disposition of former emoluments of the Temple and city, the proselyte's offering and the fourth-year fruits. None of the categories reveals decisions on legal matters, but rather on strictly religious questions which the Romans were probably content to leave to an autonomous Jewish court even during the first years after the destruction.[1] All of them were clearly made necessary by the change in the liturgical situation after the destruction, and did not represent innovations in law, so much as modifications in the face of the new and radically changed circumstances.[2] The first group reveals that Yohanan began almost immediately to try to fill the vacuum in the religious life which the Temple's destruction caused. Thus, probably very soon after August, 70, possibly even in October of the same year, he decreed a memorial to the Temple: carrying the *lulav* all seven days, in memory of the Temple; and shortly thereafter, possibly in the spring of 71, he issued a second decree on the stricter observance of the law on the day of waving, again as a memorial to the Temple. Thus he announced immediately that the commandments which had depended on the Temple would continue to be observed even though the Temple was in ruins. Most significantly, he preserved the observance of the festival of Tabernacles, and the commandment on consuming the new grain only after commencement of Passover, both of which had been dependent on the Temple rituals.[3] The other ordinances in the first group follow the same pattern. They indicate that Yohanan took account of the destruction by restoring older laws formerly abrogated on account of the Temple's needs. Thus the testimony about the new moon of the new year might be brought the entire day on which the testimony was to be expected; but the Sabbath might not be profaned in connection with bringing such testimony except for the New Year and the month in which Passover came (contrary to Rabban Gamaliel's ruling several decades earlier). The decree that the witnesses should come only to the court, despite the absence of its chief, may have represented an effort to strengthen its authority.[4]

The ordinance on the priestly benediction, like that on sounding

---

[1] Allon, *Toldot*, I, 65-71.
[2] *Ibid.*
[3] Allon, *Toldot*, I, 68; Halevi, *Dorot*, l, v, 61b-62a.
[4] Weiss, *Dor*, II, 36-7, n. 1.

the Shofar on the New Year even though it coincided with the Sabbath, brought Yohanan into conflict with the priests. Indeed, it was
likely to have been a very direct assertion of his authority over them.
In the Temple, the priests had been forbidden to go up onto the
platform in their sandals to bless the congregation.[1] By requiring the
priests to continue this respectful act when they blessed the congregation outside the Temple, Yohanan declared his intention to issue
rulings which would govern the priests as well as the laity. He thus
tried to prevent the priests from utilizing their former prestige, and
the power of their blessing to acquire such a hold over the provincial
congregations as they had had over Jerusalem. Furthermore, he emphasized that the congregation is holier than the priest, and therefore
even outside the sanctuary the priest must take his shoes off before
going near to serve it, as Moses did before the bush. Thus the priestly
blessing was made the service of a divine community, not a benefac-
tion to be dispensed by the priest as he saw fit; and this act of service
required preface in the purifying act of washing.[2] The priests were
doubtless well aware of what Yohanan's policy meant.

The last group represents Yohanan's alleged efforts to determine
the disposition of benefits the Temple and city had formerly received.
Their authenticity is open to doubt. First of all, it is difficult to understand why Yohanan ben Zakkai was referred to as Eliezer's "colleague." Furthermore, the right to redeem the fourth-year fruit of the
vineyard outside of Jerusalem was probably granted before the destruction.[3] The law concerning the proselyte's offering likewise poses
difficulties, for in another source,[4] it is taught anonymously. More
seriously, one may object that it was taught that a proselyte who
converts in this time must separate the quarter for his bird offerings.[5]

Now, when would such a law have been enforced, if Yohanan had
abrogated the necessity of separating the quarter entirely. One might

---

[1] Ex. 30.21 apparently assumes that the priests were barefoot. Cf. also Lev.
8.21. Cf. also Sotah 40a; David Philipson and Kaufman Kohler, "Blessing,
Priestly," *JE*, III, 144-6.

[2] I am grateful to Professors Baron and Smith for this interpretation.

[3] Cf. Weiss, *Dor*, I, 37, n. 1; Allon, Toldot, I, 69. It was the opinion of a late
Amora, Rav Papa, that this ordinance was by Yohanan ben Zakkai. On this cf.
S. Lieberman, *Tosefta Kipshutah* (New York, 1955), II, 783-4, 1. 44, and 784, 1,
49-50; and 785, 1. 52. Lieberman would agree that this *takkanah* preceded the
destruction.

[4] Allon, *Toldot*, I, 70. Tosefta Shekalim 3.22. Cf. also Sifre Zuta, ed. Horowitz,
p. 283, cited by Allon. Allon holds that this *takkanah* was issued by Gamaliel II.

[5] TB Rosh Hashanah 31b.

reply[1] that such a ruling might have been handed down by another
sage, before the decree of Yohanan, possibly even before the destruction of Jerusalem. One cannot assume, first, that all scholars (or even
all Hillelite Pharisees) had been in Jerusalem from 66 on. Doubtless
some were in the provinces, as Yohanan himself formerly lived in the
Galilee. As soon as Jerusalem became inaccessible, legal problems
must have confronted Jews in the land who were obligated to go to
the Temple for certain ceremonies but no longer able. These legal
problems may have been brought to whatever sages were available in
the provinces, and perhaps some sort of consensus was reached about
what to do for the time being ("at this time"), even acquiring the
force of law. Proselytes were continuing to join the Jewish faith at
this time, and the problem remained in the provinces, what to do
with the prescribed offering, which it was impossible to bring now?
They may then have given the answer, set aside the money, and bring it
later, which was congruous to the current supposition that the Temple
would be left standing. When it was destroyed and the Roman disposition made it clear that the Temple would not be rebuilt for some
time to come, then, and not before, came the time when the preceding
pro-tempore arrangement would require a *takkanah*, that is to say, not
necessarily in 70, but sometime before 75, and the earlier ruling might
have been in effect for as long as ten years, and remembered even
longer. One cannot, it must be admitted, see a parallel to this situation
in the other laws which contrast the situation before the destruction
to that at Yavneh; in reference to the day of waving, the admission of
evidence on the putative New Year, and the profaning of the Sabbath
to bring evidence, it is clearly stated that the destruction of the Temple,
and not its mere inaccessibility, necessitated the changes that were
decreed. One cannot, moreover, conceive of a situation where sages
outside of the besieged city might have enacted such changes, there
being no practical grounds for them. Whether or not these ordinances
were in fact issued by Yohanan, one may conclude that they represent
accurately problems which confronted the academy in its earliest
years, and that Yohanan very likely attempted to deal with them.

One finds, therefore, that Yohanan attempted to endow his new
court with prerogatives hitherto reserved to the sanctuary,[2] to preserve
the memory and sanctity of the Temple, on the one hand, while
providing for its temporary inaccessibility, on the other; further, that

---

[1] I am grateful to Professor Smith for the following suggestion.
[2] But compare Allon, *Toldot*, I, 68-9.

he annulled a decree of Gamaliel I, and that he apparently took into
his own jurisdiction the problems connected with the disposition of
sacred offerings which could no longer reach the altar. The traditions
preserved nine enactments in all, covering the following matters:
1. the shofar; 2. the lulav; 3. the day of waving; 4. receiving testimony
on the eve of the New Year; 5. receiving testimony even when the
head of the court is absent; 6. not profaning the Sabbath to give such
testimony, except for the New Year and Passover; 7. the priestly
blessing; 8. the proselyte's offering; 9. the four-year fruits.[1] One must
wonder whether these were the only such enactments, for the multiplicity of problems, even in the limited area of religious and liturgical
affairs, must have necessitated many others. To suppose that his
teachings and the actions of his court were limited to the handful
reported by rabbinic tradition is hardly reasonable. What is preserved
of his legal record represents clearly what the members of the court
of Gamaliel II saw fit to recall. It therefore seems likely that Yohanan
envisaged a legal reconstruction of Judaism along lines which were
subsequently modified. Thus one may speculate that Yohanan may
have proposed to declare in abeyance all those parts of the law which
depended on the Temple for their performance or importance (along
with ordinances numbered 1, 2, 3, 4, 5, 6, 8, and 9 above); modified
those laws which might still be useful in the synagogue liturgy (the
ordinances numbers 1, 2, 3, above); and rejected priestly privileges
(ordinance number 7 above). Such a policy would have been utterly
unacceptable to the priests, and disappearance of other references to
Yohanan's enactments as legally valid precedent may have been the
price which Gamaliel II later had to pay to secure priestly cooperation.[2]

One need not, however, argue entirely from silence to demonstrate
that Yohanan faced opposition to his program at Yavneh.[3] We have
already noted that of the Men of Bathyra. In addition, the priests who
survived the destruction probably avoided his new academy, gathering
at Lud and founding their own. Many of them were afterward associated with Gamaliel II, including, for example, Zadok, whom Yohanan
had tried to save.[4] Allon has speculated that among the Pharisaic

[1] TB Rosh Rashanah 31b.
[2] I am grateful to Professor Smith for this suggestion.
[3] Allon, "The Presidency of Yohanan ben Zakkai at Yavneh," *Mehkarim*, I, 253-273.
[4] This was first suggested by A. Buechler, *Priester und Cultus*, 23. Cf. also L.
Finkelstein, *Perushim ve Anshe Kenesset Hagedolah*, 22-3, who notes that the Shammaites avoided Yohanan's academy. Cf. also Allon, "Presidency," 255-259. Buechler suggested that the priests went to Lud.

sages, many opposed Yohanan's anti-war policies on *political* grouds, and therefore avoided his academy, coming to Yavneh only after the appointment of Gamaliel II as head of the court.[1] He thinks that many Pharisees opposed Yohanan's escape from the city, and considered him guilty of treason. One must note, however, that Allon argues by listing a large number of sages who were not mentioned in connection with Yohanan's hegemony at Yavneh, but who appeared afterward. This, however, may prove only the paucity of our information on that period of the academy's history. None of the names Allon mentions was ever associated with Yohanan, except for Abba Shaul, and possibly, Eleazar the Modite and Nehuniah ben Hakanneh.[2] The difficulty of the text which presents the latter in conversation with Yohanan, however, renders this inconclusive. Indeed, if one had to rely on all the available sources, one would assume that at Yavneh, only Eliezer ben Hyrkanus, Joshua ben Hananiah, and the Men of Bathyra joined in the court proceedings, a highly unlikely assumption. In truth, the sources are inadequate to sustain an argument from their silence. Second, Allon assumes that the sages he mentions might have come to Yavneh, but chose not to. It is possible, however, that some were unable to come on account of the aftermath of the war; that others were not aware of the importance of Yohanan's work until later; and that some were indeed present, but simply not recorded in the extant sources. How often, indeed, were most of the names Allon brings ever mentioned in rabbinic literature? Allon also thinks that Eleazar ben Arakh refused to follow R. Yohanan to Yavneh, but while one source[3] implies that Eleazar left Yohanan while he was still alive, another says that he left after Yohanan died.[4] One, furthermore, states explicitly that Eleazar escaped with Yohanan, but left him to go to Emmaus instead

---

[1] Allon, "Presidency," 259-263. On the opposition of the Men of Bathyra, cf. p. 164 n .4. He also raises the question of whether Yohanan ben Zakkai was actually *nasi*, and if so, to what extent was he recognized as such by the nation? Most scholars agree that he was (Allon cites Krochmal, *Moreh*, 105; Weiss, Dor, II, 34; Javitz, *Toldot*, VI, 8; Graetz, *Geschichte*, IV, 14, who say that he was *nasi*, and Frankel, *Mishnah*, 67, Bruell, *Mavo*, 50, and HaLevi, *Dorot*, I, v, 52, who deny it). Allon's judgment is that he certainly carried out the functions of the *nasi*, and holds that he was called by the title, *rabban*, which was reserved to the *nasi*. But, Allon says, he was recognized by only a small part of the people. As we have emphasized, his authority was limited both by what the Romans would permit such a group to do, and also by what could in fact be done in the first decade after the destruction.

[2] Cf. Avot 2.10 f.; TB Baba Batra 10b, Pesikta 12b.

[3] ARNa ch. 14.

[4] Kohelet Rabba 7.

of to Yavneh.[1] Allon suggests that this was in opposition to Yohanan's war policies, But, one wonders, if so, why did Eleazar leave the city at all, as this source clearly states he did? Even without considering the accuracy of these sources, one must note that the same source that says that Eleazar escaped with Yohanan, Eliezer, and Joshua, states that he went to Emmaus. Could he have opposed Yohanan's escape, and then fled with him, and finally rejected his master because Yohanan opposed the war? Allon notes that there is no mention of Simeon ben Natanel in later sources, and that Yosi the Priest was mentioned during the period of Gamaliel II and not during that of Yohanan. He suggests that this, again, was on account of political opposition. But it is, certainly possible that Simeon did not survive the destruction, and that Yosi was detained elsewhere. Allon's case must stand, therefore, not proven.

One can, in fact, suggest the opposite, that most of the sages who survived the destruction, succeeded in doing so precisely because they were not in Jerusalem when it fell.[2] According to Josephus' account, very few adult males who were in Jerusalem when the Romans conquered it survived death and escaped slavery, and so could even appear in a Pharisaic court within the next decade. Apart from the internecine strife, in which, certainly, some of the Pharisaic moderates must have fallen, Josephus records a vastly increased mortality rate,[3] famine,[4] epidemics, execution of the Temple priests,[5] thorough search lof al hiding places,[6] and indiscriminate slaughter:

> Pouring into the alleys, sword in hand, they massacred indiscriminately all whom they met, and burnt the houses with all who had taken refuge within... while they pitied those who had perished [of famine], they had no similar feelings for the living, but running everyone through who fell in their way, they choked the alleys with corpses, and deluged the whole city with blood...[7]

It seems not unreasonable, therefore, that almost everybody in the court of Gamaliel II had either fled Jerusalem during the early stages of the war, or had been absent from the first and stayed away. The dominant pro-war party of the Pharisees in Jerusalem was almost

---

[1] ARNb ch. 29. Cf. also TB Shabbat 147b.
[2] I am grateful to Professor Smith for this suggestion.
[3] *War*, V, 12, 3 (512).
[4] *War*, VI, 2, 2 (193).
[5] *War*, VI, 6, 1 (318).
[6] *War*, VI, 7, 3 (370).
[7] *War*, VI, 8, 5 (404-5).

annihilated, and this is most likely one of the reasons that there is so little reference at the court of Yohanan or of Gamaliel II to the opinions of sages of the period before 70.

One sage, however, very likely did remain in Jerusalem until the end, and only reached Yavneh with great difficulty. That was Gamaliel II, son of Simeon ben Gamaliel and heir of the prestige and authority of the house of Hillel, and, through him, it was believed, of David. His relationship with Yohanan is extremely unclear, as we have seen, and it is possible that it was characterized by considerable tension. While Yohanan may have acted to found and lead the academy because Gamaliel was unable to assume authority, some, including possibly Gamaliel himself, may have regarded Yohanan's decrees as acts of usurpation. In any case, while Yohanan was still alive, Gamaliel replaced him. Gamaliel could probably not have come to Yavneh before the close of histilities in 73, and one may suggest that he returned during the term of L. Flacius Silva, 72-80, or, at the very latest, that of M. Salvidenus, 80-86. How he regarded the achievement of Yohanan there, one simply does not know. His later relationships with Joshua and Eliezer, which were not cordial[1] would suggest, however, that Gamaliel had to cope with a certain enmity from Yohanan's old and loyal disciples, very possibly on Yohanan's account.

Whatever the opposition he faced, Yohanan clearly considered himself the possessor of the legitimate internal autonomy available to Israel. Thus he instituted the formal appointment of his disciples as *rabbis*, giving to the sages for the first time an official status within the Jewish polity:[2]

> At first each one would appoint (ordain) his own students, as Rabban Yohanan ben Zakkai ordained Rabbi Eliezer and Rabbi Joshua, and Rabbi Joshua appointed Rabbi Akiba, and Rabbi Akiva, Rabbis Meir and Simeon.[3]

---

[1] Cf. ch. 9. Cf. Allon, *Mehkarim*, I, 268. Allon cites Geiger, who thinks that Gamaliel actually forced Yohanan out; compare the view of Halevi, *Dorot*, I, v, 24a, 28a-31b, 36a, who holds that Yohanan retired to Beror Heil in order to give Gamaliel a freer hand. Cf. also Allon, *Toldot*, I, 60-65; Bacher, *Agadot*, I, i, 54.

[2] Cf. J. Goldin, "Three Pillars," 55; J. Z. Lauterbach, "Ordination," *JE*, IX, 428-30; W. Bacher, "Zur Geschichte der Ordination," *MGWJ*, XXXVIII, 122-27. Goldin explains the new title as a reflection of an authority now being bestowed on the sages, "Apparently this was part of the large, new program of Talmud Torah. Everyone must study Torah, and henceforth the man of authority, not just of influence but of authority, is the rabbi, the sage who goes through the discipline of a student of the sages and becomes a master of Torah." But compare the view of Sherira Gaon, cited by Graetz, *Geschichte*, III, ii, 472, n. 9.

[3] TP Sanhedrin 1.2. On the ordination of Yohanan's students, see also Hugo Mantel, *op. cit.*, p. 206-207.

In this action, he created a form of legitimization for Jewish leadership within the Pharisaic tradition. Before then, the sages were recognized through neither title nor official status; afterward, they constituted an authoritative and continuing class of officials in Jewish life.

Yohanan also represented the Jewish faith to gentiles with whom he came into contact.[1] He allegedly debated questions of Jewish doctrine and Scriptural interpretation, and while one cannot determine exactly with whom he debated, it seems possible that some of these discussions took place when he was in Yavneh, where there were larger numbers of gentiles, rather than at Jerusalem, where such contacts would have been limited. Certainly at Yavneh he must have come into contact with Roman authorities. The effort has been made to identify his antagonist with a Roman official, Antonius Julianus, procurator of Judah during the siege of Jerusalem, and alleged author of a book *De Judaeis*, in which the sufferings of the Jews were presented as punishment for their having abandoned God and his discipline. Unfortunately, all that is known of this book is one sentence in the writings of Minucius Felix. On so small a basis, one cannot accept such an identification.[2] The record of the conversations contains no element of reproach against the Jews for their rebellion, but rather they contain mainly the kinds of exegetical debates common in this period. The reported conversations are as follows:

---

[1] On the conversations with Roman officials, cf. Buechler, *Economic Conditions*. 57. The names include Antoninus Hegemon, Antigonos, Angatos, Kontrakos, He may have been head of the garrison at Yavneh, or some local public official. Cf. Graetz, *MGWJ*, XXXIV, 17 f.; Krauss, *Lehnworter*, II, 106; Bacher, *Agadot*, I, i, 27-8. The names are as follows:

TP Sanhedrin	–	Antonius
TP Sanhedrin	–	Angatos
Num. R. ch. 4	–	Hunntos
TB Bekorot 5a	–	Kuntrakos
Sifre Deut. 351	–	Agnitos Hegemon.

[2] Cf. D. J. Borstein, "Jochanan ben Zakkai," *Encyclopedia Judaica* (Berlin, 1932), IV, s. v.; on Antonius, cf. Josephus, *War*, VI, 4, 3 (238). Cf. Minucius Felix, *Octavian*, ch. 8. Cf. also E. Norden, in *Neuer Jahrbücher fur Greisch. Philologie*, XXXI, 664-5. The only two references to Antonius are those of Josephus and Minucius, cf. Paully-Wissowa, s. v. Antonius Julianus. Norden thinks that he was the source of Tacitus' *History*, ch. 5; dealing with the Jewish war. Cf. his article cited above. Abel, *Histoire*, II, 49, cites the Borstein article, and apparently accepts his judgment. On the nature of the *hegemon* in Talmudic and midrashic sources, cf. S. Krauss, *Paras veRome*, 137 f. Other efforts to identify Yohanan's disputant include that of Jastrow, *Dictionary*, s. v. Quitus; Krauss, *Lehnwörter*, II, 106; Bacher, *Agadot*, I, i, 27-8. Cf. also Derenbourg, *Essai*, 316. Note also the questions of the pagan on the heifer ceremony, ch. 3, p. 61-2.

It happened that a certain gentile asked Rabban Yohanan ben Zakkai, We have festival seasons and you have festival seasons. We have Calendae, and Saturnalia, and Kratesis, and you have Passover, Pentecost, and Tabernacles. What is the day on which we and you rejoice together? Rabban Yohanan said to him, "That is the day on which rain falls. How do we know? It is written (Ps. 65-13), 'The meadows clothe themselves with grain, they shout and sing together for joy.' And what is written after this? "Make a joyful noise to God, all the earth, sing the glory of his name" (Ps. 66.1).[1]

All who were numbered of the Levites, whom Moses and Aaron numbered at the commandment of the Lord, by families, all the males from a month old and upward, were twenty-two thousand... (Num. 4.46). A certain hegemon asked Rabbi Yohanan ben Zakkai, "In the specification of the Levites, you find twenty-two thousand three hundred Gershonites, 7500, Kohlthites, 8600, and Merarites, 6200, but when they are counted as a group, there were only 22,000. Where did the others go? He answered, Those three hundred were first born, and a first born cannot fulfil the obligation of a first-born (Num. 3.44), "And the Lord said to Moses, take the Levites instead of all the first born among the people of Israel, and the cattle of the Levites instead of their cattle, and the Levites shall be mine.[2]

The official had tried to demonstrate the inconsistency of the biblical narrative, but Yohanan denied that there was a contradiction. It is true, he admitted, that the number of Levites in the detailed account reaches 22,300, but the 300 omitted in the summation were the first-born, useless for the purpose for which the census was taken. As the evidence indicated, the purpose was to substitute Levites for the Israelite first-born, each Levite redeeming a male, first-born Israelite. But the three hundred first-born Levites could not themselves serve as a ransom, and therefore were not counted. (This would indicate that since there were only three hundred first-born among 22,300 Levites, each family had on the average of 74 1/3rd male children.)

And again he was asked, "With reference to the collection of the money [when every Israelite had to give half a shekel], you count two hundred and one kikkar and eleven maneh [a kikkar contains sixty maneh, and a maneh twenty-five shekels, therefore a total of one

---

[1] Deut. Rabbah 7.8. Cf. also Ber. R. 13.6, in the name of Joshua ben Korha. Cf. Numbers Rabbah 6. Midrash Tehillim to Ps. 117, likewise in the name of Joshua ben Hananiah. Midrash HaGadol on Numbers, 3.37. Cf. also Mishnat Rabbi Eliezer, ch. 15, Enelow ed. (New York, 1933), 283. Note also the holidays mentioned in Avodah Zara 1.3. Cf. also Derenbourg, Essai, 316. In Yalkut I, 117, the exegesis is in the name of Joshua ben Hananiah.

[2] TB Bekorot 5a. TP Sanhedrin 1.4. Numbers Rabbah 4.9. Cf. also Yalkut, I, 415. My comment is based on S. Fisch. Midrash HaGadol on Numbers. Numbers in Midrash HaGadol (Manchester, 1940), 197.

thousand five hundred shekels in one kikkar; 603,550 half shekels were collected, making a total of 301,775 shekels; divide one thousand five hundred into this, and one finds two hundred and one kikkar, with the remainder of 275 shekels, or eleven maneh], for Scripture states, "A bika for every man, that is, half a shekel after the shekel of the sanctuary" (Ex. 38.26), while when the money was given (by Moses), you find only one hundred kikkar, for it is written, "And the hundred talents of the silver were for casting" (Ex. 38.27). Was Moses your teacher either a thief or a swindler, or else a bad arithmetician? He gave half, took a half, and did not even return a complete half? [For a complete half would have been one hundred and a half kikkar and five and half maneh, and he only returned one hundred kikkar. And although Scripture says, "And of the thousand seven hundred and seventy five shekels he made hooks," and consequently he returned more than half, this verse was not mentioned.] He replied to him, Moses our teacher was a trustworthy treasurer and a good arithmetician, only the sacred maneh was double the common." [There were therefore one hundred and twenty maneh in a kikkar. The hundred kikkar were therefore really two hundred, and the remaining kikkar and eleven maneh were the one thousand seven hundred and seventyfive shekel mentioned from which hooks were made.][1]

And again it was asked, One scripture says, And God said, Let the waters bring forth swarms of living creatures, and let birds fly above the earth across the firmament of the heavens (Gen. 1.20). Therefore the birds were created from water. And yet it is written, "So out of the ground the Lord God formed every beast of the field and every bird of the air and brought them to the man to see what he would call them (Gen. 2.19). He said to him, From spittle they were created [which contains both water and earth]. He saw his students gazing in surprise at one another. He said to them, Is it hard in your eyes that I have turned aside my enemy with straw? They were created from water, and why did he bring them to man? To call them names. [That is, the birds were not created from dust, but were included in the verse only to indicate that they were given their names by man.][2]

Antigonos the Prince asked Rabban Yohanan ben Zakkai, "The ox will be stoned and the master also will die" (Ex. 21.29). Why? He said to him, The accomplice of a thief is like a thief. When he went out, the students asked, Master, this one you pushed away with a reed, but to us, what will you reply? He said to them, It is written, the ox will be stoned and also its master will die – the death of the ox is to be like the death of the master, for the death of the one is juxtaposed to the death of the other; just as the master dies after a fair trial with careful examination of the witnesses and twenty-three judges, so the ox dies with careful examination of the witnesses and twenty-three judges.[3]

---

[1] TB Bekorot 5a, parallel in TP Sanhedrin 1.4. Cf. also Bacher, *Agadot*, I, i, 28. Trans. I, Epstein, *The Babylonian Talmud, Seder Kodashim*, London, 1948, IV, 23-4.

[2] TB Hullin 27b. Compare Bekorot 5a.

[3] TP Sanhedrin 1.2. This follows one of Hillel's principles of exegesis. Note that this was quoted anonymously, Mishnah Sanhedrin 1.4, Tosefta Sanhedrin, 3.2.

"They teach thy laws to Jacob, and thy Torah to Israel…" This asked Agrippa the Prince to Rabban Yohanan ben Zakkai. He said to him, How many Torahs does he give you from heaven? He answered him, Two, one in writing and one to transmitted orally. He asked, And is it said "Thy Torot" [plural]? He answered, Even so, they *are* two, for it is said, *And* thy Torah to Israel.[1]

So much is known about Yohanan ben Zakkai at Yavneh: he began to build a new center of autonomous government, judging certain ritual and religious questions, teaching his disciples, and possibly debating on occasion with gentiles in the town. If Yohanan had never gone to Yavneh, he would probably be almost forgotten in Jewish history, yet the detailed record of his activity there has, paradoxically, hardly reached posterity. The course of his life during the last years is by no means certain either, but it is widely assumed[2] that he retired to Beror Heil, a village in the foothills of Judah, and remained there until his death, handing down decisions in cases that came before him, and teaching his disciples. (By this action, one may conjecture, he would have dissolved some opposition to the academy based on enmity toward himself, and cleared the way for Gamaliel II to assume the leadership of a broader part of the nation.) What is certain about his activity at Beror Heil is preserved in the following source:

"Justice, justice shalt thou pursue!" Go after a good court for justice, after Rabbi Eliezer to Lud, after Rabban Yohanan ben Zakkai to Beror Heil.[3]

---

[1] Midrash Tannaim, ed. Hoffman, 215 1.21. In Sifre, it is Rabban Gamaliel; if so, it may be Gamaliel I and Agrippa I, as Gamaliel II was unlikely to have met Agrippa II. If this is Yohanan, however, it might be a meeting with Agrippa II in Jerusalem before the destruction. Verse is Deut. 33.10. Cf. also ARNa, ch. 15, TB Shabbat 31a.

[2] Cf. HaLevi, *Dorot*, I, v, 35a. But compare Albeck, *Mavo*, 219. Cf. especially Allon, *Mehkarim*, 1, 253-273, and *Toldot*, I, 53-71, particularly 64. Cf. S. Krauss, *Sefer HaYishuv*, s. v. Cf. Kaminka, *Mehkarim*, 100, for another opinion on Beror Heil; Javitz, *Toldot*, VI, 4, thinks that Yohanan was in Beror Heil before the destruction of Jerusalem; cf. especially Derenbourg, *Essai*, 306, 307, n. 4. Derenbourg thinks that when Yohanan retired, Gamaliel II went to Syria to obtain permission from the legate for his investiture, cf. p. 310. He also suggests that the exegesis, "Happy the generation whose prince brings an offering" is an illusion of resentment at the elevation of Gamaliel II, cf. p. 312. Cf. also Bacher, *Agadot*, I, i, 54.

[3] The sources on Yohanan in Beror Heil are as follows: TB Sanhedrin 32b (quoted here); parallel in Sifre Deut. 144; Tosefta Maaserot 2.1, TP Demai 2.1, TP Maaserot 2.2.

CHAPTER NINE

FATHER OF THE FUTURE

Yohanan ben Zakkai died, probably a decade or so after the destruction of Jerusalem,[1] not a martyr, but more appropriately, in bed, surrounded by his loyal disciples. Having chosen to concern himself with day-to-day affairs, he had offered the promise contained in the moral conduct of commonplace life as Israel's true consolation; a martyr's death wo.ld have been incongruent to such a teaching. His death was reported as follows:

> In his last hours, Rabban Yohanan ben Zakkai kept weeping out loud. O master, his disciples exclaimed, O tall pillar, light of the world, mighty hammer, why art thou weeping? He said to them, do I then go to appear before a king of flesh and blood, whose anger, if he should be angry with me, is but of this world? and whose chastising, if he should chastise me, is but of this world? and whose slaying, if he should slay me, is but of this world? Whom I can, moreover, appease with words or bribe with money? Verily, I go rather to appear before the King of Kings of Kings, the Holy One, blessed be he, whose anger, if he should be angry with me, is of this world, and the world to come, and whom I cannot appease with words or bribe with money! Moreover I have before me two roads, one to Paradise and one to Gehenna, and I know not whether he will sentence me to Gehenna or admit me into Paradise. And of this the verse says, "Before him shall be sentenced all those that go down to the dust, even he that cannot keep his soul alive" (Ps. 22.30) – and should I not weep? They said to him, Master, bless us! He said to them, May it be God's will that the fear of Heaven be upon you as much as the fear of flesh and blood. They said to him, Just so much? He answered, Would that it were so. Know ye that when a man sins a sin, he says, I hope no *man* sees me. And as he breathed his last, he said, "Clear the house of uncleanness" of vessels which can receive corpse uncleanness, and prepare a throne for Hezekiah, king of Judah, who cometh...[2]

---

[1] It seems to me, as I noted earlier, that all of Yohanan's work at Yavneh could have been done within the period of seven years. Cf. J. Spitz, *Rabban Jochanan ben Zakkai* [in *Talmud and Midrash* Dissertations, Vol. IV, n. 5, at the Jewish Theological Seminary Library] (Berlin, 1883), 45-6, n. 150, for a summary of the scholarly views to that time. Most scholars date Yohanan's death at from two to ten years after 70, Spitz himself in 72 C.E., Javitz likewise. Dubnow, *Divre*, II., 13 dates it between 80 and 85, Halevi, *Dorot*, I, v, at 80, Graetz, *Geschichte*, III, ii, 58, at about 80.

[2] ARNa ch. 25, Schechter 40a, Goldin 105 f. Cf. Goldin, 198, n. 9. Goldin and Schechter do not consider that the discussion after the death scene contains the

Yohanan thus blessed his students with a blessing based on his earlier teaching to them, that the robber who steals in broad daylight is a better man than the thief who steals by night, for the one regards God and man as equals, and the other fears not God but only man.[1] He ended his life, likewise, with a characteristic reminder of the humble necessities imposed by the laws of ritual purity on those who kept them; in a moment, the house would be unclean by reason of corpse-uncleanness, therefore clear out objects which will receive it. He expressed the disquiet he felt with the prospect close at hand of going to appear before God, and one notes in his words a profound humility. One knows so little about the spiritual biography of this man, but it seems clear that on the long road from Jerusalem, through Arav, and Yavneh to Beror Heil, Yohanan ben Zakkai had passed through a valley of deep shadows and dark uncertainties. Finally, he told his students, with his dying breath, to prepare a throne for Hezekiah king of Judah, who, it was held, would herald a better day.[2] Yohanan had

---

words of Yohanan ben Zakkai. I have included in the text the additional passage added in the parallel beraita in TB Berakhot 28b, since the two comments appear to be mutually complementary.

[1] Cf. ch. five. On the idea of going before an honest judge, cf. also Philo, The Special Laws, I, 277 f. (Colson tr. VII, 261-2). Compare Yohanan's alleged death speech with Adam's, cf. Ginzberg, Legends, V, 124, and cf. the Apocalypse of Moses, 31-2, cited by Ginzberg. Cf. also J. Goldin,"Three Pillars," 55, n. 46; Allon, Mehkarim, I, 187, on the expression "Light of Israel" as applied to the sages. On the expression "to appease him with words," cf. L. Finkelstein, "On the Phraseology of the Tannaim," in J. N. Epstein Jubilee Volume (Jerusalem, 1950, in Hebrew), 96-7. On the current belief concerning the fate of the soul after death, cf. W. D. Davies, Paul and Rabbinic Judaism, 315-6; Moore, Judaism, II, 279-322; J. Bonsirven, Le Judaisme Palestinien, I, 336-40; 468-541.

[2] I follow the interpretations of Moore, Judaism, III, 201 f., II, 347 f.; Goldin, 198-9, n. 10. On Hezekiah as a messianic figure, cf. inter alia Justin Martyr, Dialogue with Trypho, in A. L. Williams ed., Adversus Judaeos (Cambridge, 1935), p. 37. Justin argues with Trypho on Ps. 110, saying that it does not refer to Hezekiah, as the Jews say, but to Christ. Cf. also Y. Ihen-Shmuel, Midrashei Geulah [Legends of Redemption] (Tel Aviv, 1954), 47-9, who thinks that this ...was a reference to an impending invasion from Parthia, and that Yohanan was warning the people to prepare for the coming redemption through the Parthian conquest. But this is not born out either by the facts of Roman-Parthian relations in this period, or by other known attitudes of Yohanan ben Zakkai toward such matters. Ginzberg, cited in Moore, III, 201 f. (cf. also Goldin, 199, n. 10) suggests that this may be Hezekiah the scholar, or the Galilean Zealot. On the death bed words, cf. also TP Sotah 9.16, and TP Avodah Zarah 3.1. Note that when Eliezer died, he said "Clear out the house... and prepare a chair for Yohanan ben Zakkai." On messianic speculations in this period, cf. A. Silver, History of Messianic Speculation in Israel (Boston, 1959), 13; Silver cites Geiger, who thinks that this refers to Hezekiah the Galilean. Cf. also J. Klausner, Messiah Idea in Israel, p. 396. Klausner interprets the saying, "If you have a sapling in your hand..." as praise of agricul-

earlier opposed the despairing trust in God's immediate intervention into human affairs, and yet he died with the messianic hope on his lips. In retrospect, it seems that Yohanan thus gave expression to his view of his own achievement. He did not regard his program of Torah, commandments, and acts of lovingkindness, nor his institution at Yavneh, as the final stages in man's salvation, but only, as we have suggested, as interim measures. He had looked forward, as did other Jews, to the Messiah's coming. Accordingly he had offered this paradigm for Judaism:

> If you have a sapling in your hand, and one comes to say that the Messiah is here, plant the sapling, and then go forth to receive him.

At Yavneh, Yohanan had planted his sapling. In the moment of death, he looked to receive him who must come.

When Yohanan ben Zakkai died, the splendor of wisdom ceased.[1] Later generations recalled Yohanan's death as a grievous loss:

> "Her adversaries saw her, they laughed" (Lam. 1.7). This refers to the death of Rabban Yohanan ben Zakkai.[2]

He was remembered as a good gift:

> "The mandrakes give forth fragrance, and over our doors are all choice fruits, new as well as old, which I have laid up for you, O my beloved" (Song of Songs 7.13). This is to be compared to a king who had a garden, and he gave it over to a gardener (to tend it). What did the gardener do? He filled fig-baskets with the fruits of the garden, and placed them at the door of the garden. When the king passed by, he saw all the glory of the garden. He said, "If all this glory is at the gate of the garden, in the garden itself how much the more so (will there be beautiful fruits). So the first generations – the men of the Great Assembly, Hillel and Shammai, Rabban Gamaliel the Elder. And in the latter generations, Rabban Yohanan ben Zakkai and Rabbi Eliezer and Rabbi Joshua, and Rabbi Meir, and Rabbi Akiba, and their disciples – how much the more so! And concerning them Scripture says, "New as well as old which I have laid up for you O my beloved (Song of Songs 7.13).[3]

---

ture (396, n. 19). He discusses the symbolism of Hezekiah, 465. Cf. also Finkelstein, *Akiba*, 70-1; Ginzberg, *Legends*, VI, 365, n. 67; compare Hillel on the messiah, TB Sanhedrin 99a. Cf. also Edershim, *Life and Times*, II, 709-6, 791-6; Kaminka, *Mehkarim*, 117. On Hezekiah as a Messianic figure, cf. also TB Sanhedrin 94b. The application of Jeremianic images (mighty pillar, Jer. 1.18 and mighty hammer, Jer. 23.29) is noteworthy.

[1] TB Sotah 9.16, Tosefta Sotah 9; TP Sotah 9.16.
[2] Lamentations Rabbati 1.7.
[3] Song of Songs Rabbah 7.18.

Yohanan's enduring memorial to his life was his students, who lived on to exemplify, each according to his own understanding, the teachings of the master.[1] When Yohanan died, Joshua and Eliezer returned to Yavneh, and it was then according to some sources that Eleazar ben Arakh went to Emmaus. Eleazar thought to found an academy there, but he did not succeed:

> When they left his presence, Rabbi Eleazar said, I shall go to Emmaus, a beautiful place with beautiful and delightful waters. But they said, We shall go to Yavneh, where there are scholars in abundance who love the Torah. Because he went to Emmaus, a beautiful place with beautiful and delightful waters, his name was made least in the Torah. Because they went to Jamnia, where there are scholars in abundance who love the Torah, their names were magnified in the Torah.[2]

Both Joshua ben Hananiah[3] and Eliezer ben Hyrcanus[4] played

---

[1] On the possibility that Eliezer and Joshua preserved Yohanan's opinions, cf. ch. 8. Cf. also Kaminka, *Mehkarim*, 103-5. There is a reference to a son of Rabban Yohanan ben Zakkai, cf. TB Niddah 15a, Tos. Niddah 3.3. If so, he must have had two sons, for one died in his lifetime, and apparently the other survived him.

[2] ARNa ch. 14, Schechter 30a, Goldin 77-8. Cf. also ch. 8. Other references to Eleazar's life at Emmaus are in TB Shabbat 147b and Kohelet Rabbah 7. Schechter says that this happened after Yohanan's death, but compare ARNb ch. 29, Schechter 30 (cited ch. 8) also:

> "Why did he not grow great in wisdom? But when they left Jerusalem, he said, where shall we go, and he it was who said, Let us go to Emmaus, to a beautiful city whose waters are sweet. His name did not grow great in wisdom, but they who said, Let us go to Yavneh, to a place where they study Torah, to a place where the disciples of the sages are abundant, their name grew great in wisdom. He who said, Let us go to Emmaus, the beautiful city, whose waters are pleasant, and whoever seeks to learn Torah will betake himself after it (to me in Emmaus), his name was diminished in wisdom..."

Cf. also Kaminka, Mehkarim, 116, and discussion in ch. 8.

[3] I have not attempted to summarize the long and interesting lives of Eliezer and Joshua, but only to cite a particularly significant incident in the life of each. Full biographies of both men are available, cf. J. Podro, *The Last Pharisee, The Life and Times of Rabbi Joshua ben Hananiah* (London, 1959), and B. Z. Bokser, *Pharisaic Judaism in Transition, R. Eliezer the Great and Jewish Reconstruction after the War with Rome* (New York, 1935). Joshua remained a staunch supporter of Gamaliel's efforts to bring about widespread acceptance of the Hillelite view on Jewish law, but he also provided the occasion for Gamaliel's temporary deposition. Cf. TB Berahot 28a. After Gamaliel's death Joshua was one of the leading figures in the decades before the Bar Kokhba war. He stood at Eliezer's death bed, and said (TB Sanhedrin 101a, cf. also Mekilta Yitro 10, Sifre Deut. 32), "O master, thou art of more value to Israel than God's gift to rain, for rain gives life in this world only, but you give life both in this wordl and in the world to come." He outlived Eliezer, and after his death, defended his opinions (TB Gittin 83a). He opposed the next rebellion against Rome, Gen. R. 44 at the end; visited the emperor in Alexandria, and conversations were reported. He was a vigorous opponent of the

leading parts in the deliberations at Yavneh during the next decades.
Joshua eventually came into conflict with Gamaliel II, and Eliezer was
a center of controversy. Thus Joshua contended with Gamaliel:

> It once happened that two witnesses came and said, We saw (the
> new moon) in the east in the morning, and in the west in the evening.
> Rabbi Yohanan ben Nuri said, they are false witnesses. But when they
> came to Yavneh, Rabban Gamaliel accepted their evidence. And two
> others came and said, We saw it at the expected time, yet in the night
> of the added day it did not appear (and hence a 30th day would have to
> be added to the lunar month of 29 days, for the new moon failed to
> appear at the expected time). And Rabban Gamaliel accepted their
> evidence. Rabbi Dosa ben Harkinas said, They are false witnesses. How
> can they say of a woman that she has given birth if the next day her belly
> is between her teeth. Rabbi Joshua said to him, I approve thy words.
> Rabban Gamaliel sent to him saying, I charge thee that thou come to
> me with thy staff and thy money on the day of atonement as it falls
> according to thy reckoning. (Gamaliel had decided that the day of atone-
> ment, according to Joshua's reckoning, and reached by ignoring the testi-
> mony of witnesses whom Gamaliel II had accepted, was not the day of
> atonement at all, and so it would be permissible to carry a staff and

---

minim (Koh. R. 1.25, Hagigah 5b). His controversies with Eliezer were on such varied
subjects as cosmology, eschatology, the future age, the resurrection, and on the
interpretation of various biblical passages, as well as on a wide range of legal
questions. Joshua generally advanced a literal interpretation of Scripture, and
historical exegisis of its contents. On his life and works, cf. W. Bacher, "Joshua
ben Hananiah," *JE*, VII, 291-2; *Agadot*, I, i, 92-141; Weiss, *Dor*, II, 74-84 (this is
on Eliezer as well); Bruell, *Mavo*, 82-8; Frankel, *Mishnah*, 87-94; Hyman, *Qgadot
HaTannaim*, II, 624-35; Umanski, *Hokhme HaTalmud*, I, 205, *Hokhme HaYerushalmi*,
II, 76.

⁴ Eliezer, who was married to Gamaliel's sister, advanced many conservative
views, which are elsewhere given in the name of the school of Shammai (likewise,
Joshua is sometimes presented as "the school of Hillel"). In later sources, Eliezer's
name is sometimes omitted in reports on his teachings. After he was excommunicated, he was visited occasionally by the sages. During the persecutions of the
Jewish-Christians, he was accused of being a Jewish-Christian, but he succeeded
in proving his loyalty to the Government. He was grieved by the accusation.
He died, apparently at Caesarea, and was buried in Lud. He is the most frequently
quoted rabbi in Tannaitic literature in his generation. Cf. S. Mendelsohn, "Eliezer
ben Hyrcanus," *JE*, V, 113-5; Frankel, *Mishnah*, 78-86; Bruell, *Mavo*, 75-82;
Braunschweig, *Die Lehrer*, 10-19; Bacher, *Agadot*, I, i, 72-114; Hyman, *Agadot*, I,
161-175; Umanski, *Hakhme HaTalmud*, 26-8, *Hakhme HaYerushalmi*, 24-5; cf. also
G. Friedlander, *Pirke de R. Eliezer* (London, 1916), xiii. Cf. also B. Toetterman,
R. Eliezer b. Hyrcanus (Leipzig, 1877, in Latin). Both Eliezer and Joshua are fully
discussed in the various general histories of the period which I have cited in
connection with Yohanan ben Zakkai. There is also a tradition that Rabbi Tarfon
studied with Yohanan ben Zakkai, cf. Tosefta Hagiga 3.36. Other posthumous
references to Yohanan include the following; TB Ketuvot 14a, Sifra Shemini 7.1,
Sotah 27b, Pesahim 18a; TP Sotah, 5.2, Tosefta Sotah 5.13. Cf. also TB Shabbat
34a.

money). Rabbi Akiba went to Rabbi Joshua and found him very perplexed. He said to him, I can teach thee from Scripture that whatsoever Rabban Gamaliel has done is done aright, for it is written "These are the set feasts of the Lord... which ye shall proclaim" (Lev. 23.4). Whether in their proper season or not in their proper season, I know no other set feasts save these (which *you* proclaim). Rabbi Joshua then went to Rabbi Dosa ben Harkinas and he said to him, If we come to inquire into the lawfulness of the decisions of the court of Rabban Gamaliel, we shall need to inquire into the lawfulness of the decisions of every court which has arisen since the days of Moses until now, for it is written, "Then went up Moses and Aaron, Nadab and Abihu, and seventy of the elders of Israel (Ex. 24.9). And why are the names of the elders not expressly set forth, if not to teach that every three judges which have risen up as a court over Israel are like to the court of Moses! (Joshua) took his his staff and money in his hand, and went to Yavneh to Rabban Gamaliel on the day which fell according to his reckoning to be the day of atonement. Rabban Gamaliel stood up and kissed him on the head and said to him, Come in peace, my master and my disciple! My master in wisdom, and my disciple in that thou hast accepted my opinion.[1]

Yohanan had taught his students the way of renunciation, when, apparently, he retired from the academy at Yavneh, and Joshua followed that way. He led the liberal wing of the academy at Yavneh, teaching "Do not put upon the people more obligations than they are capable of bearing."[2] He followed Yohanan's uncompromising policy of peace, and joined in the rabbis' missions to Rome, with Akiba, Gamaliel and Eleazar ben Azariah, in the time of Domitian and possibly also later in the time of Hadrian, in the hope of improving relations between the Government and the Jewish people.

Eliezer, for his part, was leader of the conservatives at Yavneh, strictly devoted to tradition, and opposed to allowing paraphrastic interpretation to pass as authority. He and Johua came into conflict, which produced one of the classic debates in Judaism, and Eliezer's excommunication:

> We learnt elsewhere, if he cut it (an oven) into separate tiles, placing sand between each tile, Rabbi Eliezer declared it clean, and the sages declared it (capable of becoming) unclean, and this was the oven of Aknai... On that day, Rabbi Eliezer brought forward all the arguments in the world, but they did not accept them. He said to them, If the law agrees with me, let this carob-tree prove it, – whereupon the carob tree was torn a hundred orbits out of its place. No proof can be brought from a carob tree, they retorted. Again he said to them, If the law agrees with

---

[1] Mishnah Rosh Hashanah 2.8-9. Tr. H. Danby, 190-1.
[2] TB Baba Batra 60b. Cf. also Tosefta Taanit 2.5.

me, let the stream of water prove it. Thereupon the stream of water, flowed backwards. No proof can be brought from a stream of water, they rejoined. Again he urged, If the law agrees with me, let the walls of the schoolhouse prove it, whereupon the walls inclined to fall. But Rabbi Joshua rebuked them saying, When scholars are engaged in a legal dispute, what have you to interfere? Hence they did not fall, in honor of Rabbi Joshua, nor did they resume the upright position, in honor of Rabbi Rabbi Eliezer (and they are still standing inclined). Again, he said to them, If the law agrees with me, let it be proved from heaven! Thereupon a heavenly voice cried out, Why do you dispute with Rabbi Eliezer, seeing that in all matters the law agrees with him! But Rabbi Joshua stood up and exclaimed, "It is not in heaven" (Deut. 30.12). (What did he mean by this? Said Rabbi Jeremiah, That the Torah had already been given at Mount Sinai. We pay no attention to a heavenly voice, because thou hast long since written in the Torah at Mount Sinai, "After the majority must one incline" (Ex. 23.2). Rabbi Nathan met Elijah and asked him, And what did the Holy One blessed be He do in that hour? He laughed with joy, he replied, saying, My sons have defeated me, My sons have defeated me.) On that day all objects which Rabbi Eliezer had declared clean were brought and burned in the fire. Then they took a vote and excommunicated him. They said, Who will go and inform him? I will go, said Rabbi Akiba, lest an unsuitable person go and inform him, and thus destroy the whole world. What did Rabbi Akiba do? He donned black garments, and wrapped himself in black, and sat at a distance of four cubits from him. Akiba, said Rabbi Eliezer to him, what has particularly happened today? Master, he replied, it appears to me that thy companions hold aloof from thee. Thereupon he too rent his garments, put off his shoes, removed his *tefillin* and sat on the earth, and tears streamed from his eyes.[1]

In the years that followed, Eliezer moved away, and lived in retirement at Caesarea. In these melancholy years, he may well have reflected,

> Warm thyself by the fire of the wise, but beware of their glowing coals, lest thou be burnt; for their bite is the bite of the fox, and their sting is the scorpion's sting, and their hiss is the serpent's hiss, and all their words are like coals of fire.[2]

When he died, he raised up his two arms, and laid them on his breast, and wept:

> Woe unto me, for my two arms, that are like two Torah scrolls, depart from the world. For if all the seas were ink, and all the reeds, pens, and all men, scribes, they could not suffice to write down all the Scripture and Mishnah I studied nor what I learned under the sages in the academy.

---

[1] TB Baba Beziah 59b-60a. Tr. H. Freedman, *The Babylonian Talmud, Seder Nezikin*, ed. I, Epstein (London, 1935), II, 352-3. Cf. also TP Moed Katan 3.
[2] Avot 2.15.

Yet I carried away from my teachers no more than does a man who dips his finger in the sea, and I gave away to my disciples no more than a paintbrush takes from the tube...[1]

He was said to have added,

Clear out the courtyard on account of the uncleanness, and prepare a chair for Rabban Yohanan ben Zakkai.[2]

It was said:

When Rabbi Eliezer died, the book of wisdom was hidden. When Rabbi Joshua died, good counsels and good thoughts ceased from Israel.[3]

Commenting on the crises through which they had lived, each lamented:

"From the day that the Temple was destroyed, there has been not a single day without some curse..." said Rabbi Simeon ben Gamaliel in the name of Rabbi Joshua.[4]

Rabbi Eliezer the Great said, When the Temple was destroyed, the sages began to be like school teachers, and the school teachers like synagogue-servants, and the synagogue-servants like the people of the land, and the people of the land waxed feeble, and there was none to seek and none to supplicate. On whom can we stay ourselves? On our Father in heaven.[5]

Yohanan ben Zakkai would have agreed.

---

[1] ARNa ch. 25, Schechter, p. 40a, Goldin 107-9. Cf. also TB Sanhedrin 68a.

[2] TP Sotah 9.16.

[3] TB Sotah 49b. Cf. Sotah 9.15; TP Sotah 9.16, Tosefta Sotah 15.3.

[4] Mishnah Sotah 9.12, Rabban Simeon b. Gamaliel says in the name of Rabbi Joshua, "Since the day that the Temple was destroyed, there has been no day without its curse, and the dew has not fallen in blessing, and the fruits have lost their savor." (Danby tr. 305.)

[5] Sotah 9.15, following MSS reading *Eliezer* instead of *Joshua*.

LIST OF ABBREVIATIONS

ARNa	=	Avot de Rabbi Natan, Text A
ARNb	=	Avot de Rabbi Natan, Text B
CAH	=	Cambridge Ancient History
ETal	=	Encyclopedia Talmudit
HUCA	=	Hebrew Union College Annual
JBL	=	Journal of Biblical Literature
JE	=	Jewish Encyclopedia
JQR	=	Jewish Quarterly Review
MGWJ	=	Monatschrift für die Geschichte und Wissenschaft des Judenthums
PAAJR	=	Periodical of the American Academy for Jewish Research
REJ	=	Rèvue des Etudes Juives
TB	=	Babylonian Talmud
TP	=	Palestinian Talmud

All Hebrew articles are listed by English title, the journal notation indicating the Hebrew. Hebrew journals quoted include the following:

Bizaron
HaDoar
Horeb
Sinai
Tarbiz
Zion

The translation of titles of Hebrew books is listed immediately afterward, in brackets.

BIBLIOGRAPHY

I. *Primary Sources*

A. Rabbinic Literature

Avot de Rabbi Natan. Ed. S. Schechter, Repr. New York, 1945. Trans. J. Goldin, *The Fathers according to Rabbi Nathan*, New Haven, 1955.

Babylonian Talmud. Cited according to the usual editions.

Igerret Rav Sherira Gaon. Ed. B. Levin, Haifa, 1921.

Masekhet Derekh Erez. Ed. M. Higger, New York, 1935.

Masekhet Kallah. Ed. M. Higger, New York, 1936.

Masekhet Soferim. Ed. M. Higger, New York, 1937.

Masehktot Zeirot. Ed. M. Higger, New York, 1929.

Mekilta de Rabbi Yishmael. Eds. M. Friedman, New York, 1948. J. Lauterbach, Philadelphia, 1949 (3 vols.).

Mekilta de Rabbi Shimon bar Yohai. Ed. J. N. Epstein – E. Melamed, Jerusalem, 1955.

Megillat Taanit. Ed. H. Lichtenstein, Hebrew Union College Annual, VIII-IX (1931-2), 318-351.

Midrash Hagadol. Genesis, ed. M. Margoliot, Jerusalem, 1947; Exodus, ed. M. Margoliot, Jerusalem, 1956; Leviticus, ed. L. N. Rabinowitz, New York, 1932; Numbers, ed. S. Fisch, Manchester, 1940.

Midrash Mishle. Ed. S. Buber, Vilna, 1893.

Midrash Rabbah. Repr. New York, 1942. Gen. Rabbah E. Theodor, H. Albeck, Berlin, 1912-1932; Leviticus Rabbah, ed. M. Margoliot (4 vols.), Jerusalem, 1953, 1954, 1956, 1960; Deuteronomy Rabbah, ed. S. Lieberman, Jerusalem, 1940.

Midrash Shmuel. Ed. S. Buber, Cracow, 1893.

Midrash Tanhuma. Ed. S. Buber, Repr. New York, 1946.

Midrash Tannaim. Ed. D. Hoffman, Berlin, 1909.

Midrash Tehillim. Ed. S. Buber, Repr. New York, 1947.

Mishnah. Cited according to the usual editions, Trans. H. Danby, London, 1933.

Mishnat R. Eliezer. Ed. H. G. Enelow, New York, 1933.

Palestinian Talmud. Cited according to Gilead Ed., Repr. New York, 1949, of Krotoschin ed.

Pirke de Rabbi Eliezer. Ed. Warsaw, 1852, repr. New York, 1946.

Pesikta de Rav Kahana. Ed. S. Buber, Lyck, 1868.

Pesikta Rabbati. Ed. M. Friedman, Vienna, 1880.

Seder Eliahu Rabbah and Seder Eliahu Zuta. Ed. M. Friedman, Repr. Jerusalem, 1960.

Sheva Masekhtot Ketanot, ed. M. Higger, New York, 1930.

Sifra deBe Rav. Ed. I. H. Wiess, Vienna 1861, Repr. New York, 1946.

Sifre de Be Rav, Ed. M. Friedman, Vienna, 1863, Repr. New York, 1947.

Tosefta. Ed. M. Zuckermandel, Halberstadt, 1881.

Yalkut Shimoni, Repr. Jerusalem, 1952.

B. "External" Literature.

Apocryypha. Revised Standard Version, New York, 1952.

Apocrypha and Pseudopigraphia of the Old Testament. Ed. R. H. Charles, Oxford, 1913, vols. I and II.

Eusebius, *Ecclesiastical History*, tr. C. F. Cruse, London, 1858.

Josephus, *Jewish Antiquities, Jewish War, Life*, tr. H. Thackeray, R. Marcus. Cambridge, 1956, vols. I-VII.

Megillot Midbar Yehudah. Ed A. Haberman, Jerusalem, 1959. (Texts of Megillat HaSerakhim, Megillat Brit Dameshek, Megilat HaHodaiot, Milhemet Bne Or u-Bne Hoshekh).

Philo, *Opera*. Tr. F. H. Colson, R. Marcus, G. H. Whitaker. Cambridge, 1953, vols. I-XI.

Suetonius, *Twelve Caesars*, tr. R. Graves, London, 1957.

Tacitus, *Histories*, tr. C. H. Moore; *Annals*, tr. J. Jackson, New York, 1931, 3 vols.

Biblical passages are cited, unless otherwise noted, according to the Revised Standard Version, New York, 1952.

II. *Secondary Sources, Translation, and Commentaries*

Abel, F. M., *Histoire de la Palestine*, Paris, 1952, vols. I-II.

Abelson, J., *Jewish Mysticism*, London, 1913.

Abrahams, Israel, *Studies in Pharisaism and the Gospels*, Cambridge, 1917.

Abramson, Shraga, *Baba Batra*, Jerusalem, 1958.

Albeck, H., *Mavo LaMishnah* [Introduction to the Mishnah], Jerusalem, 1959.

——, *Seder Kodashim*, Jerusalem, 1956.

——, *Seder Moed*, Jerusalem, 1952.

——, *Seder Nashim*, Jerusalem, 1954.

——, *Seder Nezikin*, Jerusalem, 1953.

——, *Seder Taharot*, Jerusalem, 1958.

——, *Seder Zeraim*, Jerusalem, 1957.

Albright, William F., *From the Stone Age to Christianity*, 2nd ed., New York, 1957.

Allegro, J. M., "Further Messianic References in Qumran Literature," *JBL* (1956), LXXV, 147-187.

Allon, Gedaliahu, "The Attitude of the Pharisees toward Roman Rule and The Herodian Dynasty," *Zion*, n. s. III (1937), 300-322.

——, *Mehkarim beToldot Yisrael* [Studies in Jewish History], vols. I-II, Tel Aviv, I, 1957, II, 1958.

——, "On the History of the High Priesthood at the End of the Second Commonwealth," *Tarbiz*, XIII (1941), 1-24.

——, "The Sons of the Scholars," *Sefer Yovel leY. N. Epstein* [Jubilee Volume to Y. N. Epstein], Jerusalem, 1950.

——, *Toldot HaYehudim beErez Yisrael beTakufat HaMishnah veHaTalmud* [History of the Jews in the Land of Israel in the Period of the Mishnah and the Talmud], vols. I-II, Tel Aviv, I, 1954 (2nd ed.), II, 1955.

Altmann, Alexander, "Gnostic Themes in Rabbinic Cosmology," *Essays Presented to J. H. Hertz*, London, 1942.

——, "Gnostische Motive in rabbinischen Schrifttum," MGWJ, LXXXIII, 1939.

——, "A Note on the Rabbinic Doctrine of Creation,'" *Journal of Jewish Studies*, VII (1956), 195-206.

Anderson, J. G. C., "The Eastern Frontier from Tiberius to Nero," *Cambridge Ancient History* (Ed. S. A. Cook et al.), X.

Avi-Yonah, M., *Bivemei Roma u-Byzantion* [In the Days of Rome and Byzantium], Jerusalem, 1946, 2nd ed.

——, *Geographia Historit shel Erez Yisrael* [Historical Geography of the land of Israel], Jerusalem, 1951.

————, *Kadmoniot Arzenu* [Antiquities of Our Land], Tel Aviv, 1955 (with S. Yeivin and M. Stekelis).

Avi-Yonah, M., ed., *Sefer Yerushalayim* [The Book of Jerusalem], 1956, vol. I.

Bacher, Wilhelm, *Agadot HaTannaim* [Legends of the Tannaim], Berlin, 1922, vols. I-VIII.

————, *Erkhe Midrash* [Midrashic Terminology], Tel Aviv, 1923.

————, "Gamaliel I, "*JE*, V, 558.

————, "Hillel the Elder," *JE*, VI, 397.

————, "Johanan ben Zakkai," *JE*, VII, 214-7.

————, "Joshua ben Hananiah," *JE*, VII, 290.

————, *Rabbanan, Die Gelehrten der Tradition*, Strassburg, 1914.

————, "La Science de la Vieille Tradition Juive," *REJ*, XXXVIII (1899, 211-219.

————, *Tradition und Tradenten in den Schulen Palästinas und Babyloniens*, Leipzig, 1914.

Baeck, Lee, *Judaism and Christianity*, Philadelphia, 1958, tr. W. Kaufmann.

Baer, Yizhak, *Yisrael Ba-Amim* [Israel among the Nations], Jerusalem, 1955.

Bamberger, B. J., "The Dating of Aggadic Materials," *JBL*, LXVIII (1949), 115-123.

Baron, Salo W., *The Jewish Community*, Philadelphia, 1948, vols. I-III.

————, *A Social and Religious History of the Jews*, vols. I-II, *Ancient Times*. 2nd ed., Philadelphia, 1952.

Barukh, Y. L., *Roshei Perakim BaTalmud* [Topics in Talmudic Studies], Jerusalem, 1953.

Ben Horim, Nahum, *Hakhme HaTalmud, Rabban Yohanan Ben Zakkai* [The Sages of the Talmud, Rabban Yohanan ben Zakkai], New York, 1928.

Bentwich, Norman, *Hellenism*, Philadelphia, 1943.

Bergmann, "Die stoische Philosophie und die Jüdische Frömmigkeit," *Festschrift zu Hermann Cohens Siebzigstem Geburtstag*, Berlin, 1912. 145-166 (no first name given).

Bergmann, H., *Jawne und Jerusalem*, Berlin, 1919.

Berlin, M. and Zeivin, S. Y., eds., *Encyclopedia Talmudit* [Talmudical Encyclopedia], Jerusalem, since 1946 et. seq., vols. I-IX.

Bertholet, D. A., *Das Ende des üdischen Staatswesens*, Tuebingen, 1910.

————, *History of Hebrew Civilization*, New York, 1927, Tr. A. K. Dallas.

Bevan, E., *Jerusalem under the High Priests*, London, 1904.

Bewer, J. A., *The Book of Ezekiel*, New York, 1954.

Blau, Ludwig, "Gnosticism," *JE*, V, 681-6.

————, "Jochanan ben Zakkai in christlicher Beleuchtung," *MGWJ* n.f. VII, 548-561.

————, "Rèvue, A. Büchler, Die Priester und der Cultus," *REJ*, XXXI (1895), 145-154.

Bloch, M., *Die Institutionen des Judenthums nach der in den Talmudischen Quellen angegeben Reihenfolge geordnet und erlautert*, Budapest, 1905, vols. I-III.

Bodenheimer, S., *HaHai BeArzot HaMikra* [Life in Biblical Lands], Jerusalem, 1955, vol. II.

Bokser, Ben Zion, *Pharisaic Judaism in Transition. R. Eliezer the Great and Jewish Reconstruction after the War with Rome*, New York, 1935.

Bonsirven, Joseph, *Le Judaisme Palestinien au Temps de Jésus Christ, Sa Théologie*, Paris, 1934, 2nd ed., vols. I-II.

————, *Sur Les Ruines du Temple*, Paris, 1928.

Bornstein, D. J., "Jochanan ben Sakkai," *Encyclopedia Judaica*, IX, 222.

Bousset, W., Gressmann, H., *Die Religion des Judenthums*, Berlin, 1926, 3rd ed.

Bousset, W., "Die Himmelsreise der Seele," *Archiv für Religionswissenschaft*, IV, 136.

Box, G. H., *Judaism in the Greek Period*, Oxford, 1953; *Clarendon Bible*, vol. V.

Brand, Y., *Klei Heres BeSifrut HaTalmud* [Artifacts in Talmudic Literature], Jerusalem, 1953.

Brandon, S. G. F., *The Fall of Jerusalem and the Christian Church*, London, 1951.

Braude, W. G., *The Midrash on Psalms*, New Haven, 1959, vols. I-II, Yale Judaica Series, XIII.

Bright, John, *A History of Israel*, Philadelphia, 1959.

Brown, F., Driver, S. R., Briggs, C. A., *Hebrew-English Lexicon of the Old Testament*, Oxford, 1955.

Broyde, Isaac, "Jose HaKohen," *JE*, VII, 243.

———, "Rabbi," *JE*, X, 194.

Brüll, J., *Einleitung in die Mishnah*, Frankfurt-am-Main, 1856.

Buber, Martin, *Israel and the World*, New York, 1948.

———, *The Prophetic Faith*, New York, 1949.

Büchler, Adolph, "Apostoli," *JE*, II, 20.

———, *The Economic Conditions of Judaea after the Destruction of the Second Temple*, London, 1912; Jewish College Publications, IV.

———, "Learning and Teaching in the Open Air in Palestine," *JQR* n. s. IV (1914), 485-491.

———, *Die Priester und der Cultus im Letzten Jahrzehnte des Jerusalemischen Tempels*, Vienna, 1895.

———, *Studies in Jewish History*, ed. I. Brodie and J. Rabbinowitz, London, 1956.

———, *Studies in Sin and Atonement in the Rabbinic Literature of the First Century*, London, 1928.

———, *Das Synedrion in Jerusalem und das grosse Beth Din in der Quaderkammer des Jerusalemischen Temples*, Vienna, 1902.

———, *Types of Palestinian Jewish Piety from 70 BCE to 70 C.E. The Ancient Pious Men*, London, 1922; Jews' College Publications, VIII.

Bultmann, Rudolf, *Primitive Christianity*, New York, 1956.

Burkitt, F. C., *Jewish and Christian Apocalypses*, London, 1914.

Burrows, Millar, *The Dead Sea Scrolls*, New York, 1955.

———, *More Light on the Dead Sea Scrolls*, New York, 1958.

Burstein, A., "Rabban Yohanan ben Zakkai's Demand from Vespasian," *Bizaron*, XXIV (1951), 34.

Cary, M., Nessiston J. D., et al., ed., *Oxford Classical Dictionary*, Oxford, 1949.

Casutto, M. D., "Ezekiel," *Encyclopedia Mikrait* [Biblical Encyclopedia], II, 390.

Chajes, H. P., "Les Juges Juifs en Palestine de l'an 70 à l'an 70," *REJ*, XXXIX (1899), 39-52.

de Champagny, Franz, *Rome et La Judée au temps de la Chute de Neron*, Paris, 1858.

Charles, R. H., *Religious Development between the Old and New Testaments*, London, 1948.

Christie, W. M., "The Jamnia Period in Jewish History," *Journal of Theological Studies*, XXVI, 347.

Cohen, A., trans., *Midrash Rabbah, Lamentations*, London, 1939, Soncino ed., VII.

Cohen, Gerson D., "The Talmudic Age," *Great Ages and Ideas of the Jewish People*, Ed. Leo Schwarz, New York, 1956.

Cohen, J., *Les Pharisiens*, Paris, 1877.

Cook, S. A., Adcock, F. E., Charlesworth, M. P., ed., *Cambridge Ancient History*, X, Cambridge, 1952; XI, Cambridge, 1936.

Cross, Frank M., *The Ancient Library of Qumran and Modern Biblical Studies*, New York, 1958.

Cullman, Oscar, *Peter, Disciple, Apostle, Martyr*, tr. F. V. Filson, New York, 1958.

Danby, H., trans., *The Mishnah*, London, 1933.

Daniel-Rops, Henri, *Jesus and His Times*, New York, 1958, vols. I-II.

Daube, David, "Alexandrian Methods of Interpretation and the Rabbis," *Festschribe Hans Lewald*, Basel, 1953, 27 f.

———, "Three Notes Having to Do With Johanan ben Zaccai," *Journal of Theological Studies*, n. s., XI, part 1, 1960, p. 53-62.

———, "Rabbinic Methods of Interpretation and Hellenistic Rhetoric," *HUCA*, XIX (1949), 239-264.

Davies, W. D., *Paul and Rabbinic Judaism*, London, 1955.

———, *Torah in the Messianic Age and/or the Age to Come*, Philadelphia, 1952.

Deutsch, Emanuel, *The Talmud*, Philadelphia, n. d.

Dill, Samuel, *Roman Society from Nero to Marcus Aurelius*, New York, 1957.

Derenbourg, J., *Essai sur l'histoire et la Géographie de la Palestine d'après les Thalmuds et les autres sources rabbiniques*, Paris, 1867.

———, "Über einige dunkle Punkte in der Geschichte der Juden: R. Jochanan ben Sakkai u. Rabban Gamaliel II," *MGWJ*, s. v. XXXVII (1893), 304.

Dubnow, Simon, *Divrei Yemei Am Olam* [History of the Eternal People], Tel Aviv, 1958, vols. I-X.

Duerr, L., *Die Stellung des Propheten Ezechiel in der Israelitisch-Jüdischen Apokalyptic*, Münster, 1923.

Duran, Simon b. Zemakh, *Magen Avot*, repr. New York, 1951.

Ebner, Eliezer, *Elementary Education in Ancient Israel during the Tannaitic Period (10-220 C.E.)*, New York, 1956.

Edersheim, Alfred, *The Life and Times of Jesus the Messiah*, New York, 1910, vols. I-II.

Efros, Israel, "Prophecy, Wisdom, and Apocalypse," *Mordecai M. Kaplan Jubilee Volume*, English Section, ed. M. Davis, New York, 1953.

Eisenstein, J. D., "Yohanan ben Zakkai," *Ozar Yisrael*, ed. J. D. Eisenstein, New York, 1951, V, 101.

Eliade, M. and J. M. Kitagawa, eds., *The History of Religions: Essays in Methodology*, Chicago, 1959.

Elliott-Binns, L. E., *Galilean Christianity*, Chicago, 1956.

Enelow, Hyman G., "The Modern Reconstruction of the Pharisees," in the *Selected Works*, IV, 117, New York, 1935.

Enslin, M. S., Christian Beginnings, New York, 1956, vols. I-II.

Epstein, A., *MiKadmoniot HaYehudim, Mehkarim veRishimot* [From the *Antiquities of the Jews:* Studies and Notes], Jerusalem, 1956.

Epstein, Y. N., *Mavo Le-Nusah HaMishnah* [Introduction to the Text of the Mishnah], Jerusalem, 1948, vols. I-II.

———, *Mevo-ot LeSifrut HaTannaim*, [Introductions to Tannaitic Literature], Jerusalem, 1958.

Farmer, William R., *Maccabees, Zealots, and Josephus*, New York, 1956.

Federbush, Simon, *BeNetivot HaTalmud* [In the Paths of the Talmud], Jerusalem, 1956.

Feldman, *The Parables and Similes of the Rabbis, Agricultural and Pastoral*, Cambridge, 1924.

Finkelstein, Louis, "Akiba, "in *Great Jewish Personalities in Ancient and Medieval Times*, Ed. S. Noveck, New York, 1960.

———, *Akiba, Scholar, Saint, and Martyr*, New York, 1936.

———, *HaPerushim veAnshei Kenesset HaGedolah* [The Pharisees and the Men of the Great Assembly], New York, 1950.

———, "Is Philo Mentioned in Rabbinic Literature," *JBL*, LIII (1934), 142-149.

———, *Mavo LeMasekhtot Avot veAvot deRabbi Natan* [Introduction to Tractates Avot and Avot de Rabbai Natan], New York, 1950.

———, "On the Phraseology of the Tannaim," *Tarbiz*, XX (1947)-9, 96-106.

————, *The Pharisees, The Sociological Background of their Faith*, Philadelphia, 1946, vols. I-II.

————, "The Pharisees, Their Origin and Their Philosophy," *Harvard Theological Review*, XXIII (1930), 185.

Frank, Edgar, *Talmudic and Rabbinical Chronology, The Systems of Counting Years in Jewish Literature*, New York, 1956.

Frank, Tenny, *Economic History of Rome*, Baltimore, 1927.

Frankel, Zechariah, *Darkhe HaMishnah* [The Ways of the Mishnah], Leipzig, 1860, repr. Tel Aviv, 1959.

Friedlander, Gerald, *Pirke de Rabbi Eliezer*, London, 1916.

Friedlander, Ludwig, *Roman Life and Manners*, tr. L. A. Magnus, London, n. d.

Friedlander, M., "La Sibylle Juive et les Partis Religieux de la Dispersion," *REJ*, XXIX (1894), 181-196.

Gardiner, Patrick, *The Nature of Historical Explanation*, London, 1955.

————, *Theories of History*, Glencoe, 1959.

Gaster, Moses, *Exempla of the Rabbis*, London, 1924.

Geiger, A., *HaMikra veTargumav* [Scripture and its Translations], tr. J. Klausner, Jerusalem, 1948.

Ginsburg, M. S., *Rome et la Judée*, Paris, 1928.

Ginzberg, Louis, "Bet Din," J E III, 114.

————, "Cabala, History and System," *JE*, III, 459.

————, "Elijah," *JE*, V. 121.

————, *Legends of the Jews*, tr. H. Szold; Index by B. Cohen, Philadelphia, 1946, vols. I-VII.

————, "The Mishnah Tamid," *Journal of Jewish Lore and Philosophy*, I, 33.

————, *On Jewish Law and Lore*, Philadelphia, 1955.

————, *Perushim VeHiddushim BaYerushalmi* [Commentaries and Novellae in the Palestinian Talmud], New York, 1950, vols. I-III.

————, "The Religion of the Jews at the Time of Jesus," *HUCA*, I, 307.

————, "Some Observations on the Attitude of the Synagogue towards Apocalyptic-Eschatological Writings," *JBL*, XLI (1922), 115.

————, *Students, Scholars, and Saints*, Philadelphia, 1928.

————, *Eine unbekannte iüdische Sekte*, New York, 1922.

Glatzer, Nahum N., *Geschichte der Talmudischen Zeit*, Berlin, 1937.

————, *Hillel the Elder: The Emergence of Classical Judaism*, New York, 1956.

————, "Hillel the Elder in the Light of the Dead Sea Scrolls," in K. Stendahl, ed., *The Scrolls and the New Testament*, New York, 1957, 232.

————, "A Study of the Talmudic Interpretation of Prophecy," *Review of Religion*, Jan., 1946.

Glover, T. R., *The Conflict of Religions in the Early Roman Empire*, New York, 1960.

Glueck, Nelson, *Das Wort Hesed*, Jena, 1927.

Goguel, M., *Jesus and the Origins of Christianity*, New York, 1960, vols. I-II.

Goldfahn, Alex H., *Die Kirchenväter und die Agada*, Breslau, 1877.

Goldin, Judah, "Hillel the Elder," *Journal of Religion*, (1946) XXVI, 263-277.

————, "The Period of the Talmud," in L. Finkelstein, ed., *The Jews, Their History, Culture, and Religion*, Philadelphia, 1949, I.

————, "Three Pillars of Simeon the Righteous," *PAAJR*, XXVII (1957), 43-57.

————, "The Two Versions of Avot de R. Natan," *HUCA*, XIX (1945), 97-120.

Goldschmidt, L., *Subject Concordance to the Babylonian Talmud*, ed. R. Edelmann, Copenhagen, 1959.

Gollancz, Hermann, *Pedagogics of the Talmud and that of Modern Times: A Comparative Study*, London, 1924.

Goodenough, E. R., *By Light, Light: The Mystic Gospel of Hellenistic Judaism*, New Haven, 1935.

———, "Philo," in S. Noveck, ed., *Great Jewish Personalities in Ancient and Medieval Times*, New York, 1960.

Gordis, "'Homeric' Books in Palestine," *JQR*, n.s. XXXVIII (1947), 359-368.

Gordon, S. L., *Sefer Yehezkiel* [The Book of Ezekiel], Tel Aviv, 1955.

Graetz, Heinrich, "Agrippa II und der Zustand Judaeas nach dem Untergange Jerusalems," *MGWJ*, XXX (1881), 481-499.

———, "Ein Arabarch Nikanor in der ersten Kaiserzeit," *MGWJ*, XXX (1881), 202-206.

———, *Geschichte der Juden*, ed. M. Brann, Leipzig, 1906.

———, *Gnosticismus und Judenthum*, Krotoschin, 1846.

———, *History of the Jews*, tr. H. Szold, Philadelphia, 1949, vols. I-VI.

———, "Das Wort Hamirom in der Talmudischen Literatur," *MGWJ*, XXIX (1880), 139.

———, "Zur Geschichte und Chronologie Agrippas II des Procuratoren unter den Hohenpriestern seiner Zeit," *MGWJ* (1880), XXIX, 337.

Grant, F. C., *Ancient Judaism and the New Testament*, New York, 1959.

———, *Economic Background of the Gospels*, London, 1926.

Grant, Robert M., *Gnosticism and Early Christianity*, New York, 1959.

Graubart, D., "Le Veritable Auteur du Traitè Kelim," *REJ*, XXXII (1896) 200-225.

Gray, George B., *Sacrifice in the Old Testament, Its Theory and Practice*, Oxford, 1925.

Greenstone, Julius H., *The Messiah Idea in Jewish History*, Philadelphia, 1948.

Grintz, J. M., "Hebrew as the Spoken and Written Language in the Last Days of the Second Temple," *JBL*, LXXIX (1960), 32.

Gross, M. D., *Avot HaDorot* [The Fathers of the Generations], Tel Aviv, 1957.

———, *Ozar HaAgadah* [Treasury of the Agadah], Jerusalem, 1955, vols. I-III.

Guignebert, A., *The Jewish World in the Time of Jesus*, New York, 1959.

Gulak, A., *Yesodei HaMishpat HaIvri* [The Foundations of Hebrew Jurisprudence], Jerusalem, 1922, vols. I-IV.

Guttmann, A., "Foundations of Rabbinic Judaism," *HUCA*, XXIII (1950), 453.

———, "Hillelites and Shammaites, A Clarification," *HUCA*, XXVIII (1957), 115-127.

Hadas, Moses, *Hellenistic Culture: Fusion and Diffusion*, New York, 1960.

HaLevi, Yizhak Isaac, *Dorot HaRishonim* [The Early Generations], Vienna, 1923, vols. I-V.

Hamburger, J., *Real-Encyclopaedie fur Bibel und Talmud*, vols. I-II.

Heilprin, Y., *Sefer Seder HaDorot* [The Book of the Order of the Generations], Warsaw, 1897.

Heinemann, I., *Altjüdische Allegoristik*, Breslau, 1936.

———, *Darkhe Hagadah* [The Ways of the Agadah], Jerusalem, 1953.

———, *Philons griechische und jüdische Bildung*, Breslau, 1932.

———, "Die Sektefrömmigkeit der Therapeuten," *MGWJ*, LXXVIII (1934), 104-117.

Helfgott, Benjamin W., *Doctrine of Election in Tannaitic Literature*, New York, 1954.

Herford, R. T., *Christianity in Talmud and Midrash*, London, 1903.

———, *Judaism in the New Testament Period*, London, 1928.

———, *Pharisaism: Its Aim and its Method*, London, 1912.

———, "Separation of Christianity from Judaism," in *Jewish Studies in Memory of Israel Abrahams*, New York, 1927, 209.

Herr, Samuel and S. Sherira, *Toldot HaSifrut HaTalmudit* [History of Talmudic Literature], Tel Aviv, 1937.

Herzfeld, L., "Chronologische Ansetzung der Schriftgelehrten von Antigonus aus Socho bis auf R. Akiba," *MGWJ*, III (1854), 221-229.

Hirschfeld, H. S., *Halachische Exegese*, Berlin, 1840.

Hoenig, Sidney B., "The End of the Great Sanhedrin in the Second Commonwealth," *Horeb*, III, 169.

——, *The Great Sanhedrin*, New York, 1953,

Hoennicke, G., *Das Judenchristentum im ersten und zweiten Jahrhundert*, Berlin, 1908.

Hoffmann, David, *Zur Einleitung in die Halachischen Midraschim*, Berlin, 1887.

Hyman, A. M., *Ozar Divrei Hakhamim u-Pitgameihem* [Treasury of the Words of the Sages and their Aphorisms], Tel Aviv, 1956.

——, *Toldot HaTannaim ve-Amoraim* [History of the Tannaim and Amoraim], London, 1909. Vols. I-III.

——, *Torah Haketuvah ve-Ha-Mesurah* [The Written and Oral Torah], Tel Aviv, 1938, vols. I-III.

Ibn-Shmuel, Yehudah, *Midrashei Geulah* [Legends of Redemption], Tel Aviv, 1954.

Jackson, F. J. Foakes, and Lake K., *The Beginnings of Christianity*, London, 1920-1933, *pass.*, vols. I-V.

Jackson, F. J. Foakes, *Josephus and the Jews*, New York, 1930.

Jacobs, Louis, "Economic Conditions of the Jews in Babylon in Talmudic Times compared with Palestine," *Journal of Semitic Studies*, II (1957), 349-359.

Jastrow, M., *Dictionary of the Targumim, Talmud Bavli, Yerushalmi, etc.*, New York, 1950.

Javitz, Z., *Sefer Toldot Yisrael* [The Book of the Generations of Israel], Tel Aviv, 1933, vols. V & VI.

Jeremias, J., *Jerusalem zur Zeit Jesu*, Göttingen, 1958, 2nd ed.

Jewish Encyclopedia, Isidore Singer, Managing Editor, New York, 1891-1906, vols. I-XII.

Joel, M., *Blicke in die Religionsgeschichte zu Anfang des zweiten christlichen Jahrhunderts, Der Talmud und die griechische Sprache*, Breslau, 1880.

Johnson, N. B., *Prayer in the Apocrypha and Pseudepigrapha*, Philadelphia, 1948.

Jones, A. H. M., *The Herods of Judaea*, Oxford, 1938.

Jost, J. M., *Geschichte des Judenthums und Seiner Sekten*, Leipzig, 1857.

——, "Über den geschichtlichen Inhalt der Mischnah Rosch Haschanah IV, 1," *Ben Hanania* (1859), II, 442.

Juster, Jean, *Les Juifs dans L'Empire Romain, Leur Condition Juridique, Economique, et Sociale*, Paris, 1914, vols. I-II.

Kadushin, Max, *Organic Thinking*, New York, 1938.

——, *The Rabbinic Mind*, New York, 1952.

Kahana, A., *Sifrut HaHistoria HaYisraelit* [Jewish Historical Literature], Warsaw, 1922.

Kahana, K., *Seder Tannaim ve Amoraim* [The Order of the Tannaim and Amoraim], Wurzburg, 1932.

Kaminka, A., "Hillel's Life and Work," *JQR*, n.s. XXX (1939), 107-122.

——, *Mehkarim BaTalmud* [Studies in the Talmud], Tel Aviv, 1951.

——, "Les Rapports entre le rabbinisme et la Philosophie stoicienne," *REJ*, LXXXII (1926), 233-252.

Karl, Z., *Mehkarim Ba Sifrei* [Studies in Sifrei], Tel Aviv, 1954.

Kassovsky, J., *Ozar Lashon HaMishnah* [Concordance to the Mishnah], Jerusalem, 1960, vols. I-IV.

——, *Ozar Lashon HaTalmud* [Concordance to the Talmud], Jerusalem, 1959, vols. I-VII.

——, *Ozar Lashon HaTosefta* [Concordance to the Tosefta], Jerusalem, 1941, vols. I-III.

Katz, B. Z., *Perushim, Zedukim, Kannaim, Nozrim* [Pharisees, Sadducees, Zealots and Christians], Tel Aviv, 1947.

Kaufman, Yehezkel, *Golah ve-Nekhar* [Exile and Alienation], Tel Aviv, 1929, vols. I-II.

———, *Toldot HaEmunah HaYisraelit* [History of the Israelite Faith], Tel Aviv, 1954-7, vols. I-VIII.

Kisch, Guido, "A Talmudic Legend as the Source for the Josephus Passage in the Sachsenspiegel," *Historia Judaica*, 1939, 105.

Klausner, Yosef, *Biyemei Bayit Sheni* [In the Time of the Second Temple], Jerusalem, 1954, 3rd ed.

———, *From Jesus to Paul*, tr. W. F. Stinespring, London, 1944.

———, *Historia shel HaBayit HaSheni* [The History of the Second Temple], Jerusalem, 1953, vols. I-V.

———, *Jesus of Nazareth*, tr. H. Danby, New York, 1953.

———, *Messianic Idea in Israel*, tr. W. F. Stinespring, New York, 1955.

Klein, Hyman, "Gemara and Sebara," *JQR*, n.s. XXXVIII (1947), 67-91.

———, "Gemara Quotations in Sebara," *JQR* n.s. XLIII (1952), 341-363.

———, "Some General Results of the Separation of Gemara from Sebara in the Babylonian Talmud," *Journal of Semitic Studies*, III, 363.

Klein, Samuel, "The Estates of R. Judah Ha-Nasi and the Jewish Communities in the Trans-Jordanic Region," *JQR* n.s. II (1911), 545-556.

———, *Ma-amarim Shonim le-Hakirat Erez Yisrael* [Selected Articles on the Study of the Land of Israel], Vienna, 1924.

———, *Sefer HaYishuv* [The Book of the Settlement], Tel Aviv, 1939.

Kohler, Kaufman, "Cabala," *JE*, III, 456.

———, "Merkabah, *JE*, VIII, 498.

———, "Zealots," *JE*, XII, 639.

Kohut, A., ed. *Aruk Completum*, New York, 1955, vols. I-XI.

Krauss, Samuel, "Etudes de Terminologie Talmudique," *REJ*, LXVII (1914), 170-177.

———, *Griechische und Lateinische Lehnworter im Talmud, Midrash, und Targum*, Berlin, 1898-9, vols. I-II.

———, *Kadmoniot HaTalmud* [Talmudic Antiquities], Tel Aviv, 1928, vols. I-III.

———, "A Misunderstood Word," *JQR*, n.s. IV (1913), 111-114.

———, *Paras veRomi BaTalmud u-va-Midrashim* [Persia and Rome in the Talmud and Midrash], Jerusalem, 1947.

———, "Die Versammlungsstätten der Talmudgelehrten," *Festschrift zu Israel Lewy*, ed. M. Brann and J. Elbogen, Breslau, 1911, 17.

———, "La Vie des Rues dans L'Antiquite," *REJ*, LXXVIII (1924), 149-155.

Krochmal, Nahum, *More Nevuhei HaZeman* [Guide to the Perplexed of this Age], Warsaw, 1894.

Lagrange, P. M-J., *Le Judaisme avant Jesus Christ*, Paris, 1931.

Landau, M., "Bilder aus dem Leben und Wirken der Rabbiner: Rabbi Jochanan ben Sakkai," *MGWJ*, I (1852), 163-176, 283-295, 323-335.

Langen, J., *Das Judenthum in Palästina zur Zeit Christi*, Freiburg, 1866.

Lauterbach, Jacob Z., "The Ancient Jewish Allegorists in Talmud and Midrash," *JQR*, n.s. I, 291.

———, "Jonathan ben Uzziel," *JE*, VII, 238.

———, "Midrash and Mishnah, A Study in the Early History of the Halakhah," *JQR*, n.s. V (1914), 503-527; VI (1915), 23-95, 303-327.

———, *The Pharisees and their Teachings*, New York, 1930.

———, *Rabbinic Essays*, Cincinnati, 1951.

———, "Shammai," *JE*, XI, 230.

————, "Simeon ben Gamaliel I," *JE*, XI, 347.

————, "Simeon ben Nataneel," *JE*, XI, 356.

Lettofsky, A., Milhemet HaYehudim BaRomaim lefi Yosifus ve-Hammekorot Ha-Talmudiim [The War of the Jews against the Romans according to Talmudic Sources and Josephus]. Unpublished bachelor's honors thesis, Brandeis University Library, 1959.

Levi, I., *La Légende de Pythagore de Grèc en Palestine*, Paris, 1927.

Levy, J., *Neuhebräisches und Chaldäisches Wörterbuch über die Talmudim u. Midrashim*, Leipzig, 1883, vols. I-IV.

Levy, Yohanan, *Olamot Nifgashim* [Studies in Jewish Hellenism], Jerusalem, 1960.

Lieberman, Saul, "Discipline in the So-called Manual of Discipline," *JBL*, LXI (1952), 199-206.

————, *Greek in Jewish Palestine*, New York, 1942.

————, *Hellenism in Jewish Palestine*, New York, 1950.

————, Light on the Cave Scrolls from Rabbinic Sources," *PAAJR*, XX (1951), 395-404.

————, "Martyrs of Caesarea," *Annuaire de l'Institute de Philologie et d'Histoire Orientales et Slaves*, VII, (1939-1944), 394.

————, *Tosefta Kifshutah*, New York, 1945, vols. I-III.

Lietzmann, Hans, *The Beginnings of the Christian Church*, tr. B. L. Woolf, New York, 1958.

Lightley, J., *Jewish Sects and Parties in the Time of Christ*, London, 1925.

Lowenstamm, S. E., "Zakkai," *Encyclopedia Mikrait*, II, 919.

Madde, F. W., *History of Jewish Coinage and of Money in the Old and New Testaments*, London, 1864.

Maisler, B., BenDor, E., Glueck, N., Klein, S., Avi-Yonah, M., Narkiss, M., *Mishar Ta-asiah, ve-Omanut be Erez Yisrael* [Commerce, Industry and Crafts in the Land of Israel], Jerusalem, 1937.

Mann, J., "Jesus and the Sadducean Priests, Luke 10.25-37," *JQR* n.s. VI (1915), 415-422.

————, "Rabbinic Studies in the Synoptic Gospels," *HUCA*, I, 323.

Marcus, J. R., and Bilgray, A. T., *Index to Jewish Festschriften*, Cincinnati, 1937.

Marcus, Ralph, *Law in the Apocrypha*, New York, 1927.

————, "Pharisees, Essenes, and Gnostics," *JBL*, LXXIII (1954), 157-161.

————, "Pharisees in the Light of Modern Scholarship," *Journal of Religion*, XXXII, 153.

————, "Philo, Josephus, and the Dead Sea Yahad," *JBL*, LXXI (1952), 207-209.

————, "A Selected Bibliography (1920-1945) of the Jews in the Hellenistic-Roman Period," *PAAJR*, XVI (1946), 97-183.

Margoliot, Eliezer, *Eliahu Hanavi besifrut Yisrael* [Elijah the Prophet in Jewish Literature], Jerusalem, 1960.

Margoliot, Mordecai, *Encyclopedia Lekahhmei HaTalmud veHageonim* [Encyclopedia of the Sages of the Talmud and the Gaonim), Tel Aviv, 1946, 2nd ed., vols. I-IV.

Margoliot, R., *LeHeker Shemot veKinuyim BaTalmud*, [On the Study of Names and Nicknames in the Talmud], Jerusalem, 1960.

Margolis, Max and Alexander Marx, *History of the Jewish People*, Philadelphia, 1956.

Marmorstein, A., *The Old Rabbinic Doctrine of God, The Names and Attributes of God*, London, 1927, Jews' College Publications, X.

————, "Rayonot Hagadah veKorot HaZeman," *Tarbiz*, V (1933), 134-147.

————, *Studies in Jewish Theology*, ed. J. Rabbinowitz and M. S. Lew, London, 1950.

Mathews, S., *New Testament Times in Palestine*, New York, 1933.

Mattingly, H., *Roman Imperial Civilization*, New York, 1959.

Mendelsohn, S., "Bet Hillel and Bet Shamai," *JE*, III, 115.

————, "Eleazar ben Arak," *JE*, V, 96.

————, "Eliezer ben Hyrcanos," *JE*, V, 113.

————, "Hanina ben Dosa," *JE*, VI, 215.

————, "Imma Shalom," *JE*, VI, 562.

Mercer, Samuel A. B., *Extrabiblical Sources for Jewish History*, London, 1913.

Mielziner, M., *Introduction to the Talmud*, Cincinnati, 1894.

Milik, J. T., *Ten Years of Discovery in the Wilderness of Judeae*, London, 1959.

Mommsen, T., *Judaea und die Juden*, Berlin, 1936.

————, *Provinces of the Roman Empire from Caesar to Diocletian*, tr. W. P. Dickson, London, 1886, vol. II.

Montefiore, E. G. and H. Loewe, *Rabbinic Anthology*, Philadelphia, 1959.

Moore, George F., *Judaism in the First Centuries of the Christian Era. The Age of the Tannaim*, Cambridge, 1954, vols. I-III.

————, "Rise of Normative Judaism," *Harvard Theological Review*, XVII (1924), 307-375, XVIII (1925), 1-39.

Morrison, W. D., *The Jews under Roman Rule*, New York, 1902.

Narkiss, M., *Matheot Erez Yisrael* [Coins of the Land of Israel], Jerusalem, 1938.

Neubauer, A. D., *La Geographie du Talmud*, Paris, 1868.

————, *Medieval Jewish Chronicles and Chronological Notes: Seder HaHakhamim ve-Korot HaYamim*, Oxford, 1887-1895, repr. New York, 1958, vols. I-II.

Neumark, D., "Dorshe Reshumot und Dorshe Hamurot," *Festschrift Professor Dr. Maybum zum 70. Geburtstag*, Berlin, 1914, 179.

Neusner, Jacob, "Does Torah Mean Law," *Journal of the C.C.A.R.*, October, 1959, 42–45.

————, "Essay on Ezekiel's Chariot," *Student Annual, Teachers' Institute, Jewish Theological Seminary*, 1961, 31-42.

————, "The Pharisaic Fellowship in the Second Jewish Commonwealth," *Harvard Theological Review*, LIII (1960), 125-142.

————, "Qumran and Jerusalem, Two Jewish Roads to Utopia, *Journal of Bible and Religion*, XVIII (1958), 284-290.

Ochser, S., "Zadok," *JE*, XII, 629.

Oesterley, W. O. E., ed., *Judaism and Christianity*, London, 1937, vols. I-III.

————, *The Books of the Apocrypha*, London, 1915.

————, *History of Israel*, Oxford, 1957.

Otto, Rudolf, *The Idea of the Holy*, Oxford, 1923.

Paltrovitch, S., *Simhat Avot* [The Joy of the Fathers], New York n.d.

Parrot, A., *Babylon and the Old Testament*, London, 1958.

————, *The Temple of Jerusalem*, New York, 1955,

Pedersen, J., *Israel, Its Life and Culture*, Copenhagen, 1953, vols. I-IV.

Perles, J., "Etudes Talmudiques," *REJ*, III (1881), 109-120.

Perowne, Stuart, *The Later Herods, The Political Background of the New Testament*, Nashville, 1959.

————, *The Life and Times of Herod the Great*, Nashville, 1959.

Pfeiffer, Robert H., *History of New Testament Times with an Introduction to the Apocrypha*, New York, 1949.

Podro, Joshua, *The Last Pharisee: The Life and Times of R. Joshua ben Hananyah*, London, 1959.

Rabin, Haim, *Qumran Studies*, Oxford, 1956.

Rabinowitz, Z. W., *Shaarei Torat Erez Yisrael* [The Gates of the Torah of the Land of Israel], Jerusalem, 1940.

Radin, Max, *The Jews among the Greeks and the Romans*, Philadelphia, 1915.

Rapaport, M. W., *Der Talmud und Sein Recht*, Stuttgart, 1900.

Reider, J., "Studies on Josephus," *JQR*. n.s. V (1914), 119-121.

Reifenberg, A., *Ancient Hebrew Arts*, New York, 1950.

——, *Ancient Jewish Coins*, Jerusalem, 1940.

——, *Israel's History in Coins*, London, 1953.

Reinach, Theodor, *Histoire des Israelites depuis la ruine de leur indépendance nationale iusqu'à nos jours*, Paris, 1903, 3rd ed.

——, *Textes d'auteurs grèces et romains rélatifs au Judaisme*, Paris, 1895.

Revel, H., "Johanan ben Zakkai," *Universal Jewish Encyclopedia*, New York, 1942, VI, 164-6.

Roberts, A. and J. Donaldson, eds., *Antenicene Christian Library*, Edinburg, 1867.

Rohden, Paulus de, *De Palaestinae et Arabias Provinciis Romanis, Quaestiones Selectae*, Berlin, 1885.

Rosenblatt, S., "The Crucifixion of Jesus from the Standpoint of Pharisaic Law," *JBL*, LXXV (1956), 315-321.

——, *The Interpretation of the Bible in the Mishnah*, Baltimore, 1935.

Rosenstein, A. M. and A. Karlin, *HaTannaim u-Mishnatam, Tekufat Yavneh*, Tel Aviv, 1952.

Rosenthal, Franz, *Vier apokryphische Buecher aus der Zeit und Schule R. Akibas*, Leipzig, 1885.

Rostovtzeff, M., *History of the Ancient World*, Oxford, 1927, vol. II.

——, *Social and Economic History of the Hellenistic World*, Oxford, 1953, vols. I-III.

——, *Social and Economic History of the Roman Empire*, Oxford, 1926.

Roth, Cecil, "A Debate on the Loyal Sacrifices, A. D. 66," *Harvard Theological Review*, LIII, 93.

——, *Historical Background of the Dead Sea Scrolls*, Oxford, 1958.

——, "The Jewish Revolt against the Romans in the Light of the Dead Sea Scrolls," *Palestine Exploration Quarterly*, July-December, 1958, 103.

——, "The Pharisees in the Jewish Revolution of 66-73." Unpublished MSS.

——, "Simon bar Giora, Ancient Jewish Hero," *Commentary*, XXIX (Jan. 1960), 52-58.

——, "Were the Qumran Sectaries Essenes? A Re-examination of Some Evidences," *Journal of Theological Studies*, X, 87.

——, "The Zealots, A Jewish Religious Sect," *Judaism*, VIII, 33.

——, "The Zealots in the War of 66-73," *Journal of Semitic Studies*, IV (1959), 332-355.

Rudy, Z., *Sociologia shel Am Yisrael* [Sociology of the Jewish People], Tel Aviv, 1957.

deSaulcy, F., "Nouvelles observations sur la numismatique Judaique," *La Revue Numismatique*, n.s. IX.

Sadowsky, Hillel, *Rabbi Jochanan ben Zakkai*, Rochester, 1932.

Schaff, Philip, ed., *Library of Nicene and Post-Nicene Fathers*, Grand Rapids, 1956.

Schalit, A., *Hordos HaMelekh, HaIsh u-Po-alo* [Herod the King, the Man and His Work], Jerusalem, 1960.

——, *HaMishtar HaRomai beErez Yisrael* [Roman Administration in the Land of Israel], Jerusalem, 1937.

——, "Roman Policy in the Orient from Nero to Trajan," *Tarbiz*, VII (1935), 159-180.

Schauss, H., *The Jewish Festivals*, Cincinnati, 1938.

Schechter, Solomon, *Seminary Addresses and Other Papers*, New York, 1959.

——, *Some Aspects of Rabbinic Theology*, New York, 1936

——, *Studies in Judaism, Second Series*, Philadelphia, 1908

Schlatter, A., "Der Bericht über das Ende Jerusalems, Ein Dialog mit Wilhelm Weber," *Beitrage zur Forderung Christlicher Theologie*, XXVIII, 1.

————, *The Church in the New Testament Period*, tr. P. P. Levertoff, London, 1955.

————, *Geschichte Israels von Alexander dem Grossen bis Hadrian*, Stutgart, 1925.

————, "Jochanan ben Zakkai, der Zeitgenosse der Apostel," *Beiträge zur Förderung Khristlicher Theologie*, III, 4.

————, "Die Kirche Jerusalems vom Jahre 70-130," *Beitrage zur Förderung Khristlicher Theologie*, II, 3.

Schlichter, B., *Masorot veEkrovot baMasekhet Avot* [Traditions and Principles in Tractate Avot], New York, 1955.

Schoeps, H. J., *Aus frühchristlicher Zeit*, Tuebingen, 1950.

Scholem, Gershon G., *Jewish Gnosticism, Merkabah Mysticism, and Talmudic Ttadition*, New York, 1960.

————, *Maior Trends in Jewish Mysticism*, New York, 1954, 3rd rev. ed.

Schopp, L., ed., *Minucius Felix, Octavius*, tr. R. Arbesmann, *Fathers of the Church*, vol. X, New York, 1950.

Schuerer, E., *History of the Jewish People in the Time of Jesus Christ*, Edinburg, 1886 et seq., tr. S. Taylor and P. Christie, vols. I-VI.

Schwabe, M., "On the Jewish and Graeco-Roman Schools in the Days of the Mishnah and the Talmud," *Tarbiz*, XXI (1949), 112-123.

Schwarz, Adolf, *Die hermeneutische Analogie in der talmudischen Litteratur*, Vienna, 1897.

————, *Die hermeneutische Antinomie in der talmudischen Litteratur*, Vienna, 1913.

————, *Die hermeneutische Induktion in der Talmudischen Litteratur, Ein Beitrag zur Geschichte der Logik*, Vienna, 1909.

————, *Die hermeneutische Quantitätsrelation in der Talmudischen Litteratur*, Vienna, 1916.

————, *Der Hermeneutische Syllogismus in der Talmudischen Litteratur*, Vienna, 1901.

Segal, M., *Sefer Ben Sira HaShalem*, Jerusalem, 1959.

Seligmann, A. I., "Revelation of God," *Encyclopeidia Mikrait*, II, 863.

Seligsohn, M., "Zakkai," *JE*, XII, 631.

Silver, Abba H., *History of Messianic Speculation in Israel*, Boston, 1959.

————, *Where Judaism Differed*, New York, 1956.

Skinner, J., *The Book of Ezekiel*, New York, 1908, in *Expositor's Bible*.

Smith, Morton, "The Common Theology of the Ancient Near East," *JBL*, LXXI (1952), 135-147.

————, Judaism in Palestine. I. To the Maccabean Revolt. Unpublished doctoral dissertation, Harvard Archives.

————, "Palestinian Judaism in the 1st Century, "in *Israel, Its Role in Civilization*, ed. M. Davis, New York, 1956, 67-81.

————, *Tannaitic Parallels to the Gospels*, Philadelphia, 1951.

Sonne, I., "Schools of Shammai and Hillel Seen from Within," *Louis Ginzberg Jubilee Volume*, English section, New York, 1945.

Sparks, H. F. D., "The Symbolical Interpretation of *Lebanon* in the Fathers," *Journal of Theological Studies*, X, 264.

Spiegel, D., *Die Kaiser Titus und Hadrian im Talmud und Midrasch sowie bei den zeitgenössischen Geschichtsschreibern*, Vienna, 1906.

Spitz, J., *Rabban Jochanan ben Sakkai*. Berlin, 1883 (in *Talmud and Midrash Dissertations*, IV, 5, Jewish Theological Seminary Library).

Stanton, V. H., *The Gospels as Historical Documents*, Cambridge, 1923, vols. I-III.

Stapfer, E., *Palestine in the Time of Christ*, tr. A. H. Holmden, London, 1886.

Stein, M., "Yavneh and Its Scholars," *Zion*, n.s. III (1937), 118-122.

Strack, H., *Introduction to the Talmud and Midrash*, Philadelphia, 1945.

Streane, A. W., *Translation of the Treatise Chagigah from the Babylonian Talmud*, Cambridge, 1891.

Tarn, W. W. and G. T. Griffith, *Hellenistic Civilisation*, London, 1953, 3rd ed.

Taylor, Vincent, *The Formation of the Gospel Tradition*, London, 1953,

Tcherikover, Victor, *Hellenistic Civilization and the Jews*, tr. S. Applebaum, Philadelphia, 1959.

Tchernowitz, Haim, *Toldot HaHalakkah* [History of Jewish Law], New York, 1950, vols. I-IV.

Thackeray, H. St. J., *The Relation of St. Paul to Contemporary Jewish Thought*, London, 1900.

——, *Josephus, The Man and the Historian*, New York, 1929.

Toetterman, C. A. R., *R. Eliezer b. Hyrcanos*, Leipzig, 1877.

Torrey, C. C., *The Apocryphal Literature*, New Haven, 1956.

——, *Documents of the Primitive Church*, New York, 1941.

——, *Lives of the Prophets*, Philadelphia, 1946.

Troeltsch, Ernst, *Social Teaching of the Christian Churches*, London, 1956, vols. I-II.

Umanski, J., *Hakhmei HaTalmud* [Sages of the Talmud, Jerusalem,] 1949.

——, *Hakhmei HaYerushalmi* [Sages of the Jerusalem Talmud], Jerusalem, 1951.

Urbach, A., "Law and Prophecy," *Tarbiz*, XXIII (1958), 1-25.

Vainstein, Y., *Cycle of the Jewish Year*, Jerusalem, 1953.

Vermes, G., "The Symbolical Interpretation of *Lebanon* in the Targums: The Origin and Development of an Exegetical Tradition," *Journal of Theological Studies*, IX, 1-15.

Vermes, G., *Scripture and Tradition in Judaism*, Leiden 1961.

Weber, Max, *Ancient Judaism*, tr. H. Gerth and D. Martindale, Glencoe, 1952.

Weber, W., *Josephus und Vespasian*, Berlin, 1921.

Weil, I., "Etudes Talmudiques," *REJ*, III (1881), 276-282.

Weiss, J. H., *Dor Dor veDorshav*, Vilna, 1904, vols. I-V, 4th ed.

Weiss, P. R., *Mishnah Horayot, Its History and Exposition*, Manchester, 1952.

Weisel, Naftali H., *Masekhet Avot im Perush Ayn Levanon*, Warsaw, 1884.

Weiss, Johannes, *Earliest Christianity*, tr. F. C. Grant, New York, 1959, vols. I-II.

Wilder, A. N., "The Nature of Jewish Eschatology," *JBL*, L (1931), 201-206.

Williams, A. L., *Justin Martyr*, Cambridge, 1930.

——, *Adversus Judaeos, A Bird's-eye View of Christian Apologiae until the Renaissance*, Cambridge, 1935.

Wolfson, H. A., *Philo*, Cambridge, 1948, vols. I-II.

——, *Philosophy of the Church Fathers*, Cambridge, 1956, vol. I.

Wynkoop, J. D., "A Peculiar Kind of Paranomasia in the Talmud and Midrash," *JQR*, n.s. II (1911), 1-23.

Yeivin, S., *Milhemet Bar Kokhba*, Jerusalem, 1952, 2nd rev. ed.

Zeitlin, Solomon, "Les Dix-huit Mesures," *REJ*, LXVIII (1914), 22-36.

——, "The Halaka in the Gospels and its Relation to the Jewish Law at the Time of Jesus," *HUCA*, I, 357.

——, *History of the Second Jewish Commonwealth, Prolegomena*, Philadelphia, 1933.

——, "The Institution of the Sanhedrin," *JQR*, n.s. XXXVII (1946), 189-198.

INDEX OF CITATIONS FROM

TALMUDIC LITERATURE

GENERAL INDEX